kwaddyft

ADVANCED QUALITATIVE RESEARCH

⑤SAGE | 50 YEARS

SAGE was founded in 1965 by Sara Miller McCune to support the dissemination of usable knowledge by publishing innovative and high-quality research and teaching content. Today, we publish more than 750 journals, including those of more than 300 learned societies, more than 800 new books per year, and a growing range of library products including archives, data, case studies, reports, conference highlights, and video. SAGE remains majority-owned by our founder, and after Sara's lifetime will become owned by a charitable trust that secures our continued independence.

Los Angeles | London | New Delhi | Singapore | Washington DC | Boston

ADVANCED QUALITATIVE RESEARCH

A GUIDE TO USING THEORY

MICHELLE O'REILLY & NIKKI KIYIMBA

Los Angeles | London | New Delhi
Singapore | Washington DC | Boston

Los Angeles | London | New Delhi
Singapore | Washington DC | Boston

SAGE Publications Ltd
1 Oliver's Yard
55 City Road
London EC1Y 1SP

SAGE Publications Inc.
2455 Teller Road
Thousand Oaks, California 91320

SAGE Publications India Pvt Ltd
B 1/I 1 Mohan Cooperative Industrial Area
Mathura Road
New Delhi 110 044

SAGE Publications Asia-Pacific Pte Ltd
3 Church Street
#10-04 Samsung Hub
Singapore 049483

Editor: Jai Seaman
Assistant editor: Lily Mehrbod
Production editor: Ian Antcliff
Marketing manager: Sally Ransom
Cover design: Jennifer Crisp
Typeset by: C&M Digitals (P) Ltd, Chennai, India
Printed and bound by CPI Group (UK) Ltd,
Croydon, CR0 4YY

Library of Congress Control Number: 2014953949

British Library Cataloguing in Publication data

A catalogue record for this book is available from
the British Library

ISBN 978-1-4462-7342-5
ISBN 978-1-4462-7343-2 (pbk)

At SAGE we take sustainability seriously. Most of our products are printed in the UK using FSC papers and boards.
When we print overseas we ensure sustainable papers are used as measured by the Egmont grading system.
We undertake an annual audit to monitor our sustainability.

Contents

List of tables and figures

TABLES

FIGURES

Preface

In recent times there has been a growth in the popularity, use and acceptance of qualitative methods in health, education, social sciences and other areas. This has been reflected in the increases in funding assigned to qualitative projects (or those with a qualitative component), a growth in qualitative publications (including the creation of journals devoted to qualitative research), and the inclusion of qualitative methods in educational curricula. Undergraduate courses have given wider recognition to the value of qualitative research, with some accrediting bodies now requiring its inclusion for course accreditation. Clearly, dissemination practices and debates have contributed to the acceptance of qualitative research, and growth in the production of qualitative textbooks has been instrumental in this. These textbooks have been an invaluable resource for novice researchers, academics and students in developing their skills and understanding the approach.

More recently, however, authors have started to move away from debating the value of qualitative research and justifying its necessity, to exploring broader methodological issues in producing high-quality qualitative work. Some of the debates emerging in the contemporary literature are those of quality criteria (see Spencer et al., 2003; Tracy, 2010), including the application of saturation for sampling adequacy (Guest et al., 2006; O'Reilly and Parker, 2013), mixing qualitative methods (Barbour, 1998; Morse, 2009), use of researcher-generated versus naturally occurring data (Potter, 2002; Speer, 2002), consequences of advances of technology for recording (Heath et al., 2010; O'Reilly et al., 2011), and the specific ethical issues that qualitative research invokes (Giordano et al., 2007; Morse, 2001; O'Reilly et al., 2011). As researchers and students become more exposed to and practised in qualitative research methods, it is essential to be well informed of the more advanced theoretical issues and debates that this kind of work evokes, and as yet there has been no single resource that draws these together.

This book, which has both a theoretical and applied focus, will be a valuable resource for all researchers, academics and students undertaking qualitative research. This timely work is important for enabling good research practice, and moves on from foundational texts by building on this knowledge. Interest in addressing the more complex issues embedded in the qualitative approach has only recently gained momentum as researchers and academics encounter them in their research practice. These issues are gradually being raised in the literature through conference presentations and journal articles, and therefore this book seeks to synthesise these debates and provide some practical guidance on how to manage them in research reality. Each chapter has been designed to enable readers to progress in their thinking and practice, through an exploration of the key theoretical issues and debates pertinent to quality in qualitative research.

AIMS OF THE BOOK

This book is not designed to give practical advice on how to conduct a particular method of qualitative inquiry, as there are many good general practical texts on qualitative research methods. Rather this book aims to help with the decision-making process and provides an overview of theoretical debates and contentions within the qualitative field.

The aim of this book is to illuminate the advanced qualitative theoretical debates that have emerged and to provide an accessible overview which will facilitate broader engagement from a wide range of audiences. Its emphasis is on explicating the theoretical aspects of the main issues in an accessible manner which is complemented by a practical focus to facilitate application. Researchers may find the task of assimilating evidence from a range of disciplines and sources complicated, particularly given the complexity of theory related to many of the issues, and therefore this book aims to amalgamate this into one accessible resource to provide a platform for understanding.

THE INTENDED AUDIENCE

We anticipate that this book will appeal to academics, researchers and students from a range of different disciplines because the issues covered are generic to all qualitative researchers, regardless of their training and background. We expect the book to be relevant to sociology, psychology, anthropology, health, social work, education, counselling, criminology, social policy, business and management, political science, law, childhood studies, human sciences, human geography and economics. We believe it will offer an important contribution as a resource for academics, researchers, postgraduate students, the voluntary sector, and practising professionals from these disciplines, and will be an essential book for anyone engaging in qualitative work, or interested in the debates more generally.

STRUCTURE AND USE OF THE BOOK

The book has been structured in such a way as to introduce the main theoretical and philosophical influences in the qualitative field, serving to provide a foundation for some of the more specific issues that are addressed in later chapters. Each chapter has been designed to illuminate a balanced argument and the breadth of contemporary thoughts within each topic area. Within the majority of chapters we have included a summary of work by one or more influential scholars in order to demonstrate the significance of their contribution to particular debates. Throughout the book we have sought to take a transparent position on our own perspective so that readers are aware of not only the wider debates but also our reflexive voice within it. Our intention has been to provide a catalyst for colleagues and peers to engage with the critical analysis of issues presented through the introduction of pedagogical case studies at the end of the majority of chapters, which focus on the key questions raised from the chapter. We recommend that the reader utilises this resource as a reference point for aiding decision-making at various junctures in the iterative qualitative process.

A central issue for qualitative research is that there are considerable differences in epistemological positions which methodological choices are informed by (and inform). Therefore it seemed essential to tackle the main foundational premises of the qualitative approach in order to set out definitions of the important concepts and terminology in Chapter 1. We also differentiate clearly between concepts that have sometimes been confused or inappropriately conflated. This has been undertaken in order to establish clarification of the core terminology as the basis for subsequent discussions.

The book concentrates on examining and explicating the heterogeneity of the qualitative field by focusing particularly on intra-paradigm (qualitative/qualitative) similarities and differences as opposed to rehearsing well-established inter-paradigm (qualitative–quantitative) debates. Our argument throughout the book is that to facilitate good-quality work it is necessary to first ensure internal consistency in the sense that there is congruence between ontology, epistemology, axiology and methodology. The concept of congruence is a central premise of Chapter 2 which focuses specifically on issues of quality. We argue that because of the different epistemological and ontological variants between qualitative approaches there needs to be a greater emphasis placed on the development of methodology-specific quality criteria. In Chapter 3, which addresses research ethics, we focus our attention particularly on those idiosyncratic issues that are particular to qualitative work such as the greater potential for deductive disclosure, coercion and discussion of sensitive issues.

In line with our thesis that good-quality qualitative work, of whichever approach adopted, needs to be commensurable with its theoretical foundations we have included chapters specifically on the importance of perspective-driven data collection (Chapter 4) and the issue of mixing qualitative methods and methodologies (Chapter 5). We highlight that pragmatically it may be possible to combine two qualitative methods, but that in so doing there may be epistemological conflicts which are likely to undermine the quality of the work. As the majority of qualitative work entails the recording and transcription of data we have addressed the core complexities related to this issue in Chapter 6. This chapter has been included not as an instructional manual on transcription and recording, but to highlight the fact that transcription is not a neutral process and decisions about the detail, notation and literalness of transcribing data are epistemologically tied and significant.

In relation to the area of primary and secondary data analysis (Chapter 7) we interrogate the conflicting use of terminology and contemporary practices. We do so by offering a new way of conceptualising the issue that is both faithful to qualitative theoretical opinion and pragmatically viable in the sense of the application to actual research practice. In relation to the importance of dissemination (Chapter 8) and the possibility of potential avenues we take an ethical position on the role of the researcher in this process. This is connected to debates regarding the relevance and application of qualitative research in more contemporary understandings of evidence-based practice. We contrast this with practice-based evidence, which is critically assessed in Chapter 9. With a growing emphasis from funding organisations on impact, we promote the benefits and value of establishing partnerships between academic communities and practitioners in order to facilitate the reciprocal gains between different kinds of knowledge generation.

Acknowledgements

We take this opportunity to thank those people who have made the process of writing this book possible. We thank our family and friends for their support. We also express our gratitude to the people working at Sage who have been a steady and consistent source of advice. Additionally, we appreciate the anonymous reviewers whose comments were valuable to developing the book.

During the process of writing this book we have been fortunate to discuss our ideas and thoughts with several people. We offer our thanks to Khalid Karim (University of Leicester) for his encouragement to take the time to write something on more advanced issues in qualitative research. We also thank Jessica Lester (Indiana University) and Tom Muskett (University of Sheffield) for taking time out of their busy schedules to comment on drafts. Their insightful comments encouraged us to develop some aspects of our arguments further. Additionally, we give special thanks to Claire Bone (University of Leicester) for reading through each draft chapter and discussing her thoughts on each issue. We note that Ejalal Jalal (University of Leicester) provided the translation for us in Chapter 6 and thank her for taking the time to do so.

Several qualitative scholars have provided us with constructive feedback on particular sections/chapters within the book and we would like to take this opportunity to express our gratitude to them. In alphabetical order (by surname) we thank:

- Charles Antaki (Loughborough University)
- Alan Bryman (University of Leicester)
- Kathy Charmaz (Sonoma State University)
- Mary Dixon-Woods (University of Leicester)
- Babak Fozooni (Open University)
- Martyn Hammersley (Open University)
- Christian Heath (King's College London)
- Alexa Hepburn (Loughborough University)
- Jon Hindmarsh (King's College London)
- Janice Morse (University of Alberta/University of Utah)

- Jonathan Potter (Loughborough University)
- Catherine Riessman (Boston College/Boston University)
- Jonathan Smith (Birkbeck, University of London)
- Teun van Dijk (Universitat Pompeu Fabra, Barcelona)

ONE

Theoretical issues in the qualitative paradigm

CHAPTER CONTENTS

INTRODUCTION

Qualitative research is not discipline-specific and its progress and application have been influenced multi-directionally by academics/researchers from a range of backgrounds. Each of these disciplines has drawn from different philosophical traditions to inform their perspectives and their research practices. The history of qualitative research is complex and has developed in different parallel strands within different disciplines and different geographical locations. As Bernard (2011) argued, methods are not specific to disciplines such as anthropology, psychology, health or sociology, rather the questions asked about the human condition may differ between and across different disciplines, but the methods belong to us all.

This chapter introduces and focuses on the intra-paradigm differences within qualitative approaches, while paying some attention to inter-paradigm differences to provide context for the chapter. The differences in style and content between different forms of qualitative research and the implications of these differences in practice will be illuminated. The chapter illustrates how different qualitative approaches are linked to different theoretical positions. To achieve this we consider some of the theories of influential scholars that have inspired qualitative researchers from different corners of the qualitative approach. Qualitative methodologies can be quite diverse, with different theoretical assumptions and epistemological standpoints underpinning them. This chapter elaborates on these core theoretical concerns and guide readers to make informed choices about their own research projects.

THEORETICAL FRAMEWORKS

A central theme of this book is our argument for the necessity of congruence between ontology, epistemology and methodology in terms of how this informs the choice of methods for data collection and analysis in qualitative research. Some scholars have argued that the different qualitative methodological approaches are underpinned by particular theoretical assumptions, and consistency between their philosophical position and methods should be clear, and we advocate this perspective. We do acknowledge, however, that other writers have argued that the different methods and philosophies offer different things and that the range of methods should be considered, with the most appropriate choice being matched to the aims of the research (Ormston et al., 2014). While we recognise that the aims of the research and research questions will guide the methods and approaches adopted, we argue that these questions will be written and developed from the researcher's perspective and interests, which are motivated and driven by their world-view. This should be acknowledged and the congruence between this world-view and methods used should be clear.

With respect to the broad range of researchers working within different ontological and epistemological positions, and acknowledging our own theoretical perspective, it is not our intention in this book to elevate the superiority of any given approach over another. Rather it is our thesis that for the credibility of qualitative research as a whole, it is essential that researchers acknowledge, illuminate, and adhere to whichever ontological and epistemological position they hold. Additionally, they need to demonstrate this position reflexively and transparently for the sake of the integrity of the study. Key introductory definitions of the core concepts are placed in Table 1.1.

Table 1.1 Definitions

Concept	Description
Paradigm	A contextual framework which provides the overarching theoretical basis for undertaking research.
Ontology	One's philosophical position relating to the nature of reality and existence.
Epistemology	Relates to the relationship between the knower and what can be known.
Axiology	Relates to the values of the researcher and the impact of these values on the research process.
Methodology	The particular research approach grounded in a particular school of thought.
Methods	The practical means by which data are collected.

PARADIGMS

The research paradigm sets the overarching context for any research project (Ponterotto, 2005). The word 'paradigm' is used by different scholars to mean different things, but the notion originated with Kuhn (1962). A fundamental idea offered by Kuhn was that a paradigm is a basic set of beliefs or assumptions adopted by a scientific community which define the nature of the world and the place of individuals within it. For the purposes of this book it is this understanding of the notion of paradigms that is adopted. In relation to qualitative work, these 'basic beliefs' define inquiry paradigms and are summarised by interconnected ontological, epistemological, axiological and methodological questions (Denzin and Lincoln, 2000). This interconnected view represents the metaphysical paradigm (Morgan, 2007) and in this context holds that the epistemological, ontological and methodological premises of the research can be referred to as a 'paradigm' or an 'interpretative framework' which is considered to be a basic set of beliefs held by the researcher guiding their actions (Guba, 1990). We acknowledge that the term 'paradigm' is used by different researchers to define slightly different concepts, including those who refer to positions within broad paradigmatic rubrics such as 'the qualitative paradigm' as paradigms. However, for the sake of clarity, our use of the word 'paradigm' is confined to overarching approaches.

The community of scholars operating within a particular paradigm share a common set of beliefs and assumptions. As such there is the possibility of flexibility due to both cultural and historical changes, and changes in technical structures and practices, resulting in paradigm shifts (Fraser and Robinson, 2003). Paradigm shifts tend to be contested and happen when a series of quantitative inconsistencies reach a critical mass and a qualitative shift occurs. For example, a significant paradigm shift in the social sciences was renewed attention to qualitative research (Morgan, 2007). Thus the typically held position of qualitative researchers is that it represents a fundamentally different paradigm from quantitative approaches (Hammersley, 1996). The paradigm informs and guides the approach taken (Guba and Lincoln, 1994).

The paradigm has a significant influence on whether the researcher chooses to undertake a project aimed at discovering general principles or individual perspectives.

Thus, within disciplines there are particular dualisms or dichotomies that create tensions regarding decisions on how best to study the human condition, which while often reflecting differences between the quantitative and qualitative approaches, can sometimes also be seen within the qualitative approach itself. We outline two of the common ones in Table 1.2.

Table 1.2   Core concepts (Ponterotto, 2005)

General	Individual
Nomothetic – focuses on uncovering general patterns of behaviour to predict and explain phenomena.	Idiographic – focuses on understanding the individual as unique and complex.
Etic – refers to the universal laws and behaviours that apply to all humans, transcending nations and cultures.	Emic – refers to behaviours or constructs which are unique to the individual and socio-cultural context and are not generalisable.

For the philosopher Windelband, the terms 'idiographic' and 'nomothetic' referred to different forms of evidence-based knowledge (Robinson, 2011). Windelband used the term 'idiographic' to signify the ontology that events are specific and unique, thus not generalisable (Carneiro, 2000). Conversely, he used 'nomothetic' to describe a kind of knowledge which locates generalities within a class of particulars, and from this, laws or theories are derived to account for those generalities (Robinson, 2011). While in contemporary practice the idiographic–nomothetic distinction is viewed as a dichotomy (Salvatore and Valsiner, 2010), originally the two terms were seen as complementary (Robinson, 2011). The dichotomous view stemmed from their application to the study of personality introduced by Allport who associated each term with particular methods (Robinson, 2011). Due to the generalisable characteristics of nomothetic research approaches they are more typically associated with quantitative research, whereas the idiographic approach tends to be typically associated with qualitative research. Importantly, however, within the qualitative approach it is possible to have either nomothetically informed or idiographically informed research.

The terms 'etic' and 'emic' refer to two different approaches to research and were developed in linguistics and anthropology during the 1950s and 1960s (Headland, 1990). These concepts originated with Kenneth Pike and were taken from the suffixes of the words 'phonetic' and 'phonemic' (Harris, 1976). The etic approach (sometimes referred to as the outsider perspective, deductive approach, or top-down position) starts from the point of theory, perspective or hypotheses. It advocates constructs such as descriptions, analyses and accounts that are expressed in terms of categories regarded as appropriate by a community of scientific scholars (Lett, 1990).

 If one is taking an etic approach and has the hypothesis that 'girls who have pierced tongues are more likely to be vegetarian', this top-down theorising provides a platform for an investigation to support or falsify this hypothesis.

Arguably, the advantage of adopting an etic approach is that it allows the researcher to compare contexts and populations (Morris et al., 1999). The emic approach (sometimes referred to as the insider perspective, inductive approach or bottom-up position) starts from the point of perspectives and words of participants, and emic constructs are the analyses, descriptions and accounts expressed as categories regarded as meaningful by particular members of a culture (Lett, 1990).

 If one is taking an emic approach to understanding the lived experiences of girls who have tongue piercings, this bottom-up theorising prefers to make participants' accounts the starting point for analysis rather than attempts to support or falsify a hypothesis.

The advantage of the emic approach is that researchers attempt to put aside their a priori theories and assumptions, allowing the participant perspective to emerge (Lett, 1990). Although qualitative work is generally emically driven, it is possible for it to be conducted etically.

ONTOLOGY

The philosophical tenet of one's ontological position is a crucial starting point for any research project. Therefore reflexive consideration of one's personal ontology is an ethically valuable position within the axiology of the research process. The concept of ontology refers to the way in which the very nature of reality and existence are conceptualised. Ontological inquiries are concerned with the nature of reality and require that questions are asked regarding what we can know about the 'real' world (Hesse-Biber and Leavy, 2004). Key ontological questions are concerned with whether or not there is a social reality that exists independently of human interpretations and conceptions (Ormston et al., 2014).

 If the researcher believes that there is a 'real' world, this directs the types of questions they ask and their conceptualisation of what kind of knowledge can be produced (Guba and Lincoln, 2004).

Broadly speaking, social science has been shaped by two overarching ontological positions, realism and relativism. Realism refers to the idea that there is a reality that exists independently of the person's beliefs or understanding of it. That is, there is a distinction between the way the world is and the interpretation of that world by individuals (Bryman, 2008a). Conversely, relativism asserts that reality is fundamentally dependent on the mind. That is, the world is only knowable through the human mind and through socially constructed meanings, and no reality exists independently of these (Smith, 1983).

While there are central characteristics of realism with the shared agreement that there is an independent reality, the position of realism has different variants:

- Naive realism advocates that reality can be accurately and directly observed (Madill et al., 2000).
- Critical realism claims that reality consists of different levels, including the empirical domain which is made up of experiences through the senses, the actual domain which exists regardless of whether it is observed, and the real domain which refers to the underlying mechanisms and processes (Ormston et al., 2014).
- Subtle realism advocates that the external reality exists but can only be known through the human mind and socially constructed meanings (Blaikie, 2007).
- Materialism is also a variant of realism and recognises that only material features, including economic relations or physical features of the world, hold reality. Values, experiences, and beliefs are features that arise from but do not shape the material world (Ormston et al., 2014).

It is often challenging for researchers, particularly within a Western cultural mind-set, to reconcile ontological positions beyond the dominant realist perspective that permeates at almost every level of their social and cultural experience. We are influenced by a realist culture, and it is only through exposure to different philosophical traditions that people challenge or broaden their thinking to consider concepts that are less easy to grasp regarding the nature of reality and the production of knowledge. However, in line with the valued process of reflexivity which characterises qualitative research, it is of immense worth to critically consider one's own ontological assumptions.

As noted, therefore, the contrasting ontological position to realism is that of relativism, and for some, extreme relativism. Relativism is not a single doctrine but does have the common theme that the central aspects of experience, thought and reality are relative to something else. Relativists argue that even if the reality described by realists does exist then it is impossible to access, as the only things that are accessible to us are our different representations of it, and none of these are truer than any other (Chen et al., 2011). Relativism deconstructs realist assumptions by arguing that there is no independent unitary reality to be accessed. This is an ontological position that many realists find difficult to conceptualise. While they put forward arguments that there is a reality which cannot be denied (such as furniture) and a reality that should not be denied (death), relativists have put forward strong counter-arguments to this assertion (Edwards et al., 2003). For example, the table from a physicist's perspective is not as solid as the realist may see it; rather its solidity is a perceptual category (Edwards et al., 2003).

─────────────── Reflective space ───────────────

Would you categorise yourself as a realist (or variant of this) or relativist in your own thinking? You might want to think about why this is the case.

EPISTEMOLOGY

Epistemology is a discipline of philosophy which is concerned with the theory of knowledge and with the fundamental relationship between the knower and what can be known (Guba and Lincoln, 2004). Thus epistemology refers to theories of knowledge (Harding, 1987) as well as means of knowledge production (Soini and Kronqvist, 2011). In a research context the interaction with the participant is the primary vehicle of knowledge production. The researcher's epistemological position will ultimately shape their conceptualisation of the participant during the research process and determine how the researcher communicates with their intended audiences (Carter and Little, 2007). The ways in which findings are portrayed influence what forms of 'knowledge' become accepted as truthful, believable, factual and publicly credible (Soini and Kronqvist, 2011). Thus epistemics is not only about the nature of knowledge, but also about how knowledge is justified and penetrates society (Schwandt, 2001).

In relation to epistemology there are many important questions and it is beyond the scope of this chapter to deal with them all. Nonetheless one important question is whether the researcher subscribes to the philosophical principles of rationalism or empiricism, and another is whether the researcher subscribes to the assumptions of science (referred to as positivism/post-positivism) or whether they favour an alternative theoretical approach (Bernard, 2011). For simplicity we set out some of the common positions in table form in Tables 1.3 and 1.4.

Rationalism and empiricism

In sum, rationalism (also referred to as nativism) is underpinned by a Platonic view of the origin of knowledge being based on innate ideas, thus experience provides occasions for knowing (Soini and Kronqvist, 2011). Soini and Kronqvist noted in contrast that empiricism takes an Aristotelian view that sees the origin of knowledge as developing from a clean slate and that experience is the source of knowledge; thus if one unique or common natural-scientific ideal of knowledge is rejected it does not necessarily follow that a new common epistemological

Table 1.3   Rationalism versus empiricism

Position	Description
Rationalism	Rationalism refers to the notion that humans can acquire knowledge because they have the capacity to reason (Bernard, 2006). Rationalism is a position that the most appropriate way of acquiring knowledge is through rational intuition (Hjørland, 2005). This kind of thinking stems from philosophers such as Plato and Leibnitz (Bernard, 2011). From this perspective there are a priori truths and with sensible preparation of the mind these truths will become evident (Bernard, 2011). Rationalism is a position that tends to adopt a 'top-down' approach in the processing of information (Hjørland, 2005).
Empiricism	The competing position is empiricism, which argues that what we know is a result of experience and that from the accumulation of experiences we make generalisations (Bernard, 2011). Empiricism is a position that observations, experiences and senses are the most important ways of achieving knowledge acquisition (Hjørland, 2005). Thus what we understand is true comes from what experiences we are exposed to (Bernard, 2011). This kind of thinking stems from philosophers such as Hume and Locke. Empiricism is based on a 'bottom-up' strategy in the processing of information (Hjørland, 2005). Empiricists argue therefore that we can never be absolutely sure that what we know is true. In social science terms we make incremental improvements to knowledge and often find that what we knew previously is now overturned by new empirical findings (Bernard, 2011).

position has to be formulated. Notably, empiricism and rationalism are often interpreted differently, with various descriptions of their nature (Hjørland, 2005). Typically, empiricism is used to mark a general approach to the study of reality which suggests that only knowledge gained through experiences and the senses is appropriate, in that ideas must be subjected to rigorous testing before they are classified as knowledge (Bryman, 2008a).

Empiricism is an epistemological position that observations and experiences ought to be regarded as the significant method for acquiring knowledge, and that controversies should be reduced to claims that can be verified through observation (Hjørland, 2005). In the social sciences, empiricists use methods such as experiments, and contemporary empiricists argue that knowledge acquisition depends on the methods of collection and analysis (Willig, 2008). Empiricism is therefore generally associated with quantitative research and is closely related to positivism, based on the assumption that the knowledge of the world is derived from scientific fact. More moderate versions of rationalism do acknowledge the role of observations and share the view of empiricism that observations are 'chemical-physical stimulations of sense organs', but rationalism is an epistemology that emphasises the role of conceptual clarity and one that looks at our concepts as inborn structures, that classify our perceptions (Hjørland, 2005).

These debates are important for those practising qualitative research, as qualitative practices vary in terms of the predefined structures and strategies – theory, constructs and operational definitions – that guide data collection and analysis (Bradley, 1993).

Objectivism and subjectivism

These issues considered above raise ontological and epistemological questions regarding objective and subjective knowing. While the objectivist–subjectivist dualism has typically been discussed as occurring between quantitative and qualitative research, it has also been debated within the qualitative approach. We outline these in Table 1.4.

Table 1.4 Objectivism–subjectivism

Position	Description
Objectivism	Objectivism makes the claim that reality exists independent of human direct contact with it through the senses. Arguably a researcher can attain objective knowledge. Objectivism advocates that the scientific method demands publicly observable, replicable facts which are only available in the area of overt behaviour (Diesing, 1965).
Subjectivism	Subjectivism makes the claim that there is no underlying existing reality that exists independently of our perception of it. Subjectivism considers different viewpoints as alternative ways of approaching things (Ratner, 2002) and advocates that the essential, unique characteristics of human behaviour are its subjective meaningfulness (Diesing, 1965).

In research terms subjectivists tend to be concerned to emphasise what is unique to humans, whereas objectivists tend to emphasise that knowledge about humans must be subject to impartial public verification (Diesing, 1965). It is clear therefore that from one perspective meanings are objective in the sense that the meanings of phenomena exist in the phenomena themselves, but that from the alternative perspective meanings are viewed as subjective and emphasise individual interpretation (Bradley, 1993).

Whether researchers take a rationalist or empiricist perspective, and whether they adopt objectivist or subjectivist ideals, is broadly related to their overall theoretical and epistemological standpoints. Positivism and post-positivism, which underpin quantitative research, typically stand in contrast to the other theoretical frameworks of qualitative research, and it is therefore essential to appreciate the meaning of these to fully appreciate the alternative, more qualitative positions.

Positivism and post-positivism

One of the first scholars credited with the use of the concept of positivism was Comte who developed two lines of reasoning: first, that society had proceeded through an inevitable evolution from the theological, via the metaphysical, to the positive; and second, that there was a hierarchy in the individual sciences (Smith, 1983). The notion of positivism has therefore dominated research in the physical and social sciences for years. Positivism advocates that there is a straightforward relationship between the world and the researcher's perception of it, claiming that there is a world that is accessible through research (Willig, 2008). On the basis of positivism, therefore, researchers are able to adopt the role of observer of an independently existing reality, and social investigation can be viewed as neutral (Smith, 1983). In this sense, positivism is an epistemological position that draws upon the natural sciences, as science is conducted in a way that is value-free and objective, with the goal of research being to produce objective knowledge (Willig, 2008), and it is viewed as anti-metaphysical. Those who operated under this positivist position promoted the practice of experimentation, measurement and reductionist thinking (Howitt, 2010).

However, there were developments in science and philosophy that undermined the notion of verification, proof and certainty implied by natural laws, and therefore researchers needed to generate ideas that were not necessarily supported by direct observation, with facts being recognised as interpreted (Fraser and Robinson, 2003). The logical limitations of positivism were beginning to be recognised and challenges to empiricism emerged (Willig, 2008). Karl Popper claimed that research was not able to demonstrate absolute truth but could be proven false (Fraser and Robinson, 2003), and he therefore developed the influential theory of hypothetico-deductivism (Willig, 2008) and the falsification paradigm (Fraser and Robinson, 2003). Falsification is the principle that states that it is not plausible to prove hypotheses and therefore researchers should seek to falsify them, and if a hypothesis withstands repeated attempts at falsification the researcher can be more confident that the theory reflects the world as it really is (Sullivan et al., 2012). This meant that objective knowledge was that which could not be disproven (Fraser and Robinson, 2003). Hypothetico-deductivism is the idea that researchers should make formal theories about the world and use these to derive testable hypotheses (Sullivan et al., 2012). Thus the positivist position has been subjected to a range of criticisms, and post-positivism represented efforts to respond to those criticisms. In contemporary practice most quantitative researchers therefore hold assumptions based on modified versions of positivism (Sullivan et al., 2012).

Typically, this objectivist epistemology of positivism/post-positivism has been contrasted against all other epistemologies and has contributed to the creation of the quantitative–qualitative divide (Staller, 2013). For qualitative research there is a broad range of different stances taken and there tends to be some confusion around these. This confusion has been further exacerbated by the treatment of qualitative epistemology as a homogeneous group when there is a great deal of diversity (Staller, 2013). This has been further hindered by some of the overlap between the different positions, and by some treating different ideas synonymously. For example, interpretivism, social constructionism and social constructivism are often used interchangeably; however, while there are some similarities, there are also important differences (Chen et al., 2011).

QUALITATIVE THEORETICAL FRAMEWORKS

There is some disagreement regarding the use of terms such as 'theory', 'epistemology' and 'paradigm'. For example, some scholars refer to notions such as interpretivism, phenomenology, critical inquiry and so forth as epistemologies (Padgett, 2008), and others position them as paradigms (Crotty, 2003). Notably some of the concepts, such as hermeneutics, symbolic interactionism and phenomenology, are considered to be at a theoretical level (Staller, 2013) and some, such as idealism, are positioned as ontologies (Ormston et al., 2014). We are not specifically advocating one label over another and thus deliberately title this section 'theoretical frameworks', while making reference to the broad discussion of 'epistemology' to reflect this tension.

It is likely that there will always be some disagreement when sorting through these ideas, and this difficulty relates to the fact that the boundaries between theory, ontology, epistemology and methodology are fluid (Staller, 2013). Furthermore, different researchers have different answers to ontological and epistemological questions which have led to divergent schools of thought, different interpretative frameworks and different qualitative approaches (Ormston et al., 2014). Each of the common positions is now discussed briefly in turn, but we acknowledge that this is a simplification of each one and only provides a very brief introduction and overview. Each of these positions has a complex history and many have a range of tensions and disagreements within them, and it is beyond the scope of this chapter to discuss these in any detail. Additional reading is therefore strongly recommended after engaging with this chapter to fully appreciate the histories, ideas and nuances of each one.

Interpretivism

Interpretivism began with the work of Kant, who argued that there are ways of knowing about the world other than through direct observation. He argued that perception relates not only to the senses but also to human interpretations of what the senses tell us, and therefore knowledge of the world is based upon an understanding that arises from reflections on what happens and not just experiences (Ormston et al., 2014). The various traditions within interpretivism take human interpretation as the initial point for generating knowledge regarding the social world (Prasad, 2005).

Interpretivists argue that it is necessary to understand how individuals' subjective interpretations of reality affect the formation of their reality, as a way of acquiring more complete explanations of social reality (Chen et al., 2011). Those operating from a position of interpretivism attempt to discover and understand how people perceive, feel and experience the social world and aim to achieve an in-depth meaning of individuals' behaviour and motivations for it (Chen et al., 2011). Thus interpretivists emphasise the importance of interpretation as well as observation in attempts to understand the social world (Ormston et al., 2014).

Hermeneutics

Originally hermeneutics was an interpretation of texts, particularly religious texts (Rennie, 1999), and in this circular process the meaning of any part of the text requires an understanding of the meaning as a whole (Smith, 1983). Within the framework of qualitative research the concept of hermeneutics is generally understood to refer to the process of interpretation of data which emphasises the importance of taking into account the context in which it was collected to inform the credibility of the interpretation. In the context of qualitative research the researcher must take a holistic approach and consider the social and historical context (Bryman, 2008a).

 When understanding an action, there needs to be an understanding of the context in which that action took place (Smith, 1983).

Philosophical hermeneutics arose through a critique of objectivity and argued that it is impossible to escape the subjective influences of culture, ideology, language, expectations and assumptions (Rennie, 1999). Importantly, therefore, a hermeneutic approach is necessary to achieve an interpretative understanding of human activity (Smith, 1983), and hermeneutics has been especially influential in the general formulation of intepretivisim as an epistemology (Bryman, 2008a). There have been claims that all qualitative research is hermeneutical, although it is questionable whether all researchers would assert this (Rennie, 1999).

Idealism

While space does not permit us to go into great detail, it should be recognised that 'idealism' is a term with many related meanings, and there are many types of idealism, including classical idealism, subjective idealism, objective idealism, transcendental idealism, absolute idealism, actual idealism, pluralistic idealism, collective idealism, conceptual idealism, ontological idealism and relativism. To summarise two of the more common:

- Subtle or collective idealism argues that the social world is made up of representations that are constructed and shared by individuals in particular contexts (Madill et al., 2000).
- Objective/transcendental idealism was presented in the work of Immanuel Kant, who argued that knowledge is constructed from the senses.

Idealism, therefore, is a cluster of philosophical ideas that assert that reality is essentially mentally constructed and immaterial (in the sense that what are perceived to be material objects are actually mental constructs). Idealism was a challenge to those scholars who supported the application of the positivist thinking inherent within the natural sciences to the social sciences. Scholars such as Weber and Dilthey were grouped together under the rubric of idealism (Smith, 1983).

Part of Dilthey's idealist argument was that understanding is a hermeneutic process advocating that human experience was context-bound and could not be context-free (Smith, 1983).

In terms of epistemology, idealism manifested as scepticism of the possibility of knowing anything that is dependent on the mind, thus emphasising how human ideas, beliefs and values shape society (Macionis, 2012). Idealism as an ontological position is concerned with the idea that reality is dependent in that we are unable to get outside of ourselves and therefore cannot conduct research which is divorced from our own place in the world, and any investigation should recognise the world with processes that are historically and socially bounded (Smith, 1983).

Symbolic interactionism

Symbolic interactionism originated as an American sociological approach and is reflected in schools of thought developing in the early twentieth century, including the Chicago School whose way of thinking was heavily qualitative (see Denzin, 1992, for an overview). This perspective was named by Blumer and originated in the work of Mead and Weber (Fine, 1993). Indeed Blumer (1969) named (amongst others) George Mead, John Dewey and William James as being responsible for the intellectual foundations of the approach. In his development of symbolic interactionism, Blumer (1969) set out three principles: first, that individuals act on the basis of a meaning that is ascribed to an event or object; second, that the meanings are derived from the social interaction with others and with society; and third, that the meanings are handled and modified through interpretative processes.

Symbolic interactionists therefore see individuals as members of society first and as individuals second (Ashworth, 2003), which is one of the core concepts that is argued to be becoming more accepted within sociology (Fine, 1993). For qualitative research, then, it is necessary to look at the symbolic systems in society, including those that are linguistic as well as those that are embedded in the forms of activities and practices of a culture (Ashworth, 2003). Symbolic interactionism informed the development of grounded theory as a methodological approach, which seeks to develop theories that explain social processes or actions through the analysis of data from participants who have experienced them (Ormston et al., 2014) and is now used in other disciplines outside sociology, including psychology and anthropology (see, for example, the work of Geertz or Malinowski).

Humanism

Humanism is rooted in phenomenological philosophy and idealised human subjectivity as a definitive source of knowledge (Sass, 1989). Humanism has been at odds with the philosophy of knowledge represented by science and has played a role in voicing the objections against positivism. While humanists do not deny the effectiveness of science for the study of non-human objects, they argue that the uniqueness of humanity requires a non-scientific method for research (Bernard, 2011). There are, however, competing definitions of humanism, with one common usage being as a synonym for humanitarian values and a commitment to the amelioration of suffering; but it has also sometimes meant a commitment to subjectivity as well as a means to appreciate the unique human experience (Bernard, 2011). For the social sciences, particularly psychology, humanism relates to an approach that studies the person as a whole and accounts for the uniqueness of the individual, underpinned by the work of Maslow (Moss, 2001).

 In clinical work, humanism has been associated with the work of Carl Rogers in his development of humanistic/person-centred therapy (Moreira, 2012).

Humanism includes theories of and aligns with other approaches with similar perspectives on consciousness and the individual, including phenomenology and existentialism. Indeed phenomenology and existentialism provided significant foundations for the development of humanistic psychology (Moss, 2001).

Phenomenology

Phenomenology as a movement was created by Edmund Husserl who emphasised the intentionality of human mental activity (Moss, 2001). Husserl was sceptical about the value of positivism and believed that through phenomenology it would be possible to be objective in a way that transcends the objectivity of positivism (Rennie, 1999). Phenomenology is a way of thinking that emphasises the need for researchers to achieve an understanding of their participants' worlds from the participants' point of view and the ways in which those participants make sense of the world around them. The aim of phenomenology was to contribute to a greater understanding of the lived experiences of individuals (Starks and Trinidad, 2007), with Husserl emphasising the validity of the everyday 'life-world' of immediate experiences (Moss, 2001). Husserl argued that perceptions are influenced by expectations, assumptions, anticipations and sensory input, and phenomenology should allow researchers to move beyond their 'natural attitude' so that reality may be perceived objectively, achieved through 'bracketing' (Rennie, 1999).

 A researcher aims to suspend or bracket their own assumptions, beliefs and pre-conceptions while analysing participants' narratives in order to enable them to see the world from the participants' perspectives.

Phenomenology has been combined with existentialism by Heidegger with a detailed examination of the structure of human existence, and developed by Merleau-Ponty, to look at behaviour as intentionally directed (Moss, 2001). Thus modern phenomenology sees reality as understood through embodied experiences (Starks and Trinidad, 2007). The influence of phenomenology also notably led to the development of ethnomethodology, the study of how people construct social order and make sense of their social world, and from this, conversation and discourse analysis emerged (Ormston et al., 2014), which moved away from phenomenology and took a more social constructionist perspective.

Existentialism

Kierkegaard is considered to be the first existentialist philosopher (Law, 2007), who 'believed that too many individual humans did not see any need to struggle with the direction of their personal existence' (Moss, 2001: 10). However, it was Sartre who coined the term 'existentialism' (Law, 2007) and who also described existentialism as 'a humanism' (Kaufmann, 1975). Existentialism is thus defined as a philosophical theory that argues that categories beyond science and morality, governed by the norm of authenticity, are necessary to grasp human existence (Crowell, 2010).

The fundamental premise of existentialism is that 'existence precedes essence' (Law, 2007). Although there are philosophical differences, existentialism is considered to be a belief that philosophical thinking begins with the human subject, who thinks, acts, feels and lives (Macquarrie, 1972). Thus, it is a perspective that considers the nature of the human condition in relation to philosophy in that humans cannot be understood as substances with fixed essences, nor can they be viewed as subjects who interact in a world of objects (Crowell, 2010).

Feminism

Feminism is generally considered to be a movement which developed mostly during the twentieth century (Friedman et al., 1987). The governing ideology of feminism is that it gives shape and direction to the women's movement which is primarily focused on women seeking equality with men (Fiss, 1994). There is some ambiguity regarding what constitutes a feminist epistemology. Nonetheless, there are some central characteristics embraced by most feminists. First, feminists have advocated that feminist research should not be carried out on women but should be for women. Second, feminists have engaged with methodological innovation by challenging conventional ways of collecting and analysing data (Doucet and Mauthner, 2006). Third, feminist research is concerned with issues related to broader social change and social justice (Fonow and Cook, 2005).

 Feminist research and feminist studies examine new subjects which can be offered to different disciplines, and this places women at the centre and as active agents in gathering new knowledge (Stacey and Thorne, 1985).

Feminists critique positivism and have played an important role in exposing a natural masculine bias in science and social science (Doucet and Mauthner, 2006). Thus feminist theoretical insights have been closely linked to qualitative methods, although it is important to recognise that there is no essential link between the two, but qualitative work can be used to address feminist questions (Finch, 2004). At this juncture we would like to note that feminism is not a homogeneous movement and within the broad rubric there are several different types of feminism, including liberal, radical, Marxist, socialist and feminism in the third world (see Friedman et al., 1987, for a good overview of these).

Critical theory

The Frankfurt School is considered the original source of what is referred to as 'critical theory'. Critical theory refutes the notion that there is an objective world and that knowledge is more than a mirror to reality. These theorists make the assumption that there is a value-determined nature to inquiry (Guba and Lincoln, 2004). Critical theory on the whole therefore is concerned with empowering individuals to overcome the social circumstances that constrain them. It is an umbrella notion that covers a range of specific movements including neo-Marxism, and subsequently, feminism, critical race theory, queer theory, and the social model of disability (Ormston et al., 2014). These theories advocate that larger social structures and processes associated with gender, social class and race shape how we understand social phenomena (Parker and Lynn, 2002).

Post-structuralism

Post-structuralism is often considered an attempt to build upon and break away from structuralism – that is, the focus on structural linguistics whereby human culture was explained as a means of structure modelled on language (Harcourt, 2007). Post-structuralism was originally a term used by American academics as a style of philosophising (Poster, 1989), although some theorists (such as Gadamer) preferred alternative phrasings such as 'neo-structuralism' (Peters, 2001). While there is some contention, it is typically associated with theorists such as Derrida, Foucault and Butler (Harcourt, 2007; Peters, 2001).

Post-structuralism is argued to be a critical reasoning style in which theorists focus on how meanings are imposed in a space that is not characterised by shared social agreement of the structure of the meaning (Harcourt, 2007). Post-structuralism asserts that all knowledge is contingent in the sense that knowledge is located within the communication shared by people; individuals construct knowledge together socially through groups and thus what we know is socially constructed (Fraser and Robinson, 2003). Thus this perspective attempts to explain how humans fill gaps in knowledge and how they come to hold their beliefs (Harcourt, 2007).

Postmodernism

Inspired by Nietzsche and Heidegger, postmodernism is a broad term (Rosenau, 2004) that is generally considered a philosophical movement that reacted against the assumptions and values of the Modern period, particularly in European history (Kvale, 1992). 'Modern' was a concept of the sixth century – 'The penultimate element, "modern", is a coinage of the sixth century' (Brann, 1992: 5) – and over time there have been many modernisms, including theological, national, literary, aesthetic and architectural; and the most important of these in shaping postmodernism were literary modernism, which was rebelling against determinism, and architectural modernism, which strove for universal technologically valid rules (Brann, 1992).

There is no consistent, coherent postmodern philosophy, but instead there are thinkers who focus on aspects of the postmodern condition (Kvale, 1992). Although there is some tension regarding the broad features, it is argued by many to have five, which include: that there is no such thing as truth; that it is anti-liberal; that it is leftist; that there is no such thing as history; and that there is a parallel with moral relativism (Lucy and Mickler, 2008). Generally, therefore, postmodernist thinkers advocate that it is necessary to seek to locate meaning rather than discover it, and it offers readings, as opposed to observations (Rosenau, 2004).

Social constructionism

According to social constructionism the human experience, including perceptions, is not a fixed and predetermined aspect of the person, but is mediated linguistically, culturally and historically. In terms of philosophy, social constructionism can be described as a loose assembly of diverse approaches including post-structuralism, deconstructionism, critical psychology, discourse analysis and discursive psychology (Burr, 2003). There is no single position of social constructionism as it is a rubric for a range of research efforts with a range of similar theoretical, empirical and methodological foundations and implications (Gubrium and Holstein, 2008). Social constructionism takes a critical position against taken-for-granted knowledge and illuminates cultural and historical specificities.

Research underpinned by social constructionism is concerned with identifying the ways of constructing social reality that are available in a culture (Willig, 2008). Micro constructionist theory and research tend to be concerned with the micro structures of language, and tend to focus on talk, situated interaction, interaction order and local culture, whereas macro constructionist theory and research tends to be concerned with the role that linguistic and social structures have in terms of shaping the social world (Gubrium and Holstein, 2008).

(e.g.) Macro social constructionists argue that knowledge is produced through daily interaction and our constructions are tied to power relations (Burr, 2003).

(e.g.) Micro social constructionists argue that knowledge is not static but is co-constructed in the detail of the mundane interactions of everyday life (Gubrium and Holstein, 2008).

Social constructivism

Social constructivism is a sociological theory that argues that groups construct knowledge for each other and thus a culture of shared meaning is created. It is argued that the world is independent of the human mind, and yet knowledge of the world is always a social construction (Crotty, 2003). The perspective of constructivism arose in cognitive and developmental psychology emphasising that culture plays a central role in the cognitive development of an individual, and was influenced by scholars such as Piaget, Bruner and Vygotsky (Young and Collin, 2004). Thus, the cognitive development of individuals is influenced by their culture.

The constructivist movement has been centrally concerned with the way in which the world is construed or constructed by the individual mind, a key concern being that actions are not based on the actual reality of the world, but rather on the meaning that those actions have for the individual (Gergen, 2009). Constructivism focuses on meaning-making and emphasises the construction of social and psychological worlds through individual, cognitive processes; the focus is on how the individual cognitively engages in the construction of knowledge (Young and Collin, 2004).

Picking up differences between social constructionism and social constructivism

In our experience one of the common confusions tends to be in relation to social constructionism and constructivism. The similarities and differences between social constructionism and social constructivism are important as these positions are often confused in the literature or the terms are used interchangeably to mean the same thing. They do have some similarities in that they both argue that the structures that exist outside cannot be grasped objectively (Franklin, 1998), but ultimately they are different positions. Notably, social constructionism gives emphasis to language and narrative and is applied largely in anthropology, psychology and sociology. Social constructivism, on the other hand, tends to be more pertinent in science, mathematics and technology studies, as well as in some branches of psychology (Gubrium and Holstein, 2008). Constructivism generally shares the commitment of positivism to a dualist epistemology and ontology whereas, as an epistemology, social constructionism advocates that knowledge is culturally and historically specific, emphasising that language constitutes, rather than reflects, reality (Young and Collin, 2004). In other words, they are different in terms of how they conceive of inner psychological structures and in terms of developmental courses versus the significance of language, culture and social processes in the creation of one's constructions (Franklin, 1998). 'In short, whereas social constructionists see the reality as a product of social processes (such as consensus and discourses), personal constructivists focusing on the person see the reality as subjectively defined and it is "beauty on the beholder side"' (Chen et al., 2011: 130). Thus, social constructionism focuses on the constructions created through the social interactions of people, and social constructivism focuses on the learning that takes place due to interactions with others (Young and Collin, 2004).

Reflective space

Consider which of these 'theoretical frameworks' you feel you need to develop a stronger understanding of and would benefit from additional reading around.

AXIOLOGY

Axiology is related to the human reflection on life, the structure of reality, the order of nature and the place of humankind in it (Hart, 1971). Axiology refers to the philosophical study of values and relates to ethics and aesthetics. Human values are concerned with judgements of what is 'good' and 'bad', and what is 'beautiful' or 'ugly' (Hart, 1971). Formal axiology is the attempt to lay out principles to measure these values with mathematical rigour (Hartman, 1967). In research terms, axiology relates to the influence of the researcher's values in the research process or how the researcher's personal moral standpoint affects their view of the world as well as the ways they conduct research (Ponterotto, 2005). An important side of axiology therefore refers to the fact that values are embedded in the world-views and perspectives of the researcher (Hill, 1984). Additionally, it is essential to appreciate that ethical and moral issues are embedded in these world-views (Morgan, 2007).

 The researcher's own personal moral framework and understanding of what they feel is morally appropriate will arguably ultimately influence the way the research is approached.

Axiological arguments are important for research, as quantitative researchers have often claimed that research must be free of values to be valid. Qualitative researchers, however, claim that it is impossible for research to be free of personal values as biases are entrenched in the researcher's culture and may go unnoticed if not brought to the fore (Arneson, 2009). Similarly, the researcher's value system has an inevitable impact on choices made throughout the research process. These values may be linked to the researcher's ontological position in relation to truth and what can be known. Discussions of epistemology and axiology do not occur in isolation but are set within an ideological arena; therefore, the wider ideology and cultural setting that the research is operating within will also have an impact (Hill, 1984).

USING THEORY IN QUALITATIVE RESEARCH

Often when novice qualitative researchers undertake their work they tend to be unaware of the many preconceptions that they hold about the nature of reality and their assumptions about the constitution and production of knowledge. Therefore it is important as a research community to foster a culture which both values and expresses the fundamental necessity of reflecting on one's personal world-view and culturally embedded assumptions before undertaking research activities. It is important to recognise and acknowledge that presuppositions exist for all researchers and that through the processes of reflexivity and transparency these can be observed. Part of this process of reflection entails careful consideration of one's own ontological, epistemological and axiological positions. From this foundational understanding researchers are in a better position to embark on their research projects with greater integrity. One of the advantages of taking time to organise one's thinking with regard to these conceptual frameworks is that it enables clarification of the process as it unfolds (Ravitch and Riggan, 2012).

Practically speaking, this process involves a series of decisions which require the researcher to reflectively examine their own ontological, epistemological and axiological perspectives. Thus, there is a need to examine the theoretical foundation on which the research builds and recognise that the notion of theory refers to a range of things (Maxwell, 2012). Ravitch and Riggan (2012) describe four domains of theory (see Table 1.5).

Table 1.5 Domains of theory (Ravitch and Riggan, 2012)

Domain of theory	Description
First domain	Theories can be causal in the sense that researchers may argue that X causes Y, or they may be relational in the sense that researchers argue that there is some form of relationship between X and Y.
Second domain	The second domain considers that it is the researcher looking at X and Y, and thus they must have accepted that there is such a thing as X and such a thing as Y.
Third domain	The third domain of theory views X and Y as a symbolic or cognitive extension of the researcher and focuses on the relationship between the world outside the room and the researcher.
Fourth domain	The fourth domain of theory focuses on the location of the researcher and how their location and characteristics affect the researcher's production of X and Y.

It is important to recognise that any research is essentially an interpretative process in which the collection and analysis of data are fundamentally a mechanism for making rather than discovering meaning (Ravitch and Riggan, 2012). The way in which a researcher understands the phenomena under investigation and the data produced from the participants is intrinsically influenced by the person the researcher is. The nature of that researcher has been and is being shaped by their personal experiences and the research context.

We recommend a number of practical research strategies to facilitate the application of theoretical frameworks throughout the research:

1. Be clear regarding which ontological, epistemological and axiological position is being subscribed to from the beginning, and be consistent and transparent throughout.
2. Read the relevant literature on theory and perspective in qualitative research and yield a general understanding of the important issues.
3. Keep a qualitative research diary and note down important issues related to theory as they arise.
4. Check for consistency at various junctures during the iterative process of the qualitative research.
5. Be reflexive throughout the research process.

METHODOLOGY

As we have shown, there are a number of theoretical positions within the qualitative approach, and thus each methodology is underpinned by and borne out of particular ontological, epistemological and axiological assumptions. With this in mind there are two ways in which a researcher may arrive at a particular methodological approach:

- The researcher has a strong personal ontological position in relation to reality and what can be known, and holds specific axiological ideals; this personal perspective will have a strong influence on the researcher's choice of methodology.
- A particular research question or area of interest seems to indicate a particular methodology, and while the researcher may not have any strong personal affiliation to the ontological, epistemological and axiological foundations of that methodological approach; nonetheless these influencing elements will be crucial to account for.

Methodology relates to how the inquirer can go about finding out what they believe can be known (Guba and Lincoln, 2004). Methodologies are procedural rules that are designed to guide researchers in their explorations of social life and human behaviour (Hill, 1984). As all methodologies are constrained by the ontological and epistemological assumptions that they stem from, the choice of methods which are appropriate to use within that given methodology is restricted (Hesse-Biber and Leavy, 2004). In other words, individual methods can only make sense if they are anchored to their methodological and epistemological frameworks (Staller, 2013).

An important aspect of methodology relates to inductive and deductive reasoning. Inherent in the quantitative–qualitative dichotomy is the view that quantitative research adopts a deductive process, whereas qualitative research adopts an inductive process.

e.g. Quantitative researchers adopting a deductive approach may be interested in finding out whether men are more competitive than women. A quantitative deductive hypothesis may predict that adolescent males are more likely than other groups to engage in competitive sports, and set experiments to test this.

e.g. Qualitative researchers adopting an inductive approach may be interested in investigating the same phenomenon. A qualitative inductive research question may be designed to explore experiences of engaging in competitive sports and feelings associated with it.

While it is often the case that quantitative research is predominantly deductive, and qualitative predominantly inductive, this position fails to account accurately for the processes adopted by researchers in practice (Hyde, 2000) and is arguably an oversimplification (Ormston et al., 2014). Within the qualitative approach, certain methodologies prefer deductive approaches, while others favour more inductive methods. The differences are outlined in Table 1.6.

Table 1.6 Deductive and inductive reasoning

Inductive	Deductive
Inductive reasoning is 'bottom-up'.	Deductive reasoning is 'top-down'.
Moves from specific observations to broader generalisations.	Moves from general observations to the more specific.
Begins to detect patterns and regularities.	Hypotheses are narrowed down so that they may be tested.
Develops general conclusions or theories.	Original theory may be confirmed or disproved.

SUMMARY AND CONCLUDING REMARKS

We have outlined the relationships between ontology, epistemology, axiology, methodology and methods. We have shown the interrelatedness of all of these positions and the essentialness of maintaining the integrity of these links between them in their contribution to the production of knowledge. As the book proceeds we make reference to the congruence between these, and while the process of qualitative research is iterative in nature, attention needs to be paid throughout to these elements of the project. This is illustrated in Figure 1.1.

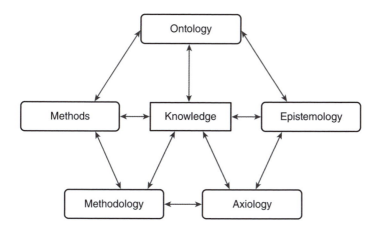

Figure 1.1 The aetiology of knowledge

The aim of this chapter has been to define some of the core theoretical terms associated with qualitative research and to contextualise those concepts inside a research framework in relation to one another. Ontology, epistemology, methodology and methods are related, and while this relationship is arguably iterative, researchers should logically reflect upon their epistemological position (Staller, 2013). It is vital to have a sound understanding of how each of these intrinsically linked concepts underpins and informs every decision made and how these connect to the research question being addressed. We encourage the reader to have a solid grounding in these issues before engaging with the controversial debates outlined in the rest of the book. We also suggest that the reader ought to take some time to consider reflectively their own assumptions about reality and the nature of knowledge and how that knowledge can be best accessed through the methods adopted.

───────── Case study and reflective questions ─────────

Rajesh is a part-time psychology PhD student who has been asked by his institution to prepare a presentation as part of the progress review process. The purpose of this review is so that a panel of experts (including his supervisor) can monitor his progress and understanding of his research project so that they can direct his next steps. He has been advised to prepare a PowerPoint presentation outlining the rationale for his decision regarding using a qualitative design for his work.

Q: How would Rajesh demonstrate an understanding of why epistemology is important in a qualitative project?

Suggestions for answering this question are available at the end of the book.

FURTHER READING

Carter, S. and Little, M. (2007) Justifying knowledge, justifying method, taking action: Epistemologies, methodologies, and methods in qualitative research. *Qualitative Health Research*, 17(10): 1316–1328.

This is a useful article for understanding the connection between epistemology, methodology and methods as it clarifies the interrelationships between these facets and presents a model for thinking about qualitative research.

Hyde, K. (2000). Recognising deductive processes in qualitative research. *Qualitative Market Research*, 3(2): 82–89.

This article focuses on the specific issue of inductive and deductive reasoning in qualitative research. The author recognises that qualitative research is typically inductive, but presents a case for how in some instances it can be deductive.

Soini, H. and Kronqvist, E.-L. (2011) Epistemology – A tool or a stance? In H. Soini, E.-L. Kronqvist and G. L. Huber (eds), *Epistemologies for Qualitative Research*. Tübingen: Center for Qualitative Psychology. pp. 5–8.

This is a useful book chapter which considers the role of epistemology in qualitative research and presents important debates in the field.

Staller, K. (2013) Epistemological boot camp: The politics of science and what every qualitative researcher needs to know to survive in the academy. *Qualitative Social Work*, 12(4): 395–413.

In the article Staller outlines the related nature of ontology, epistemology, methodology and methods and provides useful information about each of these concepts. The article has been written for researchers and students, particularly those who are new to qualitative methods, to illustrate the importance of the connection between those concepts.

TWO

Issues of quality

CHAPTER CONTENTS

INTRODUCTION

In this chapter we present debates about how to assess the quality of qualitative research. Typically the literature on quality relates to the conduct and reporting of qualitative research (Spencer et al., 2003), and yet there is no consensus in relation to how to critically appraise qualitative work. The chapter opens by exploring a history of the use of quality checklists in quantitative fields and explores the relevance of the core quality concepts of reliability, validity and generalisability. We develop this discussion in terms of how these issues have translated to a qualitative context and take a critical position on attempts to construct universal checklists in the qualitative approach. We acknowledge that any research compromises its utility where defensible rigour is not made explicit; however, we question the uncritical universal application of particular markers. While checklists have contributed to the wider acceptability of qualitative approaches, these can be counterproductive if followed too prescriptively (Barbour, 2001) and it is necessary to take into account the heterogeneity of the different methodologies. The chapter concludes with some consideration of the diversity across methodologies and that, whilst at one level there may be a small number of general principles which may be universally appropriate, it is also necessary to account for the specific and unique criteria within different methodologies.

DEFINING THE NEED FOR QUALITY CRITERIA FOR QUALITATIVE RESEARCH

In quantitative research there has been a long-standing acceptance that research should be judged against a predefined set of quality criteria. Although there is some debate about what constitutes quality markers, there is no universal acceptance of what these criteria are for qualitative work. The consensus within the academic community that scientific principles should be applied to research processes has meant that the quantitative paradigm still dominates public understanding of what equates to scientific rigour in research (Cheek, 2007). Given this dominance, it is perhaps unsurprising that these quantitative criteria have been hugely influential in appraising qualitative work. However, it is fundamentally accepted that qualitative research is different from quantitative work. The debate about whether to use the same quality criteria for both quantitative and qualitative is therefore complicated by the fact that there is a lack of uniform consensus as to precisely what qualitative research is (Mays and Pope, 2000). Although the standards offered by quantitative approaches have been used or at least adapted to judge quality in qualitative work, it is important to question how to recognise high-quality qualitative research (Easterby-Smith et al., 2008).

Qualitative researchers agree that it is necessary to evaluate their science, the quality of their analysis and their theoretical interpretations, but disagree over the terms to be used to evaluate the work (Freeman et al., 2007). These scholars argue that qualitative research should be judged on its own terms (Lincoln and Guba, 1985). Each approach has its own standards, and this makes it inappropriate to judge the merits of one by the standard criteria of the other (Collingridge and Gantt, 2008). All of the key aspects of qualitative work, including theoretical assumptions, methods, analysis, and presentation of findings, are different from those of quantitative approaches and therefore need to be judged differently. In qualitative research there is a focus on language rather than numbers, and quantifying the human experience is viewed as inappropriate (Stiles, 1993). Due to the value placed on interpretation rather than objectivity within the qualitative approach there are a number of complex issues. These include an appreciation of non-linear causality (Stiles, 1993), the necessity to illuminate the research process (Onwuegbuzie and Leech, 2007), the acknowledgement of the role of the researcher as integral to the study (Stenbacka, 2001), and an appreciation that there are multiple realities rather than a single objective one (Kisely and Kendall, 2011).

Consequently there has been a surge of interest from within the qualitative community in developing appropriately specific quality frameworks. As already mentioned, this need has grown from concern that research studies were being judged by the quality standards of quantitative work (Anastas, 2004; Muecke, 1994). The rationale for this need was that qualitative methods cannot be judged in the same way as quantitative methods because they are non-standardised, flexible, unstructured and open to amendment (Davies and Dodd, 2002). Unfortunately, until more recently, there has been little literature to guide scholars in their evaluations of the quality of qualitative research. This is despite an ethical obligation of the qualitative researcher to illustrate the integrity and rigour of their study (Angen, 2000).

The imposition of experimental criteria therefore led to a sense of urgency to create qualitative standards (Denzin, 2008). This has been particularly important as the credibility of qualitative research as an authoritative 'science' has been under threat (Morse et al., 2002) due to the lack of clear guidelines for appraisal. The drive for credibility has led to four interrelated arguments:

- First, there are arguments that qualitative researchers should use adaptations of quantitative quality criteria to judge the value of qualitative work.
- Second, some argue that there is a need for distinctive but universal markers of quality that would be applicable to all qualitative work.
- Third, there are those who argue that due to the heterogeneity and diversity within the qualitative paradigm it is necessary to have specific and individualistic markers for quality.
- Finally, there are those scholars who argue that due to semantics and theory, there is no need for any quality criteria for qualitative work.

THE ARGUMENT OF QUANTITATIVE ADAPTATION

A prominent way of thinking about measuring quality in qualitative research has been to transpose the terms used in quantitative work onto qualitative research. The premise of this argument has been that the concepts of reliability, validity and generalisability can be adapted for the purpose of assessing qualitative research. Research is arguably worthless without rigour as it loses utility, and therefore attention needs to be paid to the ways in which terms relating to reliability and validity are ascertained, and these may be used in a different way for qualitative approaches (Morse et al., 2002).

Adaptation of the marker of validity

In both quantitative and qualitative research, validity relates to the credibility of claims made; however, this credibility is achieved differently for qualitative approaches. It is important to bear in mind that the notion of a 'unitary reality' onto which 'facts' can be unproblematically mapped is contestable within many qualitative methodologies within the approach. Therefore, the translation of the realist notion of validity into qualitative work hinges on whether the claims to knowledge made are an accurate representation of reality (Spencer et al., 2003), or whether reality exists in an objective way. In quantitative research there are many different types of validity, but fundamentally, within a realist frame, validity relates to whether the researcher has measured what they set out to measure: whether the means of measurement are accurate (Golafshani, 2003). Two important areas therefore where validity becomes a particular concern for qualitative research are within the realms of data collection and interpretation.

 When disseminating their work qualitative researchers tend to use direct quotations from the data so that the claims they make can be verified by the audience. Therefore, validity in relation to interpretation is accomplished by providing access to segments of the data.

Validity from some perspectives is therefore most relevant at the points of data collection and during the process of interpretation, with validity being concerned with the trustworthiness of interpretations (Stiles, 1993). Trustworthiness as a marker of quality tends to mean different things within different epistemological traditions. For example, within the micro-social constructionist epistemology, notions of trustworthiness, validity, and reality are understood to be interactionally constructed rather than measures of pre-existing external facts. In terms of interpretation, validity and trustworthiness, this issue is dealt with reflexively by application of data extracts in disseminated work in order that audiences have the necessary information to evaluate the data-driven claims. Thus the notion of validity fails to fully reconcile for some qualitative approaches, whereas for others adaptations of validity are more readily accessible.

For those who adapt the marker of validity, there is an argument that during data collection the interaction between the researcher and respondent is essential to improve the possibility of good data (Stenbacka, 2001). This reflects the epistemological concern of accessing the 'true' thoughts, feelings and opinions of one's participants, which is thought to be improved by a positive research relationship and is dependent upon the acceptance of this theoretical viewpoint. This is strongly linked with the interpretation of the data produced. This perspective advocates that the validity of interpretations can be tested. One mechanism for achieving this is through member checking, which is the process of corroborating findings with participants (Corden and Sainsbury, 2006). The premise of this process is that member-checked findings will have greater validity.

Foster (2004) used four levels of member checking in his analysis: first, during the pilot stage; second, during the interview process to feed back ideas to participants; third, in an informal post-interview; and finally, participants were asked for feedback on the transcript of the interview.

An alternative way in which attempts are made to establish the credibility of the claim and thus its validity is through the process of triangulation (Seale, 1999; Silverman, 2013). One way of achieving dependable coding is through inter-rater reliability which seeks to establish consistency of findings by employing more than one researcher (Armstrong et al., 1997). Inter-rater reliability or multiple coding is important for qualitative research as it encourages thoroughness by interrogating the data and providing an account of how the analysis was developed (Barbour, 2001). However, while this does offer some level of reliability and validity for semi-structured interviews, where similar questions are asked in roughly the same order, it is less appropriate for unstructured interviews or when little is known about a topic or issue (Morse, 1997).

One of the main arguments directed against adapting validity as a marker of quality for qualitative research is that qualitative research is non-linear. The iterative nature of qualitative work means that it is difficult for any conceptualisation of validity to account for the iterative process, but the concept of validity is arguably necessary (Onwuegbuzie and Leech, 2007). A more fundamental critique of the use of realist markers of quality, including validity, is that it is based on an assumption that a reality can be uncovered and social life can be accurately represented, which is an epistemology which is not congruent with all in the qualitative approach (Hammersley, 2007).

Adaptation of the marker of reliability

In quantitative research, reliability is concerned with the replicability or repeatability of results (Golafshani, 2003). It is argued that even in qualitative research, there can be no validity without reliability (Lincoln and Guba, 1985). In qualitative research, however, reliability is a complex concept and relates to the extent to which replication is possible (Spencer et al., 2003). For this approach, therefore, reliability has been adapted to consider the degree of consistency with which instances are assigned to the same category by the same researcher on different occasions or by different researchers on the same occasion (Silverman, 2013).

For those who adopt this perspective, there is an assumption that a participant's thoughts, feelings and opinions can be accessed and interpreted, and arguably all researchers should draw similar conclusions from those data. On the basis that it is this viewpoint that makes it possible to accurately access participants' inner words, reliability in qualitative work relates to the consistent production of rich and meaningful descriptions of phenomena (Collingridge and Gantt, 2008). However, this notion of 'truth' is questionable and arguably in qualitative work there should not be a link to 'truth' but rather to trustworthiness (Sandelowski, 1993), although for some the notion of reliability is inherently concerned with the trustworthiness of the observations of data (Stiles, 1993). Reliability is therefore typically achieved by having a clear audit trail, giving a clear account of how the research was conducted, so that audiences are able to see how the findings were derived (Sandelowski, 1993; Spencer et al., 2003).

e.g. In qualitative research a marker of good-quality work is that the authors demonstrate a comprehensive degree of transparency regarding the research process
so that the interpretations of the data are clearly grounded. Reliability is therefore
achieved through this process.

Problematically, however, while audits provide evidence of the decisions made,
they do not necessarily identify the quality of those decisions or the rationale
behind them (Morse et al., 2002). Furthermore, the notion of reliability in qualitative research is potentially misleading and instead quality is arguably better
indicated by enabling intersubjectivity through a description of the research process
(Stenbacka, 2001).

Adaptation of the marker of generalisability

In quantitative research, generalisation rests on statistical representativeness (Mitchell,
1983), relating to the extent to which the study results can be related to the broader
population. In qualitative research, however, research is not considered generalisable
in this sense, but it is argued that it is possible to make connections across studies to
establish the applicability of the research (Freeman et al., 2007). Thus, in qualitative
research, generalising is based on assertional rather than probabilistic logic (Kvale,
1996). This use of assertional logic has been referred to as 'analytical generalisation'
(Collingridge and Gantt, 2008). Collingridge and Gantt illustrated that qualitative
generalisation relies on assertional logic whereby the researcher illuminates the similarities and differences between situations and draws upon relevant theoretical frameworks for interpretative understandings that support their generalisation claims,
allowing others to ascertain the soundness of argument made and applicability of
generalisations made.

In line with this viewpoint, generalisations in qualitative research are limited
to a specific culture and time-frame (Payne and Williams, 2005). This approach
has been referred to as 'moderatum generalisation' (Williams, 2000) and confines
its claims of applicability to other participant groups rather than making sweep-
ing statements that hold over a period of time or range of cultures (Payne and
Williams, 2005). One mechanism for achieving generalisation in qualitative
research therefore is 'representational', whereby the researcher cannot make wider
inferences to other settings but can consider those findings as representative of
the phenomenon being studied (Lewis and Ritchie, 2003).

However, despite attempts to apply generalisation in modified ways to qualitative research, this notion has received some criticism. Predominantly it has
been argued that generalisation is not possible in qualitative work because evaluation is context-specific and meaning is not context-free (Schwandt, 1997).
In reality, therefore, qualitative researchers tend to explain their findings in
terms of transferability rather than generalisability. In order for a credible argument

for transferability to hold there is an onus on the researcher to provide a detailed description of the research context, including the physical setting (see Devers, 1999).

--- Reflective space ---

It is worth stopping at this point and reflecting on these arguments. What do you think about the application of concepts such as validity, reliability and generalisability for qualitative work?

THE ARGUMENT OF DEVELOPING A UNIVERSAL SET OF QUALITY MARKERS

One of the difficulties for assessing the quality of qualitative work has always been the degree of ambiguity about which quality criteria are appropriate to use. This becomes particularly relevant in situations where researchers are engaged in the critical synthesis of qualitative work for review or funding purposes. It is a necessary part of the review process to critically evaluate the quality of the individual pieces of qualitative research which are incorporated in the review. While each methodological approach should ideally be assessed against specific quality markers for that particular methodological approach, it is arguable that it may be pragmatically beneficial to develop a universal set of quality criteria which are appropriate across all qualitative methodologies. Although there may be some merit in adapting quantitative markers of quality, a more general consensus has been to develop a universal set of criteria specifically for the qualitative approach. One of the main proponents of this perspective is Yvonna Lincoln, and we summarise her contribution to the debate in Box 2.1.

--- Box 2.1 Quality and universal criteria ---

Yvonna Lincoln

Yvonna Lincoln is a distinguished professor within the Educational Administration and Human Resource Department at Texas A&M University. She has written extensively (often in collaboration with other authors) on the topic of research methods and particularly in relation to the issues of quality in qualitative research.

In her early work alongside Egon Guba, Lincoln argued that there was a need to convince the dominant scientific community that there were merits to qualitative

(Continued)

(Continued)

research. A fundamental way of achieving this for naturalistic inquiry was to translate the quantitative quality markers into appropriately applicable qualitative criteria. They translated internal validity into *credibility*, external validity into *transferability* (*applicability*), reliability into *dependability*, and objectivity into *confirmability* (Lincoln and Guba, 1985). Lincoln and Guba proposed therefore that to establish the trustworthiness of a qualitative report the researcher must have credibility and applicability of findings, and the naturalistic inquirer must be mindful of the uniqueness of each local context. Guba and Lincoln (1989) added a fifth marker of *authenticity* in order to capture the truth value of multiple perspectives and illustrate the dependability of findings in broader contexts.

This early work is recognised as being influential in contemporary thinking about quality in qualitative research. Lincoln herself notes that this early work recognised that the usual requirements for scientific inquiry could not be met, but argued that it is important to be rigorous without the assumptions of science (Lincoln, 2010). While the notion of rigour is one borrowed from positivism for qualitative work, rigour is important in the application of methods and should be based on defensible reasoning that is plausible alongside some sense of reality known to the author and audience (Guba and Lincoln, 2005). An issue relating to validity which Guba and Lincoln caution against is the potential conflation of method and interpretation, as no singular method or collection of methods can lead to ultimate knowledge (Guba and Lincoln, 2005).

Despite their attempts to develop quality guidelines which are generally applicable to the qualitative paradigm, Guba and Lincoln point out the potential difficulties with a complete set of universal standards against which qualitative research can be measured because of the diversity of approaches (Guba and Lincoln, 2005). Nonetheless, while they recognise that different qualitative methodologies operate from different ontological and epistemological assumptions, they note that it is important not to completely reject the use of quality criteria. A pragmatic reason for this is that researchers who fail to conform to the conservative methodological powers operating are more likely to be denied resources (Cannella and Lincoln, 2004). Additionally, there is an ethical discourse created through the desire for the 'good' social researcher (Lincoln and Cannella, 2004), which is facilitated by a demand that researchers interrogate themselves in terms of how the research is shaped around contradictions, binaries and paradoxes that form their lives, referred to as 'reflexivity' (Guba and Lincoln, 2005). Thus, reflexivity is a process of critically reflecting on the self as a researcher (Guba and Lincoln, 1981).

An important aspect of reflexivity, and ultimately quality, is for a researcher to focus on producing their own high-quality work without resorting to dismissing the work of others. Lincoln acknowledges that discussions relating to quality criteria are not merely practical or theoretical, but often also political: 'Politics and complexity are embedded within research as a construct that generates power for some and can be used to discredit others' (Cannella and Lincoln, 2004: 168). In her more recent work Lincoln argued against researchers adopting oppositional identities and instead advocates that the qualitative community should be proud of the range of different work that has been generated (Lincoln, 2010).

The argument for developing a set of universal criteria for qualitative research has led to a proliferation of frameworks being developed; Spencer et al. (2003) identified 29 different ones, and obviously more have been created since then. A number of these rubrics unproblematically treated all qualitative research methodologies to some extent as homogeneous in the sense that they argued for holistic criteria that would span all approaches. Others, however, recognised the heterogeneity within the qualitative paradigm and sought to develop different criteria for different methods/methodologies. Nonetheless all frameworks were recognised to have a primary concern with identifying good practice in qualitative research (Spencer et al., 2003). From their review, therefore, Spencer et al. developed four overarching principles to guide quality, outlined in Table 2.1, noting that many writers prefer the notion of guiding principles as opposed to fixed standards.

Table 2.1   Overarching principles (Spencer et al., 2003)

Principle	Description
Contributory	To advance wider knowledge and understanding.
Defensible	The design of the research should include strategies which address the research question posed.
Rigorous	The research should be rigorous in conduct through a systematic and transparent collection, analysis and interpretation of data.
Credible	The claims made should be credible, with well-founded and plausible arguments that are related to the significance of the evidence generated.

The synthesising heuristic across these four overarching principles was that the research is professionally conducted in an ethical manner. An additional element added by Spencer et al. to this was that the relationship between the researcher and the researched should be accounted for and transparent in the reporting. The contentious nature of quality in qualitative research is, however, marked by the continued efforts to establish a gold standard of universal quality criteria with a definitive and accepted set of markers. This is evident in more recent attempts to establish a common language for assessments of quality. For example, eight markers were promoted by Tracy (2010) as an effort to unite and engage in dialogue with those involved in these debates. We outline these in Table 2.2.

Table 2.2   Eight universal markers of quality (Tracy, 2010)

Principle	Description
Worthy topic	The research should be relevant, timely, interesting, significant or evocative.
Rich rigour	The researcher should consider if there is enough data to support claims made and the findings should be rich and interesting.
Sincerity	Can be an end goal that is achieved through transparency, honesty and data auditing.
Credibility	Relates to the trustworthiness and plausibility of findings, achieved through thick description.
Resonance	The researcher's ability to meaningfully translate to audiences by engaging in practices that promote empathy. Resonance also refers to the transferability of findings.
Significant contribution	The importance of the study in extending knowledge or improving practice.
Ethics	That there are a number of practices that attend to the iterative process of ethics.
Meaningful coherence	The study accomplishes the stated purpose using methods that relate to relevant theory and paradigms and connect to the literature reviewed.

A common trend in the frameworks developed and arguments proposed is that qualitative research should be rigorous. However, what constitutes a rigorous study has been contested and debated (Caelli et al., 2003). Nevertheless, there are three quality markers which are generally agreed upon by qualitative researchers for promoting rigour: transparency, reflexivity and trustworthiness.

One important aspect of transparency involves giving an honest account of the research through a full description of what was done and an explanation and justification for all decisions (Spencer et al., 2003). Perhaps the most significant of these decisions relates to sampling adequacy. There should be transparency regarding sampling, and particularly claims of saturating data (Caelli et al., 2003); where saturation is an inappropriate measure of quality, the rationale for this should be made explicit (O'Reilly and Parker, 2013). It requires the researcher to carefully document all the steps with an assumption that comparison of the original findings can be used to reject, sustain or challenge the original interpretations (Armstrong et al., 1997). This relationship between the data and the claims made is typically demonstrated through the dissemination process by offering appropriate information for the audience to re-examine and assess the researcher's assertions and interpretations (Freeman et al., 2007). One way in which this transparency can be achieved in reporting data is through the use of verbatim quotations from research participants, and indeed this is a particularly common way of representing data (Corden and Sainsbury, 2006). Additionally, to ensure transparency, researchers need to make explicit their theoretical position and provide evidence for the congruence between their methodology and their methods (Caelli et al., 2003). Transparency can also be achieved by being clear about separating evidence from interpretation and ensuring reflexivity when reporting methods (Seale, 2004).

As well as transparency, the quality marker of reflexivity is considered by most qualitative researchers to be particularly important for ensuring quality. This is because the methods used unavoidably 'influence the objects of inquiry', and it is therefore essential that the researcher gives a clear account of both the process of data collection and analysis (Mays and Pope, 2000: 89). In other words, reflexivity requires the researcher to reflect on their own role in the research process and consider the ways in which they have impacted on a project from inception to dissemination (not that we are suggesting a linear process).

(e.g.) Qualitative researchers need to be mindful of how their own epistemological world-view both shapes and influences the research conducted. Additionally, personal characteristics such as status, ethnicity, age, gender and so on are known to have an impact on how participants respond in research settings. Reflexivity encapsulates the process of being self-aware of how these attributes influence participant responses.

Reflexivity has therefore become one of the key markers indicating the trustworthiness of a qualitative piece of research. This is a skill that most researchers need to cultivate in conducting qualitative work.

The notion of trustworthiness has been a core priority spanning all these debates about how to measure quality in qualitative work, which have evolved from concerns about how qualitative work can successfully compete with quantitative studies. This notion of trustworthiness was therefore promoted by early work, such as Lincoln and Guba (1985), as a way of illustrating the value of qualitative research. From these debates ostensibly it appears as though checklists for quality have become an inherent aspect of qualitative work despite concerns regarding the appropriateness of these measures. Potentially, however, 'if we succumb to the lure of "one size fits all" solutions we risk being in a situation where the tail (the checklist) is wagging the dog (the qualitative research)' (Barbour, 2001: 1115).

THE ARGUMENT OF ACCOUNTING FOR HETEROGENEITY OF QUALITATIVE APPROACHES

One solution to the problems posed by the general qualitative quality criteria argument is that each methodology should be judged against the specific quality criteria of that particular approach. A fundamental difficulty for developing appraisal criteria is that it has tended to treat the qualitative approach as unified at both the level of data collection and the level of methodology, which is clearly flawed (Dixon-Woods et al., 2004b). The qualitative approach, however, is a paradigm of fragmentation and has limited consensus regarding frameworks and methodological propositions and a wide range of techniques and theoretical traditions employed (Buchanan and Bryman, 2007). The heterogeneity argument thus emphasises the diverse nature of qualitative approaches and the need to acknowledge this formally in the quality criteria used to judge each study. The rationale for this argument is that there is greater within-group diversity in qualitative research than in quantitative, and the assessment of quality of these methods must account for this diversity (Meyrick, 2006).

One reason why it has no so far been possible to agree on universal criteria is the complexity of the debate, because qualitative research is neither monolithic nor static (Devers, 1999) and the epistemological scope of qualitative research is simply too broad for a single set of quality criteria (Sandelowski and Borroso, 2002). It is arguable that any generic criterion for quality would fail to adequately appreciate the wide range of methodologies that fall under the rubric of qualitative research and should therefore be evaluated against quality markers that are congruent with the epistemological origins (Caelli et al., 2003). Furthermore, the expansion, evolution and proliferation of qualitative approaches have extended the tensions (Whittemore et al., 2001).

Arguably the qualitative approach cannot be viewed as unified due to the fact that underpinning the methods used there is a fundamental diversity in philosophical, ideological, ethical and political assumptions (Moccia, 1988). While some advocates of universal markers have acknowledged the importance of recognising the diversity of ontological and epistemological research (Spencer et al., 2003), 'the continued failure to agree on universal criteria for judging quality in qualitative research is symptomatic of an inability to identify a coherent "qualitative" research paradigm' largely due to the fact that this notion of a homogeneous qualitative paradigm does not exist outside of textbooks (Rolfe, 2006: 308). This need for clarity regarding epistemology and ontology arose from the metaphysical paradigm during an era where qualitative research was competing for credibility in a quantitatively dominated scientific pursuit. This purist movement thus facilitated and advanced the status of qualitative research (Whittemore et al., 2001).

Problematically, authors often fluctuate between the philosophical and methodological meanings without being fully clear about which they are referring to and without specifying the relation between the two (Devers, 1999). Admittedly, this further complicates the process of judging the quality of that specific piece of research. Therefore research of high quality should ensure that the theoretical and epistemological position of the research is clearly stated in the study (Meyrick, 2006). This is particularly important because qualitative researchers acknowledge that we perceive the world from particular viewpoints, and in turn this world-view constrains the points of view that are possible (Seale, 1999). According to the heterogeneity argument, quality criteria can only be idiosyncratically applied (Caelli et al., 2003). Notably, researchers ought to resist demands for a fully explicit set of universal quality criteria as the nature of the research dictates that the criteria cannot operate in a way that is frequently assumed by those who demand them (Hammersley, 2007).

THE ARGUMENT THAT NO CRITERIA ARE NEEDED

Resisting demands for a full set of universal quality criteria has led to the argument that it is in fact inappropriate to develop criteria at all (Hammersley, 2007). One of the main pioneers of this argument was Smith (1990), who proposed that qualitative research is philosophically distinct from quantitative and rejected the need for associated quality criteria. Smith argued that the generation of criteria is based on an assumption that correct procedures can be followed; however, no epistemological privilege can be attached to specific procedures and therefore developing criteria is logically impossible. This argument hinges on what is meant by the concept of 'criterion' which by definition refers to observable and sufficiently explicit and concrete indices (Hammersley, 2007). These arguments have led to a call for the ending of 'criteriology' which is claimed to stifle the creative aspects of qualitative research (Schwandt, 1996) and eliminate the need for judgement (Hammersley, 2007). Extreme relativists argue that any criterion is a construct designed to account for a reality which does not exist, and therefore quality criteria as assessments are not only impossible but also irrelevant (Smith, 1984).

While these arguments have some sociological merit at a metaphysical level, in daily practice qualitative researchers are faced with the very real pragmatic issues of publishing and funding their work. It is obvious that policy-makers and commissioners need to have confidence in the quality of qualitative findings (Dixon-Woods et al., 2004b). Similarly reviewers of qualitative work have responsibility to assess that methodological practices are consistent with the tradition in which the work was conducted (Easterby-Smith et al., 2008). It is argued, therefore, that there is a need for criteria in some form to evaluate qualitative evidence in order to foster a willingness to fund and publish qualitative studies (Devers, 1999).

───────────────── Reflective space ─────────────────

There are strengths and limitations to all four of the arguments we have presented in this chapter about the potential application of quality markers in qualitative research. We recommend that you consolidate your thinking at this point by writing your own summary of the arguments and highlighting any areas for additional learning.

SUMMARY AND FINAL THOUGHTS

The modern emphasis on evidence-based practice has heavily influenced the funding and publishing of research. This has led to an imposition of standards for reporting research, and such top-down efforts to legislate scientific practice and mandate research design threaten the boundaries of what is regarded as science and may devalue qualitative work (Freeman et al., 2007). While efforts to dictate quality standards in the evidence-based movement have been well intentioned, we would argue that researchers themselves are better placed to suggest appropriate quality standards against which particular qualitative methodologies may be judged. One of the characteristic strengths of qualitative work is its ability to examine notions of truth and knowledge, objectivity and subjectivity, science and evidence (Freeman et al., 2007). The analytic skills required of qualitative researchers are not only in writing, critiquing and revising their proposals but also an ability to defend their work and review the work of others (Kuyper, 1991). Therefore the responsibility for scientific rigour lies with researchers themselves (Morse et al., 2002).

From synthesising the arguments it seems evident that there are some practical merits for researchers in adhering to a small number of core guiding quality principles in both designing and evaluating the quality of their work. Drawing upon the influential work of scholars such as Lincoln and the review of Spencer et al. (2003), we propose that these should be:

- Transparency (including auditability, trustworthiness, rigour, credibility)
- Reflexivity (being aware of the constructed nature of findings and impact of the researcher)
- Transferability (degree of relating to other contexts)
- Ethicality (risk and benefit assessment, significance of contribution, worthiness of topic)
- Integrity (epistemological congruence, authenticity, sampling adequacy)

While we suggest that these are useful guiding principles for those operating within the qualitative approach, we argue that it is essential that colleagues from each methodological framework explicate how these general principles might be applied in their specific context and the particular additional markers that are necessary to evaluate work using that methodological perspective. We therefore invite influential scholars from each discipline to put forward clear guidelines for commissioners, reviewers and less experienced researchers to use as a quality control mechanism in order to preserve and progress both the intrinsic and perceived value of their methodology. In doing so, experts in the field will helpfully initiate and set the standards for particular methodologies. This will redress the current top-down mandate and give control back to researchers themselves. In doing so there is potential to promote the usefulness of qualitative research and inform evidence-based practice in a way that accounts for the heterogeneity of the paradigm.

──────────── Case study and reflective questions ────────────

Lukas has been asked to conduct a review of an article submitted to a psychology journal. The journal is one that accepts research using both quantitative and qualitative research and has a wide readership. In his own research speciality Lukas has tended to favour using grounded theory as an approach that he feels best fits his epistemological perspective. The article submitted, however, uses interpretative phenomenological analysis (IPA) and Lukas has been asked to conduct a review based on his expertise related to the topic of the article.

Q: Are there any general qualitative criteria that apply to both grounded theory and IPA studies that Lukas could draw upon to inform his review?

Q: Do you think that he needs to take anything else into consideration when assessing the quality of the method and the interpretation of findings?

Suggestions for answering these questions are available at the end of the book.

FURTHER READING

Barbour, R. (2001) Checklists for improving rigour in qualitative research: A case of the tail wagging the dog? *British Medical Journal*, 322(7294): 1115–1117.

In this article Barbour considers the value of qualitative quality checklists and argues that their uncritical use can be counterproductive. The main argument presented is that reducing qualitative research to a list of technical procedures will make it overly prescriptive and as such there is a risk of compromising the unique contribution that qualitative research can make.

Guba, E. and Lincoln, Y. (1989) *Fourth Generation Evaluation*. Newbury Park, CA: Sage.

This is an interesting and useful text presented by two authors who have an extensive experience in qualitative methods and debates about quality. The book considers a range of problems that have been faced by qualitative researchers and shows the differences between positivist and constructivist paradigms alongside practical processes for evaluating research.

O'Reilly, M. and Parker, N. (2013) 'Unsatisfactory saturation': A critical exploration of the notion of saturated sample sizes in qualitative research. *Qualitative Research*, 13(2): 190–197.

This is a useful paper when considering the quality issue of sampling adequacy as it provides a critique of the taken-for-granted marker of saturation. It also provides some context for the debate by guiding the reader through different definitions of saturation and how it applies to qualitative research.

Seale, C. (2004) Quality in qualitative research, in C. Seale, G. Gobo, J. Gubrium and D. Silverman (eds), *Qualitative Research Practice*. London: Sage. pp. 409–419.

This is a very useful book chapter with a clear discussion of some of the key issues faced by qualitative researchers when considering the issue of quality in qualitative research.

Spencer, L., Ritchie, J., Lewis, J. and Dillon, L. (2003) *Quality in Qualitative Evaluation: A Framework for Assessing Research Evidence*. London: Government Chief Social Researcher's Office, Prime Minister's Strategy Unit. http://www.civilservice.gov.uk/wp-content/uploads/2011/09/a_quality_framework_tcm6-38740.pdf

This is a specific framework that was developed to promote effective evaluation of qualitative work and give criteria for the critical appraisal of qualitative research. It provides a discussion of some of the issues.

Tracy, S. (2010) Qualitative quality: Eight 'big-tent' criteria for excellent qualitative research. *Qualitative Inquiry*, 16(10): 837–851.

This is also a specific version of universal criteria for qualitative research which proposes a set of eight quality markers that link to the general quality terms that can be found in the literature.

THREE

Research ethics and researcher safety

CHAPTER CONTENTS

INTRODUCTION

As we have noted, it is fundamentally accepted that qualitative research is different from quantitative. It is perhaps therefore unsurprising that the way in which ethics is thought about and implemented within the qualitative approach is also different. In this chapter we present four core interrelated arguments that this difference invokes. First, we discuss the debates about the relevance and appropriateness of adopting ethical principles commonly considered in the quantitative approach. Second, we consider arguments about how qualitative protocols are treated by ethics committees and how tensions may be resolved. Third, we present and discuss arguments that the core ethical principles used in research may be and potentially ought to be operationalised differently in qualitative work. Finally, in relation to the implementation of these principles, we explicate the arguments existing regarding the potential implications for the safety of researchers.

ETHICAL FRAMEWORKS

Ethics is associated with intra-professional specialities, and each of these disciplines has developed ethical guidelines to inform the practice and research of most major professional organisations (Hoagwood et al., 1996). These guidelines tend to be grounded in one of three major approaches to ethics emerging from philosophy, as noted by Brinkman and Kvale (2005):

- Consequentialism – deriving from utilitarian thought, which argues that ethics should be based on the actual and potential consequences of actions.
- Deontology (also known as principlism) – deriving from Kantian thought, which offers four guiding principles for researchers to follow.
- Virtue ethics – deriving from Aristotle, which engages in the phenomenological task of describing the moral particulars of persons, actions and communities. This puts emphasis on the moral character of the researcher.

Although there are philosophical arguments that these are discrete ethical approaches, there is usually an experience in practice of some integration of all three. This means that it is expected that researchers will operate under their own moral framework (virtue) and pay attention to the possible outcomes and consequences of their actions (consequentialism); however, most of the official guidelines in many disciplines follow the deontological approach. This requires they utilise the key principles of respecting autonomy, advocating justice, and ensuring beneficence and non-maleficence (Beauchamp and Childress, 2001).

THE EPOCH OF ETHICAL ENLIGHTENMENT

While the history and conceptualisation of ethics and morality lies mostly with philosophy, the practical application of ethical principles in research has been heavily influenced by health and medicine. Although most Western researchers from a wide range of disciplines would now consider the submission of their research protocol to an ethics committee fairly standard procedure, it is only fairly recently that universities began to develop governance systems to review research applications (Hunter, 2008). This has been influenced by the inclusion of social research projects in the field of health among those to be reviewed by ethics committees, which is now a mandatory requirement (Cave and Holm, 2002).

Debates about ethical guidelines for health research ostensibly date back to the Nuremburg trials, but evidence suggests that the emergence of ethical research practice actually pre-dates this time (Ashcroft, 2003). This is evidenced through a number of ethical scandals which happened previously (European Commission, 2010). Nonetheless, the scandal of the Nazi experiments occurring during the Second World War precipitated the development of three major documents: the *Belmont Report*, the Declaration of Helsinki and the Nuremberg Code. The development of the Nuremberg Code and a heightened awareness of the Nazi experiments created an expectation that medical researchers would conform to the guidelines (Hunter, 2008), but neither the Nuremberg Code nor the subsequent Declaration of Helsinki had much immediate effect on the ways research was regulated in Britain (Brierley and Larcher, 2010). It was following a public crisis of confidence in the 1960s that medical research became subject to particular ethical scrutiny (Hazelgrove, 2002). During this period of time ethics committees were being set up in America in response to the requirements of American funding bodies (Hedgecoe, 2009).

The lessons learned from historical events heightened both public awareness and researcher concern regarding the potential risks to research participants. Although research was oriented to providing evidence for the benefit of others, a tension was created as researchers also became conscious of their obligation to protect participants from harm (Orb et al., 2001). It is this combination of the micro-ethics of protecting individual participants and the macro-ethics of producing knowledge beneficial to the wider culture that has become central to ethical debates and illuminations of risk (Brinkman and Kvale, 2005). This concept of risk is thus central to the organisation of the social world (Dickson-Swift et al., 2008), and it is argued that we now live in a 'risk society' (Beck, 1992) where everyone is thought of as a potential victim (Dingwall, 1999). In research terms the notion of risk relates to a potential, but not fully known, harm (Shaw and Barrett, 2006). While guidelines for protecting participants from harm and mitigating against risk were originally intended for biomedical research (Gunsalus et al., 2007), risk also became a central component of research ethics in social science research (Richards and Schwartz, 2002).

THE VALUE AND UNIQUENESS OF ETHICS IN QUALITATIVE RESEARCH

Throughout the development over the last two decades of mandatory ethical guidelines there has been an emphasis on research using quantitative approaches. The primary concerns of qualitative researchers in response to this emphasis have been to question the inappropriateness of judging qualitative work against quantitative standards, and to complain that committees were made up of predominantly quantitative advocates with limited understanding of qualitative issues.

While the fundamental ethical principles are shared between approaches, the ways in which they are accounted for and applied do differ. This has led to a critical discussion about how ethics should be uniquely viewed in qualitative research. Due to there being virtually no data on complaints from participants coming to harm in qualitative research little is known about the risk it invokes (Morse et al., 2008). Notably, within the qualitative community, differences of opinion exist within these debates regarding the nature and content of the ethicality of qualitative work.

One argument that has been advocated by some members of the qualitative community is that qualitative research is less risky than quantitative. For example, Kvale (2008) recognised that within this community there has been a tendency to display the nature of the inquiry as inherently ethical, or, at the very least, more ethical than quantitative research. This viewpoint is known as 'qualitative ethicism' (Brinkman and Kvale, 2008) and has led to some objections to undif-ferentiated ethical review by social scientists who argue that the levels of risk are not the same as in quantitative research (Hedgecoe, 2008). These arguments have contributed to the popular and widely accepted view that qualitative methods pose fewer risks to participants (Ensign, 2003). While this may be the case to some extent, qualitative ethicism does not suggest that no harm can be caused by quali-tative research, and thus social scientists may naively overlook the potential harms that can occur from their work (Hedgecoe, 2008). There are therefore dangers in adopting this perspective as it can lead to an uncritical romanticising of qualita-tive research and can direct attention away from meaningful ethical discussions in relation to this approach (Kvale, 2008). Thus there are several differences between quantitative and qualitative research that impact on ethical implementation; these are illustrated in Table 3.1.

At a simplistic level a key difference for ethics between quantitative and qualita-tive approaches relates to breadth versus depth of information about participants'

Table 3.1 Characteristics of qualitative ethics

Uniqueness	Description
Depth	Qualitative research requires depth of individual participants' information and experience at both data collection and analysis.
Researcher involvement	The researcher is inevitably embedded in the research process and is an integral mechanism for data collection.
Iterative process	The qualitative research process is iterative rather than linear and evolves throughout, making its impact on participants and researchers difficult to predict.
Visibility	There is greater emphasis on participant anonymity in qualitative research due to higher risks of identification.
Data management	There is a particular onus within qualitative research on ethical management of disseminating large amounts of personal data.

experiences. Those practising qualitative research favour depth throughout the research process and therefore have some level of prolonged contact with participants, and also they elicit more personal and potentially sensitive information. However, the 'sensitivity' of topics covered may not be immediately apparent at the start of the project but may emerge as culturally and contextually dependent (McCosker et al., 2001). Thus the potentially intrusive nature of the work raises special ethical considerations (Hewitt, 2007). In light of this, some argue that qualitative researchers have ethical obligations to ensure they provide a sound justification for the research question and tools of investigation which should extend beyond simple curiosity (Thorne and Darbyshire, 2005). This becomes particularly important when investigating the experiences of more vulnerable groups (Flewitt, 2005) as there is potential for additional stigmatisation, pathologisation, misrepresentation, and/or the invitation of voyeurism (James and Platzer, 1999). Although there may be an unhealthy voyeuristic interest from the wider community in marginalised or minority groups, some researchers may also feel guilty about the more voyeuristic aspects of conducting qualitative research (Malacrida, 2007).

A second fundamental difference for qualitative research is the role and impact of the researcher in the process. Unique to qualitative research is the premise that the researcher acts as the research instrument, and neutral, unbiased administration of data collection tools is not possible (Connolly and Reilly, 2007). This has a number of specific ethical implications that do not arise in the same way in quantitative research, such as issues of power.

> (e.g.) There are arguably issues of power inherent in the qualitative relationship, which could be based on characteristics such as status, gender or age. From an ethical point of view it is important that researchers be cognisant of the interactional power dynamic between themselves and the participants, which may result in the inadvertent coercion of cooperation.

The necessity to build rapport in order to collect high-quality data may encourage participants to open up more than they feel comfortable with, and also may create an environment from which they find it difficult to withdraw (Duncan et al., 2009). Furthermore, this closeness and relationship building may have detrimental effects on the researcher due to the emotional impact, and this is an issue which is important for ethical consideration. It is important, therefore, that the researcher remains aware of these issues and takes steps to counter any possible harms arising. One way that researchers have recently tried to bring power dynamics more into equilibrium is to do research 'with' rather than 'on' populations (see, for example, Doucet and Mauthner, 2006; O'Reilly et al., 2013).

A third core difference relates to the iterative and unpredictable nature of qualitative research. Qualitative research is not by nature a linear and predictable process as the research evolves throughout the circular stages. Research questions may be modified and recruitment may be extended, alongside developments in data collection and analysis. This means that informed consent should be constantly negotiated and ethics itself needs to be treated as an iterative aspect of the work. Possible changes to open questions and changes in the consent process have the potential to increase the risks to which the participants are exposed (Hadjistavropoulos and Smythe, 2001). This evolutionary quality of qualitative research means that intended research agendas may veer away from what was anticipated. Risk assessments in qualitative research must therefore be reflexive and iterative (Morse et al., 2008).

A fourth concern in qualitative research ethics is the increased visibility of participants, not only literally in terms of the presence of audio or video recordings, but also indirectly in terms of the use of direct quotations in dissemination practice. This raises three issues for qualitative researchers. First, there is the potential issue of data protection, ensuring that the 'live' recordings are kept safe. Second, there is a greater risk of deductive disclosure of participants' identity which is heightened by the use of direct quotations. Third, there are debates about empowerment and the use of real identities of participants.

> (e.g.) Some participants value the importance of retaining utter anonymity, and therefore keeping recordings of data stored securely and rigorous anonymisation of transcripts, including potentially identifiable features, is essential. However, for some participants the possibility of using their real names in transcripts offers a welcome opportunity for sharing their stories openly (see Giordano et al., 2007).

A final issue for qualitative research ethics relates to data management and the ethics of dissemination. Although the ethicality of appropriate dissemination of participant information in quantitative research is important, due to the depth and volume of personal information collected in qualitative research there is a greater ethical obligation to appropriately disseminate data collected. There is an onus on the researcher not to collect narratives from participants from personal curiosity, but with the intention of using the material in ways consistent with ethical practice for the benefit of the wider society. While there is always a pressure on qualitative researchers to collect sufficient data to ensure credibility of the claims made, equally there is an ethical constraint not to gather more data than is necessary.

It is clear, therefore, that there are several ethical issues that are either unique to qualitative research or more significant in this type of work, and several scholars have contributed to this issue. Among them is Janice Morse, whose contribution we outline in Box 3.1.

influential **voices**

——— Box 3.1 The uniqueness of qualitative ethics ———

Janice Morse

Janice Morse* is a professor and presidential-endowed chair at the University of Utah College of Nursing, and professor emeritus at the University of Alberta, Canada. She has written extensively on issues pertinent to qualitative methodology, including qualitative research ethics.

The notion of risk in qualitative research is contentious, and this has broader implications for the theoretical discussion and practical implementation of ethics. Morse (2007) argued against the idea that qualitative research is inherently safer than medical drug trials just because it is not invasive physically, as there are ethical considerations that need to be accounted for when undertaking qualitative work. In relation to this, Morse (2001) acknowledged that some approaches and methods within the qualitative paradigm may present more potential dangers than others. She argues, however, that it is not inherently harmful, and that, with due consideration and reflexive awareness, quality ethical research can be produced. In particular, qualitative research necessitates carefully developed informed consent procedures and measures to ensure anonymity/confidentiality so as to protect and safeguard participants (Morse, 2001). Nonetheless, one of the risks of eliciting detailed personal information from participants is that even where confidentiality has been assured there may still be situations where the researcher is legally obligated to breach this ethic, which may have social, financial, legal or political consequences (Corbin and Morse, 2003).

A particular risk for those practising qualitative research is emotional, as the discussion of sensitive topics may lead participants to become distressed as they narrate events (Corbin and Morse, 2003). Participants are free to divulge their innermost emotional lives should they wish to, and some methods provide an emotional space for participants to relive the experiences that they are narrating (McIntosh and Morse, 2009). From her own perspective, Morse has written extensively using the grounded theory approach, and the method of interviewing. Morse notes that when interviewing people about sensitive topics the researcher should express caution in relation to participants being asked to share intimate aspects of their lives (Corbin and Morse, 2003). However, subjectivity and emotion are the hallmarks of good qualitative inquiry (Morse et al., 2008), and although research may provide the emotional context for the distress to occur, it is not necessarily the cause of it (McIntosh and Morse, 2009).

While it is essential that the ethics of qualitative research remains open to scrutiny, particularly when involving vulnerable or disempowered participants (Morse, 2007), Morse (2003) argues that it is somewhat problematic that evidence suggests

(Continued)

(Continued)

that some ethics committees have a limited understanding and knowledge of the methodological practice and epistemological assumptions of qualitative research. This has implications for qualitative researchers submitting proposals for ethical review. A common concern for ethics committees has been that participation may cause re-traumatisation, but this is not necessarily the case (McIntosh and Morse, 2009). Indeed, McIntosh and Morse noted that in the retelling of the experience, the emotional distress is integral, signalling the worthiness of the research, and this does not necessarily cause harm, as distress can coexist with beneficence and can feel therapeutic rather than harmful. Reviewers of ethics thus need to be aware that when qualitative research is carried out with sensitivity and care it can provide opportunities for reciprocity, and therefore any risks may be mitigated by the benefits of taking part (Corbin and Morse, 2003). While it can be difficult for ethics committees to judge the level of competency of researchers to respond to distress, if researchers are prepared and knowledgeable of their ethical responsibilities and remain aware of the changing emotional manifestations they can take steps to debrief participants and take care of them emotionally (Morse et al., 2008).

*We thank Professor Morse for taking the time to read an earlier draft of this chapter.

ETHICS COMMITTEES AND QUALITATIVE RESEARCH ETHICS

As discussed earlier in this chapter, formal ethics committees are a relatively recent development (Alderson, 2007). This review process provides an important framework for the assessment of risk of harm that may be introduced by research, and thus the role of the ethics committee is to weigh risk against benefit (Shaw and Barrett, 2006). Typically ethics committees are made up of individuals with a range of experience, knowledge and expertise whose role is to consider the research proposal in terms of the potential risks involved (Alderson, 2007). This risk assessment tends to be underpinned by the precautionary principle, which advocates a largely risk-averse position (McGuiness, 2008). Thus the work of an ethics committee is to provide sound research governance to protect participants from dubious research (Elliott, 2004). This position has been criticised as being overly paternalistic in its attempts to protect the interests of vulnerable groups (Smith, 2008). Unfortunately this rhetorical tactic, of assuming that researchers are potentially inherently unethical, positions the researcher and participant as binaries in terms of the vulnerable participant needing protection from the theoretically unscrupulous researcher (Halse and Honey, 2007).

In practice, ethics committees have considerable power to refuse approval and put an end to any given project (McGuiness, 2008). The practices of ethical review, therefore, have come under criticism (Robinson et al., 2007), with particular complaints relating to apparent capriciousness and inconsistency (Lux et al., 2000), and ethics committees/boards have been accused of impeding or hindering important research (Academy of Medical Sciences, 2011). Specifically problematic for qualitative researchers is that some committees seem to have a limited knowledge or understanding of the methodological practices and epistemological assumptions of qualitative research (Morse, 2003). Because of the iterative, cyclical and inductive nature of qualitative research, researchers are often unable to provide the level of detail about likely outcomes that is desired by ethics committees (Morse et al., 2008). In addition, the static formalised guidelines that guide decisions may render invisible the inherent nature of tensions, fluidity and uncertainty of ethical issues that can arise in qualitative research (Denzin and Giardina, 2007). Thus it is risky to assume an ethical universalism which ignores the complexity of qualitative social research (Miller and Boulton, 2007). It is argued, therefore, that ethics committees in the social sciences need more flexible ethical standards which incorporate practical judgement (Hornsby-Smith, 1993) and an ethical perspective which includes context and emotion (McIntosh and Morse, 2009). Nonetheless, while this lack of familiarity with qualitative methods is acknowledged by committee members, there is often an attempt to address it by the presence of an expert member on any given panel (Hedgecoe, 2008).

One of the difficulties for ethics committees is that qualitative research tends to evolve as the project unfolds, making it difficult to predict the exact trajectory. Nonetheless, many qualitative projects are granted approval and it is recognised that any significant changes in the life of the project can be revisited with the committee (Alderson, 2007). That said, a large number are also rejected, particularly when researching sensitive or emotionally charged topics (Lincoln and Tierney, 2004). There has therefore been some objection from social scientists who disagree with the process of ethical review for social research. Due to changes in funding body policies, social researchers are now required to undergo ethical review, which has led to complaints from the social science community that ethical review is unable to address moral philosophy questions and does little to improve the quality of qualitative research (Hammersley, 2009). Arguably, however, these criticisms have misrepresented what ethics committees do in terms of how they treat qualitative research and have distorted our understanding of how ethical review impacts on research relationships (Hedgecoe, 2008). Researchers themselves must be accountable for their research practices and engage with committees in order to move forward (Balen et al., 2006), as well-intentioned researchers may not be best placed to judge the ethicality or benefits of their own proposed research (Hedgecoe, 2008). Some of these debates are outlined in the work of Mary Dixon-Woods which is summarised in Box 3.2.

influential **voices**

─────────── Box 3.2   Issues relating to ethical review ───────────

Mary Dixon-Woods

Mary Dixon-Woods* is a professor of medical sociology in the Department of Health Sciences at the University of Leicester. She has written extensively in the area of research ethics, with a particular focus on the role and function of research ethics committees operating within the area of health research. Dixon-Woods has achieved this by analysing communication (in the form of letters) between committees and research teams, and by interviewing researchers to ascertain their views.

One area that Dixon-Woods has particularly illuminated is the process of communication between ethics committees and the research community regarding the ethicality of their proposed works. In particular, Dixon-Woods et al. (2007) argue that the analysis of ethics committee letters can offer important insights into how they operate, and it is through these texts that they establish and position their authority (O'Reilly et al., 2009a). They argue that the main important social functions that these letters perform are to:

1. Define what is ethical practice through the committee and convey authority.
2. Provide an account of their work.
3. Specify the nature of the relationship between the committee and the applicant, putting the applicant in a supplicant role.

The outcome of the ethical review process is that committees will issue an opinion that is either favourable, provisional or unfavourable (Angell et al., 2010). Often these letters outline changes that are required relating to issues of potential physical/emotional risk, informed consent procedures, confidentiality and recruitment processes (Angell et al., 2007).

Inevitably the process of judging the ethicality of a study is not unambiguous and judgements about morality may be contestable (Dixon-Woods and Ashcroft, 2008). There are several good examples of this ambiguity, and Dixon-Woods highlights two of these as being research with children and research with managers/staff of public services. The issue here is risk. In health research there has been a strong focus on the potential harm and risk that children may be exposed to as research participants (Dixon-Woods et al., 2006b), with ethics committees emphasising the process of informed consent and the language used to communicate research to children (Angell et al., 2010). In research with public services employees there is a risk that the process of data collection may cause them undue stress or anxiety and they may feel that the data threaten their interests (Dixon-Woods and Bosk, 2011).

It is perhaps unsurprising therefore that over the last few decades, regulation of research has significantly tightened within a community that previously enjoyed relative autonomy (Dixon-Woods and Ashcroft, 2008). Although ethics committees

are accountable for their decisions and the process of arriving at these decisions, being formally accountable through their institutional structure (O'Reilly
et al., 2009b), some researchers still expressed dissatisfaction with the burdens of
regulation and governance (Dixon-Woods and Ashcroft, 2008). This has led some
in the research community to express concern over what constitutes ethicality and
morality, which arguably results in unnecessary bureaucracy and the imposition
of 'sameness'. However, despite some difficulties and debates, participants themselves have viewed ethics committees as a form of reassurance as they tend to
make assumptions that research is regulated (Dixon-Woods and Tarrant, 2009)
and ethical review is essential to secure moral licence (Dixon-Woods and Ashcroft,
2008). It is important nonetheless to recognise that to be effective the ethics committee must act as 'an honest broker, not as defender of procedure' (Dixon-Woods
and Bosk, 2011: 270).

*We thank Professor Dixon-Woods for taking the time to read an earlier draft of this
chapter.

MARKERS OF ETHICAL PRACTICE IN QUALITATIVE RESEARCH

We have noted that qualitative research is potentially ethically risky, although
not inherently so, and that the ethics of this approach deserves consideration. We
have highlighted that qualitative research, while adhering to the general ethical
principles guiding all research, does have some inherent differences from quantitative research that require attention, and that the ethically practising researcher
has the potential to produce very worthy research. It has been demonstrated that
ethics committees are grappling with these differences and that a greater understanding may be necessary. Broadly, the concerns for qualitative research ethics
relate to four general areas: informed consent; anonymity and confidentiality;
power, coercion and responsibility; and the problem of positionality.

Informed consent

The aim of informed consent is to empower participants to enable them to make
decisions and choices that promote their self-interest (Cox-White and Zimbelman,
1998). For a person to be able to give this consent freely and behave autono-
mously, they should be able to weigh up the information and make a decision
(Steinke, 2004). Thus, providing informed consent is the explicit agreement by the
participant to actually take part in the research (Tee and Lathlean, 2004). However,
because of the nature of risk, researchers are inevitably only able to offer participants reasonable, not absolute, protection (Shaw and Barrett, 2006).

Informed consent is a communication process and is more than simply gaining a written signature (Field and Behrman, 2004). In other words, consent should not be viewed as a one-off isolated event but reviewed throughout the process and integrated within the professional relationship (Barnett, 2007). One aspect of qualitative research is typically the proximity of the researcher and the development of a research relationship with the participant. This may potentially inhibit the participant from exercising their right to withdraw from the study, which is an essential aspect of giving informed consent (Mishna et al., 2004). This is particularly important in qualitative research because of the fact that the precise course of the research is unpredictable (Flewitt, 2005), partially due to the fact that it is not possible to specify an exhaustive list of all possible questions (Pope and Mays, 1995). We argue therefore that informed consent should be considered to be an iterative process which it is essential to revisit throughout the research (O'Reilly et al., 2011).

The consent process therefore needs to be designed adequately to accommodate individuals from various social, educational and cultural backgrounds (Field and Behrman, 2004) and of different ages and intellectual capabilities. In addition, it is essential to account for the issue of capacity to express autonomy in this process, as for consent to be valid the individual must have capacity and be free from inducement (Tee and Lathlean, 2004). The issue of capacity for vulnerable groups such as those with mental health difficulties and children is a legal matter. For example, children do not have the legal capacity to provide consent and therefore parental permission is required (Field and Behrman, 2004), and this can complicate the process if the children do not wish to have their parents involved or have no contact with parents (such as homeless children). In these cases a legal guardian, social worker or otherwise involved adult may need to be a gatekeeper. Informed consent in qualitative research therefore needs to be multi-factorial in its design and process in order to take all of these specific issues into account.

(e.g.) Loyd (2013) undertook an interpretative study using interview, observation, documentation and survey methods with children diagnosed with autism. Although the purpose of the research was to identify outcomes for these young people from participation in drama education, the informed consent process caused some challenges and was necessarily iterative and revisited at several stages.

Anonymity and confidentiality

Importantly, anonymity and confidentiality refer to different ethical elements. Confidentiality refers to the management of private information, whereas anonymity refers to the removal of identifying information about the participants (Tilley and Woodthorpe, 2011). Nonetheless, anonymity is one of the mechanisms through which confidentiality is realised (Wiles et al., 2008). One of the characteristics of qualitative research is the collection of a significant volume of personal information about participants (Richards and Schwartz, 2002). The way such data are disseminated typically involves the use of verbatim quotations from participants (Hadjistavropoulos and Smythe, 2001), and this may extend the risk of identification. Therefore it is important that participants are informed about how results will be published, including how quotations will be represented (Orb et al., 2001), and note that because of this, absolute confidentiality cannot be guaranteed (Robinson, 1991).

A particular risk in qualitative research is that of deductive disclosure (Tilley and Woodthorpe, 2011). Deductive disclosure refers to the possibility of a confidentiality breach in the sense that the rich detail in the dissemination may be recognised by other people known to those participants (Sieber, 1992). This is because transcription often contains multiple clues regarding the identity of the participant even after the process of anonymisation (Richards and Schwartz, 2002). For example, qualitative researchers have noted an underestimation of the extent to which individuals may be able to identify other participants when from the same community (Stein, 2010), which may result in sanctions, prejudice, stigma or reprisals (Kylmä et al., 1999). The increasingly prolific use of the internet as a medium for dissemination further exacerbates the potential risk of deductive disclosure as research publications are more readily available to a wider population (Tilley and Woodthorpe, 2011).

Qualitative researchers rely on providing rich descriptions and narratives which make the research vulnerable to deductive disclosure. The challenge, therefore, is to maintain confidentiality while providing rich detailed accounts of social life (Kaiser, 2009). If characteristics are changed too much it may blunt the power of the narrative (Stein, 2010), and the removal of identifying features runs the risk that the meanings of the stories may be altered (Kaiser, 2009). In addition to deductive disclosure is the risk of forced disclosure. While researchers do assure participants of confidentiality, there are cases where political or legal pressure means that researchers are required to breach this agreement. See Box 3.3 for a contemporary example.

Box 3.3   Breaching confidentiality: The Irish Republican Army study

Between 2001 and 2006 academics from Boston College conducted research interviews with members of the Irish Republican Army (IRA). Those individuals who were interviewed were assured that their identities would be kept confidential (Zezima, 2011). Recently, however, a US appeals court mandated that the College must hand over some of the interviews (Giglio, 2012). The retribution from the release of these

(Continued)

(Continued)

research interviews is, however, potentially damaging to those who participated, and the College appealed against the decision, fighting to maintain the confidentiality of the research participants. The case has been closely watched by academics, journalists and historians who are fearful of the long-term consequences for the world of research if the breach of confidentiality is forced by the court (Zezima, 2011), and indeed a number of arrests have been made, including that of Gerry Adams (Arsenault et al., 2014).

In addition, research has shown that some participants do not desire anonymity (Bass and Davis, 2002) and thus we should question the assumption that all participants do (Corden and Sainsbury, 2006). Some argue that just because participants have the right to anonymity, researchers should not necessarily impose it: if participants choose to identify themselves then this is their right (Kelly, 2009). Participants in qualitative research are active agents, and thus there is a case for allowing them to make choices on such ethical matters (Giordano et al., 2007). Despite these debates, anonymity is still and arguably should be the default position (Kelly, 2009).

Power, coercion and responsibility

Researchers often inhabit professional roles in addition to that of researcher, which have their own specific ethical frameworks. While there may be overlap between the ethical guidelines for these different roles, some ethical principles may come into conflict and these differences need to be acknowledged and recognised. The most common area of research where the ethical guidelines of different professional roles may conflict is in the area of health research. While health professionals are concerned with pursuing the client's best interests, researchers may be more concerned with issues of scientific integrity (Hart and Crawford-Wright, 1999). The professional background of the researcher also impacts on the participant, in that participants respond differently to researchers depending on their perception of the role of such individuals (Richards and Emslie, 2000). Richards and Emslie found that when the researcher was introduced as sociologist/researcher rather than doctor, participants were more open and talkative and less likely to seek medical opinions. Therefore the separation of research and clinical roles can be challenging (Attkisson et al., 1996; Johnson and Macleod Clark, 2003). While power and role are important considerations in health research, the role of the researcher is also an important feature of social research.

(e.g.) An individual inhabiting the dual role of probation officer and researcher may particularly benefit from considering the ethical implications of being known to the participants in both roles. In this situation the possibility of unintentional coercion due to the inherent power differential may unduly influence the participants' engagement with the study.

Power is not inherent in people, and it is not a fixed concept, but resides in the research process (Christensen, 2004). In research terms, however, it is typically assumed that the researcher holds the power (Brinkman and Kvale, 2005), with the risk of coercing or exploiting individuals that this entails (Orb et al., 2001). However, participants do have power, and this lies with their consent to participate and their engagement in the process (Etherington, 2001). However, it may still not be possible for researchers to achieve completely balanced power relations (Aluwihare-Samaranayake, 2012), particularly as qualitative research is often conducted with vulnerable populations in order to accumulate knowledge about their lives and experiences (Ensign, 2003). There is an ethical risk that participants may respond to qualitative questions that they would prefer not to answer as they may feel under some obligation, or may lack the assertiveness to withdraw (Duncan et al., 2009). The onus of responsibility therefore rests with the researcher to be sensitive to the impact of questioning. They should bear in mind that extensive questioning in qualitative research may leave the participant experiencing emotional stress (Hadjistavropoulos and Smythe, 2001). Researchers have a moral obligation in these circumstances to refer the participants to sources of support such as counselling (Orb et al., 2001).

Positionality

One of the characteristics of qualitative research is its iterative and unfolding nature. Inevitably, therefore, as the research progresses there are likely to be countless ethical dilemmas which arise, requiring the researcher to maintain an ethically reflective position (Flewitt, 2005). Part of the process of this reflexivity is to consider the nature of the relationship between the researcher and participant, referred to as 'positionality'. The focus of qualitative research is on exploring, examining and describing people, and inherent within this is the relationship between the researcher and researched (Orb et al., 2001). The ethically reflexive researcher will take into account the cultural context of the research (Brinkman and Kvale, 2005) and be sensitive to language and cultural factors (Liamputtong, 2007).

Qualitative researchers engage with their participants and immerse themselves in the participants' narratives (Fossey et al., 2002). There is therefore a potential risk embedded in this intimacy, which may take the guise of mutuality (Sinding and Aronson, 2003). Establishing relationships may encourage participants to disclose information and trust the researcher (Orb et al., 2001). An important boundary for researchers is that of differentiating friendship from the research relationship (Dixon-Woods et al., 2006b). Indeed, there is a risk in qualitative research of 'faking friendships' (Duncombe and Jessop, 2002). Qualitative research is likely to require the engagement of the personal and sometimes distressing details of individuals' lives, and this can place researchers in an ambiguous relationship with their participants (Warr, 2004). For some the inclusion of emotions allows a richer and deeper analysis of the data (Blakely, 2007), but for others it is argued that there should be a balance between objectivity and sensitivity (Strauss and Corbin, 1998). However, in practice, researchers often find it difficult to maintain an objective position in relation to their participants (Malacrida, 2007), and where researchers have developed close working relationships they may have misgivings about the ending of such relationships, particularly when a longer time-frame is involved (Dixon-Woods et al., 2006b).

RESEARCHER SAFETY

Researcher safety is a pertinent issue for all research but is of particular importance for those practising qualitative methods. This is because qualitative research by nature can impose different types of risk on the safety of researchers. First, qualitative researchers usually have a closer proximity to their participants due to the data collection methods used, and this may be upsetting (Fincham et al., 2008). Second, the nature of qualitative research is to explore participants' experiences in depth, often over a long period of time (Bloor et al., 2010), which can create a cumulative impact on the researcher (Warr, 2004). This leads to a greater risk of burnout for the researcher, although it impacts on people in different ways (Coles and Mudlay, 2010). Third, qualitative research requires an immersion of the researcher in the data, often involving repeated listening to data and reading of transcripts. This repeated exposure to the distressing narratives increases the intensity of the experience (Woodby et al., 2011). In addition, qualitative research data collection often takes place in the field, frequently in participants' own homes, and the risk of physical threat to the researcher is potentially higher than in quantitative data collection processes. The evolutionary nature of qualitative work thus means that while some risk can be predicted at the outset and thus mitigated, there are usually unanticipated events and reactions that occur during the process that can be planned for (Bloor et al., 2007).

Despite the importance of researcher safety, historically risk in research has been limited to an examination of risk to participants (Dickson-Swift et al., 2008). The safety of the researchers is often barely considered by ethics committees (Lee-Treweek and Linkogle, 2000), and current ethical guidelines do not fully take into account the emotional risks experienced by qualitative researchers (Aluwihare-Samaranayake, 2012). This is hindered further by the limited literature on the management of risks to researchers (Bloor et al., 2007). However, the importance of researcher safety should not be underestimated and we therefore consider both the emotional and physical threats to safety that may be encountered.

> In addition to the greater propensity for extracting an emotional toll on researchers, qualitative research also has greater physical safety risks as it is often conducted outside of controlled, 'safe' institutional settings.
>
> (Ensign, 2003: 48)

Emotional risks

As qualitative research requires the development of close relationships with participants there is a greater possibility of emotional impact on the researcher (Ensign, 2003). The emotional experiences of the researcher thus can range from the mildly uncomfortable to the personally disturbing or traumatic and may affect them long after data collection is concluded (Hubbard et al., 2001). Irrespective of the content of the participants' narratives, the labour-intensive, personally demanding process of qualitative data collection can be stressful for researchers (Johnson and Macleod Clark, 2003). Data collection can be very demanding, and unstructured interactive interviews in particular can be exhausting to conduct (Corbin and Morse, 2003). In addition, the requirements of confidentiality limit the opportunities for offloading stress (Johnson and Macleod Clark, 2003) and the stress experienced can lead to increased emotional impact.

e.g. Dickson-Swift et al. (2007) interviewed qualitative researchers to investigate what issues arose during the course of the research process. They found that researchers did experience emotional impact, related to rapport development and listening to participants' stories; they experienced guilt and vulnerability and found leaving the research relationship challenging; and ultimately sometimes they felt exhausted by the process.

Of particular relevance for qualitative research is the often sensitive or emotional nature of participants' narratives. Hearing such emotional and sensitive information can be distressing for researchers, leaving them feeling helpless or hopeless (James and Platzer, 1999). Even just reading the transcripts has been found to be emotional for researchers (McCosker et al., 2001). Often research with vulnerable or marginalised participants produces data which are emotional in content, and listening to these narratives can be akin to witnessing (Malacrida, 2007). The impact of listening to these traumatic stories can therefore lead to vicarious traumatisation (Etherington, 2007). Over a period of time the gradual accumulation of emotion that this creates can lead to 'researcher saturation', which is a form of emotional overload characterised by distress, headaches and anxiety (Wray et al., 2007).

Physical risks

The literature discussing physical threats to researchers is limited (Paterson et al., 1999) as researchers are usually less concerned with physical risk than with emotional risk (Sampson et al., 2008). Often physical risk only becomes an issue for researchers when someone in their institution is confronted with a threatening event (Paterson et al., 1999). A distinction has been made, therefore, between ambient and situational danger (Lee, 1995). According to Lee, ambient dangers are those that are inherent in a setting and thus can be anticipated, whereas situational dangers are those that are evoked by the presence of the researcher and cannot be predicted. This may lead to researchers finding themselves in risky situations that have not been planned for (Dickson-Swift et al., 2008). While physical risk is rare, there have been instances plotted throughout history. Much of our evidence of these threats, however, is anecdotal (Bloor et al., 2007), with empirical reports emerging only recently (see Parker and O'Reilly, 2013).

―――――――――――――――― Reflective space ――――――――――――――――

In your own research practice consider proportionally how much attention you pay to your own emotional safety compared to your physical safety. Think about what measures you currently take to ensure your safety and whether there are any changes that it may be beneficial to make.

Managing risk

Due to the increasing awareness of researcher safety and risk, in 2007 an inquiry was conducted in order to make recommendations to institutions for protecting researchers (Bloor et al., 2007). These included recommendations such as including researcher safety as an issue in general research methods courses, and that this should be a criterion for course recognition. The inquiry also proposed that supervisors and senior investigators should receive training and that in university health and safety audits there should be a section on researcher safety. The inquiry placed emphasis on the responsibility of the funding body which should require compliance with the Social Research Association (SRA) safety guidelines and should ask referees to comment specifically on researcher safety issues. While institutions clearly have a requirement to take some responsibility for their employees, in practice researchers themselves have to be accountable for their own safety by considering the specific issues pertinent to their own research context. We present in Table 3.2 an overview from a paper of ours of some practical recommendations both for institutions and researchers in effectively managing researcher risk.

Table 3.2 Parker and O'Reilly's (2013) recommendations for managing risk

Recommendation	Description
Raising awareness	There is a need for more visible discussions relating to safety issues within the research community. Researchers, managers, funding bodies and ethics committees need to be more aware of the physical and emotional threats to qualitative researchers.
Need for training	Specialist training workshops need to be available and offered to researchers conducting qualitative research on how to predict and manage risk.
Transparent risk assessment	Researchers and institutions should conduct a clear risk assessment during the planning stages of the research which includes consideration of researcher safety as well as participant safety.
Debriefing	Due to issues of confidentiality it is important that institutions offer formal mechanisms of support and supervision for researchers to allow them the opportunity to offload emotional experiences.
The team approach	Researchers may find themselves isolated and stress/distress may accumulate over time. A more team-centred approach can allow opportunities for discussions and shared decision-making. It also provides a forum for reflexive practice.

By planning their research in advance, researchers may be able to anticipate and manage risk (SRA, 2010). This will involve appraising the potential threat of each individual field visit in relation to their own life experiences, personality attributes and/or prior experiences in similar situations (George, 1996). This will in turn require taking account of the cultural norms of the participant, the gender dynamics and the use of appropriate body language (SRA, 2010). This process of risk assessment – unique to qualitative research – involves awareness not only of participants' demographics but also of the researcher's own personal strengths, vulnerabilities, and current life circumstances. Reflexivity is important in qualitative research as this can facilitate the emotional wellbeing of the researcher (Connolly and Reilly, 2007) and help manage the delicate boundaries between researcher and participant to help prevent emotional overload (Dickson-Swift et al., 2006). This reflects the dilemma for researchers in that some may feel that showing their emotions may make them more vulnerable, but emotional detachment may reduce the rigour of the study (Dickson-Swift et al., 2009). Furthermore, in an effort to remain objective a researcher may inadvertently invalidate a participant's experience by failing to respond empathically to their distress.

SUMMARY AND FINAL THOUGHTS

The application of ethical principles in qualitative research is clearly an important consideration for researchers and ethics committees. Debates and controversies surrounding the judgement of qualitative research proposals illustrate that the ethical concerns for qualitative work need to be applied in different ways to quantitative approaches. In particular, the characteristics of qualitative ethics relate to depth of data, the proximity of researcher involvement with participants, the iterative process of qualitative work and a greater emphasis on visibility, requiring careful consideration of anonymity and the need for ethical management in the dissemination of participants' narratives. Our critical discussion has identified the key markers of ethical practice in qualitative research. We have paid particular attention to the iterative nature of informed consent, the risk of deductive disclosure and the broad issue of responsibility and positionality. We have proposed that researchers, ethics committees and funding bodies need to extend discussion of the distinctiveness of qualitative research ethics to appreciate these specific characteristics. This has the potential to enhance ethical practice and also promote confidence in the rigour of qualitative research. These discussions have implications too for the management of researcher safety in the field, which we propose is a topic that requires more attention.

Case study and reflective questions

Eduardo is a senior lecturer of sociology who is interested in comparisons of virtual identities in social networking sites. He plans to recruit a selection of his own students and request access to their Facebook accounts, Twitter feeds and LinkedIn pages. His intention is to use discourse analysis to look at the socially constructed nature of identity in a virtual environment.

Q: How might the process of iterative consent be applicable to this research project?
Q: What might Eduardo need to consider in relation to power and positionality?

Suggestions for answering these questions are available at the end of the book.

FURTHER READING

Brinkman, S. and Kvale, S. (2008) Ethics in qualitative psychological research, in C. Willig and W. Stainton-Rogers (eds), *Handbook of Qualitative Research in Psychology*. London: Sage. pp. 261–279.

Although this book chapter is set in the context of psychology, its discussion is also pertinent for other disciplines as it provides a useful and practical discussion of the issues of ethics specifically in qualitative research.

Dixon-Woods, M. and Ashcroft, R. E. (2008) Regulation and the social licence for medical research. *Medicine, Health Care and Philosophy*, 11(4): 381–391.

This article is written in the context of health and sociology, and the authors provide a discussion of ethical regulation and the criticisms that such governance has received from the research community in general.

Hammersley, M. (2009) Against the ethicists: On the evils of ethical regulation. *International Journal of Social Research Methodology*, 12(3): 211–225.

Hammersley proposes an argument that takes issue with the regulation of research, particularly qualitative research. Hammersley acknowledges the increase in ethical regulation of research from funding bodies, educational institutions and regulatory bodies and calls into question the legitimacy of such regulation.

Liamputtong, P. (2007) *Researching the Vulnerable: A Guide to Sensitive Research Methods*. Thousand Oaks, CA: Sage.

This book focuses specifically on vulnerable populations and considers the sensitivities of being a researcher exploring the worlds of groups at the margins of society. Throughout the book the author takes an interest in the ethical, practical and methodological implications of working with vulnerable groups.

Morse, J. (2001) Are there risks in qualitative research? *Qualitative Health Research*, 11(1): 3–4.

This is a short critical discussion that provides an overview of some of the risks that are considered to be specific to qualitative approaches.

FOUR

Perspective-driven data collection

CHAPTER CONTENTS

INTRODUCTION

This chapter debates issues related to prospective research planning versus retrospective decision-making and potential consequences related to this. The overall argument relates to advocating congruence between the ontological, epistemological and methodological levels of research design, which informs choices regarding the data collection methods and analytic frameworks. We contextualise this by discussing some of the most common methodologies within qualitative work and highlighting the relevance and importance of maintaining methodological boundaries. One of the most important decisions to be made at an early stage is whether data will be researcher-generated or naturally occurring. This decision hinges heavily on the methodological protocol. In this chapter we use an example of the popular method of interviews to illustrate the necessity of congruence at different theoretical and practical levels.

DEBATING CONGRUENCE AND THE INFLUENCE OF PERSPECTIVES

The purpose of qualitative research is to yield an appreciation of how people's experiences are shaped by their subjective and socio-cultural perspectives (Wilkinson et al., 2004). Qualitative research should be viewed as a process of decisions, and arguably these should be intrinsically connected to the underpinning assumptions of the theory driving the research. The different aspects of the research process should be congruent with the underlying traditions of the research approach selected (Wimpenny and Gass, 2000). What this demonstrates is that the perspective chosen should drive the choices made about data collection as well as the type of analysis conducted. For example, in qualitative research there are two types of reasoning informed by the epistemological framework of the researcher (see Chapter 1). There are those who use inductive reasoning whereby the data are used to generate ideas, and those who favour deductive reasoning which starts with an idea and uses the data collected to confirm it (Thorne, 2000). Inevitably the agenda and aims of the researcher will thus direct the choices made that inform the data collection methods.

Notably the importance of beginning with ontology and mapping this onto epistemology and methodology creates some tensions between academic thinkers. Some argue that ontology and methodology may be separated (see Ten Have, 2002), while others view them as inseparable (Speer, 2002). We argue that it is essential that there is congruence between ontology, epistemology and methodology, for reasons of quality and consistency. Inevitably these underlying ways of viewing the reality of the world influence decisions made as each stage of the research process involves active selection. Any method of documenting social interaction is a culturally biased, human, interpretative and selective process (Hamo et al., 2004). For example, if the ontological premise argues that there is an objective reality (realism) which can be accessed, then the researcher will make assumptions that their mode of data collection will be a tool to reflect the reality of the participants (Morse, 2000). However, if the ontological premise argues that there is no objective reality (relativism) then the mode of data collection cannot be simply a neutral method for accessing an objective reality but is a social action in its own right. Ultimately, therefore, the ontological premises adhered to by researchers affect and reflect the nature of the data collection tools employed. This then affects how the data themselves are regarded and treated in the analytical process.

Reflective space

Before going any further with this chapter, we suggest that you take a few minutes to consider your own personal ontological position. Most people favour a perception of the world in which either there is an objective reality (realism) or alternatively reality is a relative construct (relativism).

THE DILEMMA OF RETROSPECTIVE DECISIONS

A motivating factor influencing our development of this argument relates to frequent personal experiences of supervising students or practitioners looking for advice on qualitative analysis after they have already collected their data. Problematically this inevitably means that many of the considerations about why the particular data collection method was chosen have not been given sufficient attention. This therefore limits the possibilities for analysis and dissemination. We give an example of this in Box 4.1.

─────────── Box 4.1   Personal case example ───────────

A clinical practitioner had collected eight qualitative interviews with parents of children with autism. This was an independent project, and therefore the practitioner had sought little guidance during the planning stages. At the point of asking for advice related to undertaking analysis of the data a number of problems became apparent. These problems included:

- The research question was weak.
- There was no rationale for sampling adequacy, and for many approaches eight interviews would be deemed insufficient. Additionally, some approaches require concurrent, rather than sequential or linear, data collection and analysis.
- The type of interview conducted was not pre-considered or defined, and some aspects of the interview seemed semi-structured whereas other parts were more unstructured.
- The purpose of the research was not entirely clear, and there was little determination of an inductive or deductive approach.
- There was an unacknowledged underlying realist ontology which had not been made transparent or reflected on by the practitioner.
- During the interviews the researcher did not anchor their style of interviewing to a particular perspective, and as such did not consider relevant aspects such as considering issues of bracketing, power, role, relationships, context, and so forth, which are critical in most approaches.

It is essential for the quality of a piece of work that there is congruence throughout the process. Any qualitative researcher working from a particular analytic approach who read the disseminated research of this practitioner would critique the findings and trustworthiness of the interpretations because of the lack of integrity. By failing to adhere to the specific methodological markers of quality through the process, the research would be considered weak or even invalid. The consequence, therefore, of applying an analytic technique to general interview data is that the choice is limited to those methods with epistemological flexibility. Any other choice risks lacking credibility.

THE VALUE OF PROSPECTIVE PLANNING

The risks to credibility can be addressed through prospective planning. This means that from the outset the researcher will ensure epistemic compatibility in all phases of the research project. As qualitative research is by nature a cyclical iterative process, prospective planning is not limited temporally. While decisions are driven by the research question and aims of the project, decision-making will be revisited throughout the early stages of the project, ahead of data collection. Note that for some the research will begin with a problem, and the researcher selects an appropriate approach which facilitates addressing this problem (Howitt, 2010). However, this is not necessarily as straightforward as it may appear, as the way in which the researcher conceives of the problem already involves several assumptions regarding the nature of the world (Potter, 1998). The methodology chosen and methods used to implement it must, therefore, be ontologically and epistemologically congruent.

Perspectives are underpinned by theoretical and philosophical frameworks and thus based upon ontological and epistemological assumptions. Evidence shows, however, that researchers in practice are often unaware of the importance or relevance of epistemology and ontology (Bryman, 2007). What this means is that in qualitative work there are a number of traditions, and these vary in relation to theoretical and philosophical frameworks, data collection and analysis, and standards of quality (Creswell, 1998). Thus, qualitative researchers must be particularly aware of the choices they make. This is because the position taken and perspective chosen will have an effect on the content, style and substance of design and implementation of methods. To ensure consistency in the process it is essential that researchers consciously consider perspectives as they develop their ideas.

By investing time to consider the importance of epistemological integrity in qualitative work there will be a greater acceptance of both the individual disseminated piece, but also a greater respect for the discipline. We argue, therefore, that congruence is inextricably linked to quality in qualitative research. While acknowledging our preference for the methodologies of discursive psychology and conversation analysis, as these fit with our personal relativist ontological and social constructionist epistemological stance, we are not arguing for the superiority of any specific methodological approach in this book. Rather we are clear that the data collection and analytic methods employed in *any* project should be borne out of a transparent theoretical framework in order that the work has veracity. This should not be tokenistic or ignored.

CONGRUENCE WITHIN THEORETICAL FRAMEWORKS

The different methodological approaches are informed by different ontological and epistemological foundations, and these fundamentally influence everything about how the research is conceptualised, actioned and analysed. The theoretical framework informs the research question, data collection and analysis, and we therefore guide readers through some of the core approaches within the qualitative approach to demonstrate how epistemological and ontological concerns matter in specific areas. We make no attempt to provide detail regarding the specifics of each approach, rather our aim is to demonstrate how methods and analytic approaches are selected with reference to the coherence of the methodology, and thus only a brief summary of each is provided. We recommend that readers take the time to read further on those that they are considering for use in their own work.

Grounded theory

The term 'grounded theory' refers to both the method of inquiry as well as the product of inquiry (Charmaz, 2005) and offers a qualitative approach for exploratory investigations (Charmaz, 1995). The grounded theory methodology emerged from the collaborative work of Glaser and Strauss (1967), who created an approach which transcended the boundaries between data collection and analysis that pervaded research at that time (Willig, 2008). In the early stages of the development of grounded theory as a methodology the aims were to develop an inductive approach which additionally proposed a way to conceptualise the data collected, the ultimate goal being to formulate an explanatory theory of the social processes in the environments in which they have taken place (Glaser and Strauss, 1967). In more modern versions, the aim is to explore basic social processes as well as understanding the multiplicity of interactions that produce variations in that process (Heath and Cowley, 2004). One contemporary version is interpretative grounded theory which emphasises more abstract understandings (Charmaz, 2006).

(e.g.) The epistemological premise of grounded theory assumes that the theoretical knowledge that will be gained through research cannot be presupposed. Therefore, the methodological approach is congruent with this premise and regards knowledge production as something which can only be gained through an inductive procedure. Furthermore, due to this unfolding procedure the methodology promotes iterative cyclical processes of simultaneous data collection and analysis.

Since its original inception, grounded theory has diversified, with Glaser and Strauss advocating slightly different versions – Glaser staying faithful to the original version (Heath and Cowley, 2004) and Strauss and Corbin reformulating the classic version (Annells, 1996). While these different versions share an ontological position, there are slight epistemological variations (Heath and Cowley, 2004). Ontologically Glaser and Strauss offered a compromise between extreme empiricism and complete relativism, arguing that knowledge claims made by analysts are based on how individuals interpret reality (Suddaby, 2006). However, other grounded theorists contend that the analyst's knowledge claims are more predominant. The premise of some grounded theorists grew from symbolic interactionism (Starks and Trinidad, 2007) and may operate from social constructionist (Burck, 2005) or constructivist (Charmaz, 2000) epistemologies, although there is some tension regarding this (see Glaser, 2007).

Because the objective of grounded theory is to generate an overarching encompassing theory (Biggerstaff, 2012), its method involves the identification and integration of categories within the data (Willig, 2008) using constant comparative analysis (Charmaz, 2006). It should be noted, however, that prominent researchers working within grounded theory have developed and evolved their positions (see, for example, Corbin and Strauss, 2008). Grounded theorists (like many other qualitative researchers) tend to favour interviews as the data collection method, differentiating between formal and informal interviewing (Chenitz and Swanson, 1986), and in this approach the questioning is responsive to the emerging theories (Wimpenny and Gass, 2000). In terms of theoretical congruence, therefore, both the methods of data collection and analysis are integral to the ideal of theory generation, which includes the simultaneous process of collection and analysis, as well as debates regarding when the literature should be consulted.

Interpretative phenomenological analysis

Generally speaking, phenomenology is 'a philosophical approach to the study of experience' (Smith et al., 2009: 11). There are, however, different ways of performing phenomenological analysis. There is a tradition that developed from Husserl's ideas on phenomenology, and others that lean more on Heidegger's development of those ideas. Interpretative phenomenological analysis, pioneered by Smith, is an approach influenced by both Husserl and Heidegger (Smith et al., 2009). IPA aims to explore in depth the personal lived experiences of participants and how they make sense of those experiences, and is thus idiographic, inductive and interrogative (Smith, 2004). IPA relates to phenomenology in the sense that it has a core concern with the individual's perceptions of objects or events, and is hermeneutic in that it is interested in how the participant makes sense of their personal and social world (Smith, 2004). Additionally, Smith (2004) draws attention to the experience of the 'double hermeneutic' where the researcher is trying to make sense of their participants' sense-making of their experiences.

(e.g.) The fundamental epistemological position of IPA is that the knowledge gained through the research process should be a reflection of the participant's perspective on how they make sense of the world and is seen as more important than the researcher's understanding of their experience. Although the methodology is referred to as 'interpretative' the congruence to the epistemological foundation ensures that the interpretation provided is the participant's rather than the researcher's.

IPA rejects the idea that objective knowledge is attainable, and therefore could be described as a form of relativism. However, IPA resists taking a strong relativistic stance, instead advocating an interpretative position (Sandberg, 2005). For data collection most IPA studies use the method of semi-structured interviews. This method is preferred because this approach requires 'thick description' of the lived experiences of its participants (Sokolowski, 2000). In order to interpret the data in a way that is consistent with the approach and reflects the participants' perceptions, for some phenomenological approaches, the interviewer must 'bracket off' their own presuppositions about the world in order to adopt a detached position (Wimpenny and Gass, 2000). However, other phenomenological approaches, including IPA, do not subscribe to a straightforward bracketing process, viewing it instead as a 'hermeneutic circle' where there is a dynamic changing relationship between the researcher's understanding and the phenomenon (Smith et al., 2009). The methods of data collection and analysis reflect congruence with the underlying epistemologies of the approach by attempting to remain faithful to the subjective experience of those participating.

Ethnography

Ethnography does not have a standard defined meaning, due to its complex history, but is generally viewed as a long-standing form of social research which looks at how people make sense of their everyday lives (Hammersley and Atkinson, 2007). Ethnography originated in Western anthropology in the late nineteenth century but has become popular in other disciplines, and is considered both a method and a product: 'an ethnography' (Fetterman, 2010). Ethnography is an approach to research that involves immersion within, and investigation of, a culture or social world (Thorne, 2000). Notably there are different types of ethnography, including classical, critical and autoethnography (Grbich, 2013), and the method of ethnography has also been used by other methodological approaches, such as discourse analysis (Hamo et al., 2004).

(e.g.) Due to the inherent diversity within the methodology of ethnography, it is important for researchers working within this approach to be clear about which epistemological position is informing their work. One of the unifying features of ethnographers is a supposition that the authenticity of the knowledge gained through the research process is enhanced by using methods which favour immersion in the field.

The underpinning epistemological positions of ethnographic approaches are varied. For example, Staller (2013) claimed that classical ethnography is linked to objectivism, critical ethnography is underpinned by social constructionism, and autoethnography is associated with subjectivism. Importantly, notions of objectivism and subjectivism, and other theoretical frameworks, have not been universally accepted by the research community (refer to Chapter 1). Ethnography, therefore, as a product in broad terms has been influenced by a range of different positions including sociological functionalism, philosophical pragmatism, symbolic interactionism, hermeneutics, post-structuralism, feminism, Marxism and postmodernism (Hammersley and Atkinson, 2007). In terms of the methods favoured by ethnographers, fieldwork is at the heart of ethnography (Fetterman, 2010). Ethnographers tend to favour observation but may also use interviews, documents and artefacts (Hammersley and Atkinson, 2007); and for analysis, the ethnographer may adopt a range of different analytical approaches. In relation to congruence, therefore, ethnography should be carried out in line with the relevant underpinning position, in relation to the particular type of ethnography being conducted, which should be made transparent by the ethnographer and will vary according to the discipline and the problem (Fetterman, 2010).

Narrative analysis

Narrative analysis is a form of qualitative analysis that recognises the extent to which the stories people tell provide insight into their lived experiences and how they understand and make sense of their lives and worlds (Thorne, 2000). Narrative analysis is the systematic study of narrative data (Riessman, 2008) and is underpinned by narrative theory, which advocates that individuals are born into a 'storied world' (Murray, 2003). Narrative theorists argue that storytelling is a pervasive human activity (Crossley, 2000), and consequently oral narrative has been the subject of much social research. It is important, however, to note that there are different types of narrative analysis, but all are informed by narrative theory (Burck, 2005) that originated in narratology (Clandinin and Rosiek, 2007). For example, Riessman (2008) outlines four of the main types:

- Thematic narrative analysis: The focus is on 'what' is said or the content of the narrative. Common thematic elements are identified but analysis remains 'case-centred', unlike grounded theory.
- Structural narrative analysis: The focus is on 'how' a narrative is spoken, narrative form including the function of clauses, organisation into units of discourse, and other structural features.
- Dialogic narrative analysis: A broad interpretative approach, the focus is on the contexts shaping narrative, including how it is 'multi-voiced' from past language use and 'co-constructed' in the present conversation. Attention is paid to performative features and reflexivity.
- Visual narrative analysis: The focus is on images, how and why they are produced, and how they can be made and interpreted with participants.

Notably, narrative inquirers hold a range of different ontological and epistemological positions, including symbolic interactionism, constructivism, and different forms of realism (Riessman, 2008). While there is great diversity in narrative inquiry, many favour interview methods as the primary choice because interviews provide 'narrative occasions' (Riessman, 2008: 23). Arguably they offer a basis for sharing power, allowing participants to tell their story in their own way (Crossley, 2000). Of central importance for structural narrative analysis is a concern with how narrative is organised to explicate meaning (Murray, 2003). Meaning is created using linguistic devices to access the structural elements of language, including 'stanzas' (the basic building blocks), which form 'strophes' that make up the story as a whole (Gee, 1991). Under the broad rubric of narrative theory, each of the various analytic approaches retains an integrity which permeates through methodology, data collection and analysis. As such, there is an internal congruence which honours its theoretical roots.

Discourse analysis

Discourse analysis is an umbrella term for a number of language-based approaches. The overall premise is an interest in how social processes inform the ways in which the scientific community come to consider particular knowledge claims as objective, factual representations of the world (Wooffitt, 2005). There are several different types of discourse analysis, including traditional, critical, Foucauldian, Bhaktian, and discursive psychology. While operating from different theoretical perspectives, they share a conviction that language is performative, not just reflective of mental processes. However, they differ in terms of their epistemological and ontological assumptions.

> **e.g.** Discursive psychology is informed by a relativist ontological position and a social constructionist epistemology. It embraces the key concerns of ethnomethodology and Wittgenstein's ideas that there is not a single universal meaning of language, but rather that language is a medium of social interaction (Wooffitt, 2005).

Critical discourse analysis tends to be informed by a critical realist ontological position and a post-structuralism epistemology, although some scholars prefer the term 'critical discourse studies' to distinguish it as an applied broader critical practice (van Dijk, 2008). The theoretical framework of critical discourse analysis seems 'eclectic' and 'unsystematic' (Weiss and Wodak, 2003), but the plurality is considered a strength (Wodak, 2002). In practice, therefore, researchers adopting this methodology attempt to investigate the role of discourse in the production of power within social structure, looking at how discourse manages to sustain and legitimise social inequality (Wooffitt, 2005). Specifically, they take an explicit socio-political position focusing on the role of discourse in the (re)production of the dominance of elite groups and institutions as they are legitimated and reproduced by talk and text (van Dijk, 1993, 2008).

Despite a shared interest in discourse practices in social interaction, due to the different types of questions posed and assumptions made, data collection methods vary quite widely. For example, discursive psychology researchers utilise naturally occurring data for many reasons. One of these is due to the belief that any speech act produced can only be meaningfully analysed by reference to the situated nature of the talk and the specific characteristics of the interlocutors (Edwards and Potter, 1992). Additionally, talk is organised interactionally and thus it is essential to capture the authenticity of the details of that interaction (Potter and Hepburn, 2012). Other forms of discourse analysis do not necessarily share this perspective, and may be willing to use researcher-generated methods such as interviews and focus groups. When reviewing or critiquing a discourse analysis study, it essential to bear in mind the parameters of the methodology in relation to its adherence to appropriate data collection methods which are congruent with underpinning epistemological and ontological foundations.

Conversation analysis

Conversation analysis is the study of talk-in-interaction (Schegloff, 1987). Conversation analysis was pioneered by the sociologist Harvey Sacks who was concerned with how people use language to accomplish social actions, with a focus on general day-to-day interaction (Wooffitt, 2005). While different conversation analysts have slightly different foci, with some favouring more applied approaches (Antaki, 2011), the central tenet of conversation analysis is to examine the social organisation of activities produced though talk via the detailed analysis of sequential patterns of interaction (Hutchby and Wooffitt, 2008). Thus conversation analysis is an emic and inductive methodology which prioritises a particular form of empirical evidence that involves the participants' understanding of social phenomena (Bolden and Robinson, 2011). Conversation analysis is underpinned by a relativist ontological position and a social constructionist epistemology.

(e.g.) In practice, those who adopt this methodological position take a world-view that knowledge is co-constructed and socially situated. The premise behind this kind of investigation is one of unmotivated looking, followed by data-driven analysis, seeking to discover what new understandings of social action can be discovered by neutral examination of talk (Hutchby and Wooffitt, 2008).

It is essential for conversation analysts to collect data considered naturally occurring (Hutchby and Wooffitt, 2008). Data are frequently divided into the two broad categories of mundane and institutional. Mundane conversation is that which occurs in everyday face-to-face or telephone interactions, while institutional conversation refers to talk occurring within institutional contexts for institutional purpose (Wooffitt, 2005). The markers of quality for a conversation-analytic piece of work are that it has internal integrity in that all parts are rigorously justified through sequential analysis which is transparent for the audience. While analysis is performed from the recorded data, this is facilitated by the detailed and comprehensive transcription notation (Jefferson, 2004). Congruence between ontology, epistemology and methodology is achieved inherently by the explicit tightly defined parameters of the approach.

Thematic and template analysis

Although there are differences between thematic and template analysis, there are many commonalities. Thematic analysis is a methodology used to identify, analyse and report patterns within a data set, allowing for the descriptive organisation of the data in a way that facilitates interpretation of various aspects of the research topic (Boyatzis, 1998). In this process the researcher takes an active role in selecting and categorising the data into themes (Braun and Clarke, 2006). Similarly, template analysis provides a framework for thematically organising and analysing textual data, producing a set of codes which represent themes (King, 2004). However, template analysis starts with the first transcript and builds a template which is applied to subsequent transcripts (King, 2012).

(e.g.) Both thematic and template analysis are considered 'epistemologically flexible' in the sense that they regard themselves as methodologies that are compatible with a range of epistemological positions (Braun and Clarke, 2006; King, 2004). Therefore, it is important to acknowledge that this does not mean that they are epistemologically free, and it is important that the researcher is transparent regarding their epistemological perspective in performing the thematic/template analysis.

Theoretical thematic analysis is driven by the theoretical interest of the researcher, and coding maps directly onto a specific research question (Braun and Clarke, 2006). Inductive thematic analysis, however, is when the themes are viewed to emerge from the data (Patton, 1990). Often template and thematic analysis are performed on interview data, but can also be usefully applied to qualitative questionnaires, focus groups, documents and video-recorded materials (Joffe and Yardley, 2004). Where the researcher is careful to be explicit about their ontological and epistemological assumptions in relation to the thematic or template analysis, this congruence makes the research more credible. When researchers exhibit 'some or all of the characteristics' of the qualitative endeavour but fail to focus their research with a congruent theoretical framework, they tend to be classified as 'generic' qualitative research studies (Caelli et al., 2003: 4). This means that critical audiences have insufficient information to judge the quality of the work.

Facet methodology

Facet methodology is a new methodology linked with the qualitative approach, and thus there is currently only a limited literature that discusses or uses this approach. However, its scope is potentially far-reaching and multidisciplinary, and further developments are likely in this field. Facet methodology has been developed by several researchers at the Morgan Centre, University of Manchester (UK), and its leading proponent is Jennifer Mason. The purpose of facet methodology is to research the multidimensionality of lived experience, and this represents a new way of practising and thinking about research (Mason, 2011). It seeks to illuminate the sets of facets that are linked to specific research questions, with facets being methodological and substantive and 'strategically and artfully designed investigations into particular aspects of the object of concern' (Mason, 2011: 79).

(e.g.) Davies and Heaphy (2011) used facet methodology to investigate the experiences of personal interactions amongst lesbians and gay men. They found that each method applied in a different context enabled them to look at the topic from other angles.

This approach requires the researcher to be creative and have a 'playful' approach to epistemology, and it is noted that ontology and epistemology are closely bound together (Mason, 2011). Therefore, the importance of congruence is recognised as integral to the approach. Mason further argued that facet methodology draws upon a range of epistemologies that require a different way of thinking, and this approach is not tied to any singular methodological tradition or paradigm.

Action research

Action research has a complex history and is not a single discipline; rather it is an approach to research that has emerged over time within a broad range of areas (Brydon-Miller et al., 2003). There is, however, some consensus that action research originated in the 1950s within the work of Kurt Lewin (Huang, 2010). Action research is a qualitative approach that associates research with practice (Avison et al., 1999) and is participatory in nature (Koshy et al., 2010). There is no universally agreed definition of action research, but it has been described as an approach that is used in designing studies that seek to inform and influence practice; it is a particular orientation and purpose of inquiry as opposed to being a research methodology per se (Reason and Bradbury, 2001). Thus action research is a form of cooperative inquiry and action science that tends to be used for improving conditions and practices within organisations such as healthcare (Lingard et al., 2008), with four key types outlined by Avison et al. (1999):

- Action research, which focuses on reflection and change.
- Action science, which tries to resolve conflict between espoused and applied theory.

- Participatory action research, which emphasises participant collaboration.
- Action learning, designed for programmed instruction and experiential learning.

The strength of action research is argued to be its focus on generating solutions to practical problems and its ability to empower those working in practice-based environments by allowing them to engage in the research process (Meyer, 2000). This is why the most influential theoretical framework for action research is critical theory as it aims to encourage those who are often excluded from the research process to inform it and because it is participatory (Waterman et al., 2001). It has been argued that critical theory made the work of action researchers possible as it enabled the framing of issues of identity and power in the suggestion of strategies for action and explanations for outcomes (Brydon-Miller et al., 2003). However, although most strongly associated with critical theory, it has been argued that the researcher should position themselves with a world-view that they feel is compatible with their own beliefs (Koshy et al., 2010), and some argue that action research can be utilised within both quantitative and qualitative approaches (Waterman et al., 2001).

―――――――――――――――――― Reflective space ――――――――――――――――――

Our list of examples has only been intended to be a brief overview of each methodology and we therefore recommend that you take some time out at this point to engage in some further reading.

NATURALLY OCCURRING VERSUS RESEARCHER-GENERATED DATA COLLECTION

Methods of data collection are an important aspect of the issue of congruence, and there have been lively debates about the value of different tools of collection. An issue that has been epistemologically and methodologically pertinent is the naturally occurring versus researcher-generated debate.

What are generally understood to be naturally occurring data are those conversations which would have occurred regardless of the intervention of the researcher. These data are therefore those that would satisfy what has been referred to as the 'dead social scientist test' (Potter, 1996). Thus an interaction is said to be naturally occurring if it would still occur even if the researcher had never been born (Potter, 1997) or if researcher was unable to collect it (Potter, 1996).

e.g. Raymond and Heritage (2006) conducted a conversation-analytic study with naturally occurring data of a telephone conversation between two friends. The analysis demonstrated that the identity of 'grandparent' was socially constructed and made relevant and consequential to that particular interaction.

Alternatively, researcher-generated data are those which are 'set up' by the researcher and are deliberately contrived in order to address a research question. Speer (2002) argues that the status of a piece of data as naturally occurring or researcher-generated is not dependent upon the researcher's intentions about what they will do with the data.

 Example of naturally occurring data: Recordings of police interrogation of interviews with their suspects.

 Example of researcher-generated data: A semi-structured interview with members of the police force about their interrogation of suspects.

Some of the literature presents a polarised position whereby some scholars advocate the superiority of naturally occurring data, with others favouring researcher-generated modes. However, there are some researchers who caution against this competitive stance and suggest the distinction between natural and contrived data should not be taken too far (Silverman, 2011). Our position in this debate is that neither approach to data collection is superior per se, rather the issue relates to consistency and congruence, and the choice of data collection should be driven by the ontological and epistemological position of the research. The choice regarding the use of either one of these approaches should depend on how the researcher intends to study phenomena (Ten Have, 2002). We consider this debate further in Box 4.2.

Reflective space

Consider how the benefits of using naturally occurring data may offset the potential difficulties in collecting data of this kind.

influential **voices**

Box 4.2 Favouring naturally occurring data

Jonathan Potter

Jonathan Potter* is a professor of discourse analysis and dean of the School of Social, Political and Geographical Sciences at Loughborough University. Professor Potter has made significant contributions to debates on naturally occurring versus researcher-generated data.

Jonathan Potter is a co-founder of the discipline of discursive psychology, the premise of which is that, rather than starting with a predefined research question, naturalistic data allow novel questions to emerge (Potter, 2012). Central to arguments of naturally occurring versus researcher-generated data collection is the popular method of research interviewing. Potter has consistently challenged the uncritical adoption of interviewing as the preferred method for data collection in qualitative research. His argument is that interviews should only be used when they are the most appropriate tools for collecting data and, when employed, should be studied as an 'interactional object' (Potter and Hepburn, 2012). The underlying premise for those using interview methods is that they are a tool for accessing what is inside people's heads. However, Potter (2002) argues that what is presented in the interview by the participant is situated and designed for that interaction and should be recognised as a co-constructed reality. Interviews ought not be viewed as a vehicle for acquiring data, rather as an arena for interaction, where the interviewer is not neutral but actively engaged in the production of talk (Potter, 2004a). In other words, it is legitimate to study interviews which can be a rich source for analysis; however, it is important to acknowledge their limitations and the interactional and situated nature of their occurrence (Potter, 2002). From this perspective one way of exploring interview data is to identify the discursive resources drawn upon in the interview (Potter, 2003).

Within the discursive psychological framework, Potter prefers the use of naturally occurring data, by far the most commonly occurring discourse, both in everyday interaction and institutional settings (Edwards and Potter, 1992). His perspective is that everyday talk is in its own right creative, challenging and fascinating to study. This is because it captures the actual interaction and most easily retains the action-oriented and situated nature of the talk, showing how participants orient to their setting without abstraction from the researcher's agenda and thus avoiding cognitive reifications of the research (Potter, 2004b). A general concern within qualitative research is with how to minimise the impact of the researcher on the participants so as not to 'contaminate the data'. Reflexivity is proposed as the main way in which this can be managed. However, Potter argues that this is impossible to achieve in reality, and he advocates that the researcher is either embraced as a co-participant in the data creation or completely absent from data generation (Potter, 2002). His preference for this is predicated on the basis that talk must be analysed with reference to the context of the interaction within which it occurred. He does, however, acknowledge that naturalistic material may not be most appropriate in all cases, and interviews can be an appropriate choice for some research issues (Potter and Hepburn, 2012).

*We thank Professor Potter for taking the time to read an earlier draft of this chapter.

QUALITATIVE INTERVIEWS

Interviewing is a particularly popular technique of data collection (Brinkman and Kvale, 2005). Commonly, general methods texts divide interview types into three categories – structured, semi-structured and unstructured – although there are other types of interviewing that are often unacknowledged such as the naturally occurring interview or the narrative interview. The boundaries between these three common types are, however, more complex than is often considered and the terminology is understood differently by researchers from different approaches. Nonetheless, this categorising remains a helpful heuristic to guide the researcher in broad terms. Thus the aim of the research will guide the interview's nature, style, content and substance. However, researchers often do not make clear the relationship between their method of data collection and the underpinning theoretical framework, which may result in the interview being treated as a generic research tool (Wimpenny and Gass, 2000). Nonetheless, different epistemological perspectives favour different interview approaches, whether it be semi-structured or unstructured interviews (or, for some, naturally occurring interviews). The choice between different interview methods is often dictated by fundamental concerns such as whether the premise of the research is inductive or deductive, and the methodological approach being taken.

Part of this distinction relates to the nature and type of relationship they hold with the interviewee. For example, some approaches advocate that the interviewer takes a detached position, 'bracketing' off and suspending prior assumptions and knowledge (Husserl, 1970). In addition to this, inherent in the interview process is an asymmetry between the two parties as the interviewer's interest sets the agenda and directs the conversation (Brinkman and Kvale, 2005). In this way interviews are not neutral tools for gathering data but are active interactions (Fontana and Frey, 2003), and therefore it is important to appreciate the researcher's place in the production of the data (Potter, 2002). In other words, the types of questions asked, the ways in which those questions are asked and the relationship between the interviewer and interviewee will shape its outcomes. All of these factors therefore should be dictated by the underpinning theoretical framework informing the interview schedule and process. For example:

- If one adopts a social psychoanalytic perspective the interviewer will be seeking to elucidate from the participant free association and will be attending to transference and countertransference issues during the interview.
- In contrast to this, a phenomenologist is more likely to bracket off their personal involvement in the interview to focus on eliciting narratives about the lived experiences of the participant. What this demonstrates is that the nature of the relationship built between the interviewer and interviewee is guided by the assumptions underpinning the perspective.

- For grounded theory the interviews tend to be less open and more structured in style than for some other approaches (Wimpenny and Gass, 2000), and the direction of grounded theory interviews sets the tone in order to seek information, feeling and reflection (Charmaz, 1994).
- However, conversation analysts see the interview as jointly constructing meaning, with the interaction's status as an interview with a turn-by-turn accomplishment, and therefore the interview cannot be a standardised instrument (Speer, 2002).

It is important, then, to note that the perspective chosen will inform the development of the schedule, including the questions asked, the nature of the relationship and the ways in which questions are delivered. Arguably, the researcher is like a research instrument in the sense of being the mechanism through which data are collected (Sorrell and Redmond, 1995). In some philosophical traditions this acknowledgement of the synthesis of method and relationship to the researcher is integral to the research process (Wimpenny and Gass, 2000).

Sampling adequacy

The perspective adopted and the theoretical assumptions made have implications not only for the type of data collection strategy, but also for the number of participants required for an adequate sample. In Chapter 2 we referred to the issue of sampling adequacy in relation to the broad issue of transparency which is considered by most to be a core quality indicator for qualitative research. Transparency is the mechanism through which the researcher is able to illustrate to intended audiences the trustworthiness of the findings; and transparency regarding how congruent the methods adopted are with the informing perspective is an essential part of this. Because there is no fixed minimum number of participants for quality, sufficient depth of information needs to be gathered to fully appreciate the phenomenon (Fossey et al., 2002).

A frequently used measure of sample size sufficiency is saturation. The notion of saturation has become embedded in the methodological cultural discourses and is usually understood to mean that sampling should continue until the themes emerging from the research are fully developed so that all diverse instances have been explored (Kuzel, 1992). Problematically this process is potentially limitless, and the concept of saturation is something routinely reported in research but questionably ever actually reached (Green and Thorogood, 2004). The issue, however, extends beyond whether saturation is possible, to the legitimacy of the reification of the use of saturation as a concept in such a general way. This, therefore, relates to attempts to homogenise qualitative research by trying to develop the same quality criteria for all approaches, and this fails to account for the diversity in ontology and epistemology of those perspectives. One result of this is that saturation has become not only accepted but also expected.

This taken-for-granted expectation ignores the fact that saturation is a perspective-tied concept (O'Reilly and Parker, 2013). The notion of saturation actually emerged from grounded theory, which advocates simultaneous data collection and analysis with the objective of developing abstracted generalisable theory from individual cases (Charmaz, 2005). The legitimacy of using the concept of saturation is thus intrinsically bound to the purpose and objectives of this particular perspective. Although the meaning of saturation has transformed in a way to be useful for other theories, it is important to recognise that different perspectives have different purposes and objectives, so that saturation is not an appropriate measure of validity for all qualitative approaches (O'Reilly and Parker, 2013). While saturation is an essential marker for sampling adequacy for some methodological perspectives, for others it is wholly inappropriate, and entirely unachievable.

In a single case design it is entirely legitimate to assume that one participant is an adequate sample.

In conversation-analytic studies the methodology advocates that the minute nuances of small pieces of interaction are pertinent and analysable in their own right.

SUMMARY AND FINAL THOUGHTS

In this chapter we have advocated the importance of prospective planning of methods choices which take into consideration appropriate and congruent analytic decisions. We acknowledge that due to the iterative nature of qualitative work, this process cannot be conceptualised as purely linear; however, the necessity to avoid retrospective decisions enhances the quality of the research. One of the significant areas in which the congruence between ontology, epistemology, methodology and data collection methods is illuminated is within the naturally occurring versus researcher-generated data debate. While we personally favour the use of naturally occurring data as this is compatible with our epistemological position, our main argument is that the debate should not focus on whether one is superior to the other but on which is most appropriate to the perspective driving the research.

With this in mind we have advocated that there is no such thing as a generic neutral interview. We have taken the position that researchers need to carefully plan their research projects and consider a number of important methodological issues prior to embarking on their journey. Particularly noteworthy and significant here is the sometimes ignored matter that theoretical perspectives drive the interviewing method in different ways and, therefore, the researcher needs to engage in a number of informed choices. This is not to say that post-hoc analysis is impossible or inferior, but if done this way it needs to be performed reflexively and with full acknowledgement of its limitations. One of the problems with generic uses of interview materials and limited consideration of perspectives prior to analysis is that they lead to overgeneralisations and inappropriate application of theory-specific terminology. Each analytic perspective utilises different vocabulary, has different historical roots and is employed for different purposes (Honan et al., 2000). This is important in the context of quality frameworks and judgements.

Case study and reflective questions

Bruce and Caroline are both undertaking a degree in nursing. Bruce has recently collected 26 interviews with his diabetes patients. Caroline is at the planning stage of her research and is unsure which form of data collection to use. They have both recently attended a nursing conference where they participated in a methods workshop on interpretative phenomenological analysis. They both plan to utilise this approach for their projects.

Q: What problems may Bruce face in his retrospective decision to use IPA?
Q: How will having attended the workshop help Caroline to plan her data collection?

Suggestions for answering these questions are available at the end of the book.

FURTHER READING

Potter, J. (2002) Two kinds of natural. *Discourse Studies*, 4(4): 539–542.

This article is part of a series focusing on the distinction between naturally occurring and researcher-generated data. The author responds to earlier articles that raised inconsistencies in the distinction. Notably the author also provides some sense of what constitutes naturally occurring data.

Potter, J. and Hepburn, A. (2012) Eight challenges for interview researchers, in J. F. Gubrium and J. A. Holstein (eds), *Handbook of Interview Research* (2nd edition). London: Sage. pp. 555–570.

In this book chapter the authors challenge the popularity of interview research in qualitative methods and provide a critical discussion that presents some of the limitations of this approach to research. This is a useful and interesting discussion that critiques some of the more taken-for-granted ideas within qualitative approaches.

Speer, S. (2002) Transcending the 'natural/contrived' distinction: A rejoinder to Ten Have, Lynch and Potter. *Discourse Studies*, 4(4): 543–548.

In this article the author attempts to bring together some of the core issues in relation to distinguishing naturally occurring and researcher-generated data collection methods.

Wimpenny, P., and Gass, J. (2000). Interviewing in phenomenology and grounded theory: Is there a difference? *Methodological Issues in Nursing Research*, 31(6): 1485–1492.

In this article the authors consider the similarities and differences between two methodological approaches to interviewing. They argue that the interview method of data collection should be consistent with the underlying principles of the methodology and should be clearly connected to the methodological framework.

FIVE

Research design and mixing qualitative methods

CHAPTER CONTENTS

INTRODUCTION

In this chapter we present a focused overview of the different strands of theoretical debates within the arena of 'mixed methods'. We advance discussion in this area from more familiar arguments concerning inter-paradigm (qualitative–quantitative) conflicts to explore the nuances of intra-paradigm (qualitative-qualitative) challenges. The chapter opens with a critical discussion of the traditional mixed methods debate (quantitative/qualitative). This incorporates an overview of the key elements of what is understood by the notion of a paradigm (see also Chapter 1). This is necessary to set the scene for the second part of the chapter, which contextualises and explicates the historical development of the metaphysical arguments relating to paradigm purity and superiority. We move on to detail the phases of development within what is known colloquially as the 'paradigm wars', finishing with the most recent move towards evidence-based science. This provides a platform for the development of these discussions as they relate to intra-paradigm arguments, of qualitative–qualitative designs. The premises that characterise the possible difficulties inherent in this debate relate to the decision to mix *methods* or *methodologies*. This relates to several issues, including the potential incompatibility of the philosophical foundations; the different viewpoints and understandings of the place of contextual information in informing analysis; and the specific and generic criteria for judging quality within each approach. We offer some considered reflections on these important issues and propose some possible trajectories of inquiry to engage the reader in progressing these theoretical deliberations forward.

CONTEXTUALISING THE MIXED METHODS DEBATE

The fundamental claim of the mixed methods community is that the use of two or more methods within a single study increases confidence in the findings (Dixon-Woods et al., 2004a). The rationale of this type of research has been the ability of this approach to compensate for any weaknesses in a single research design (Bryman, 2008a). Additionally, it is argued that the integration of two different methods allows the researcher to obtain a more rounded and complete set of results, thus making the most of the complementary strengths of both the quantitative and qualitative approaches (O'Cathain and Thomas, 2006). Therefore the goal of the mixed methods approach is not to replace either of the two approaches, but to draw upon their strengths and minimise any limitations (Johnson and Onwuegbuzie, 2004).

The language used by scholars involved in the 'mixed methods debate' has typically been characterised by metaphors of combat and warfare, although this metaphoric discourse is disliked by some scholars. Most notably the phrase 'paradigm wars' has been adopted in some circles as a way of encapsulating the conflict between those who argue from either a theoretical or pragmatic viewpoint about the compatibility or incompatibility of combining quantitative and qualitative approaches within a single research study.

Within research communities a variety of terms have been used, often interchangeably, to describe mixed methods studies; these include 'mixed-methods', 'multi-methods', 'multiple-methods' as well as 'mixing-methods' (O'Cathain and Thomas, 2006). The term 'pluralism' has also been used to indicate the mixing of quantitative and qualitative methods in a single study (Barker and Pistrang, 2005), a term which has been applied to intra-paradigm (qualitative–qualitative) combined methods approaches as well (Nolas, 2011).

Central to the mixed methods debate are disagreements regarding the definition of the concept of 'paradigms' (as we discussed in Chapter 1). The philosopher Thomas Kuhn is often credited as being one of the original writers on the issue of scientific paradigms. In his early work Kuhn (1962) proposed four characteristics of paradigms which are outlined in Table 5.1.

Table 5.1 Characteristics of scientific paradigms (Kuhn, 1962)

Characteristic	Description
Problems focus	Paradigms centre on sets of problems that are important for the advancement of knowledge.
Shared practice	Paradigms require a shared understanding about research techniques and their appropriateness for investigation.
Shared identity	Paradigms involve a shared sense of 'identity' which is reinforced through the process of exchanging information.
Groups	Paradigms operate through groups as they function as a 'research community', which exist at a number of different levels.

However, even within his original work, at least 22 different uses of the concept were identified (Masterman, 1970). It is evident, therefore, that the term 'research paradigm' has multiple meanings (Morgan, 2007). Over the last half century the way the term 'paradigm' is understood and used has become more sophisticated and divergent. These changes have been usefully categorised by Morgan (2007) who identifies four core ways in which the notion of a paradigm has been conceptualised in social science research, listed in Table 5.2.

Table 5.2 Four notions of paradigms in social science (Morgan, 2007)

Paradigm	Description
Paradigm as world-view	This is the broadest understanding of the concept and is the version most frequently referred to in the social sciences. This includes beliefs about values, morals and aesthetics.
Paradigm as an epistemological stance (metaphysical paradigm)	This view takes a narrower approach linking the researcher's world-view with the philosophy of knowledge. It treats paradigms as distinctive belief systems which influence how research questions are asked and answered.
Paradigm as a system of shared beliefs	This view considers that within a particular research community, paradigms are systems of shared beliefs where there is a consensus about which questions are most meaningful and which methods are most appropriate to address them.
Paradigm as a model example of research	This approach proposes model case studies as exemplars of the paradigm which researchers use to demonstrate and reflect sets of shared beliefs about questions asked and methods used to answer them.

Paradigm debates

The historical phase that was referred to at the time as the paradigm wars emerged in the 1970s with the rise of post-positivism challenging the dominant positivist position in social science research (Denzin, 2010). The dissatisfaction with positivism, coupled with the rise of qualitative approaches, led to paradigm discontent. For qualitative research to be accepted as a legitimate form of inquiry operating on an equal footing regarding knowledge claims, the debate was moved to a metaphysical level (Morgan, 2007). Over time there have been a number of debates within the mixed methods community which retrospectively have been conceptualised chronologically as a series of four paradigm phases. We begin by outlining these in Figure 5.1.

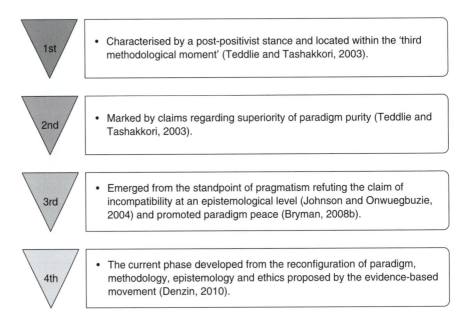

Figure 5.1 Paradigm historical chronology

Beginning in the 1980s, the central issue within the second phase of paradigm shift was related to the incompatibility of mixing quantitative and qualitative approaches in a single study (Howe, 1988). This was based on the original works of Kuhn who argued that two paradigms that have their own language and rules of justification are fundamentally incompatible, referred to as the notion of incommensurability. This second phase grew out of dissatisfaction with the overemphasis on quantitative methodology and a renewed interest in qualitative approaches, which illuminated the need to question prevailing metaphysical assumptions (Guba and Lincoln, 1994).

Based on Kuhn's proposition that two scientific paradigms are fundamentally incommensurable, purists argued that it is theoretically impossible to combine the two approaches (Denzin and Lincoln, 2005).

Proponents of this metaphysical paradigm took a strong position on incommensurability. They asserted that researchers should accept one paradigm and reject all others, thus creating communication barriers between the knowledge produced by each of the paradigms (Morgan, 2007).

Purists within the research community at this time promoted their preferred paradigm as superior and advocated the 'incompatibility thesis' that quantitative and qualitative approaches could not be mixed (Howe, 1988).

This argument of incompatibility was based on the belief that different research paradigms were underpinned by radically different assumptions about the nature of reality, and therefore researchers within the different approaches utilised specific language which made it impossible to translate research between them (Morgan, 2007). However, researchers who were frustrated with the constraints imposed by incommensurability sought to argue an alternative position, which was proposed as a resolution to some of the ongoing debate. The emergence of the third phase was therefore characterised by the rise of pragmatism. This pragmatic movement was based upon ideas of methodological eclecticism, which held that a practical approach should be sought using whatever combination of methods seemed appropriate (Yancher and Williams, 2006).

Pragmatism is typically considered to be the philosophical underpinning of the mixed methods approach (Johnson and Onwuegbuzie, 2004), and for some, mixed methods is considered to be the 'third paradigm' (Denscombe, 2008). Thus there are those who argue that mixed methods is a new paradigm that always requires the mixture of quantitative and qualitative approaches (Johnson et al., 2007), although some disagree with this (see Morgan, 2007, for a discussion).

Pragmatism focuses on the compatibility of combining 'methods', rather than the incommensurability of competing 'epistemologies'. Thus, in this 'third methodological moment' (Teddlie and Tashakkori, 2003) mixed methods research is argued to have its own epistemology (Freshwater, 2007). The arguments from the first, second and third movements are well reflected in the writings of two core contributors to the debate and we outline these positions below in Box 5.1.

influential **voices**

Box 5.1   Epistemological incompatibility
and pragmatism in mixed methods research

Epistemological incongruence of mixing methods	A pragmatic approach to paradigm peace
Thomas Kuhn	Alan Bryman

Thomas Kuhn was a professor of philosophy at Massachusetts Institute of Technology (MIT). Kuhn unfortunately passed away in 1996, but his work on the vocabulary of the philosophy of science continues to have enormous impact in many disciplines.

The central premise of Kuhn's argument was that different scientific paradigms are fundamentally incompatible and therefore cannot be reconciled (Kuhn, 1962). In social science research this 'paradigms approach' is characterised by a reflexive understanding of the research process, and a belief that a new mode of thinking will replace the old (Morgan, 2005). The paradigms approach treats paradigms as fixed, externally defined systems; however, Kuhn emphasised that for any shifts in paradigms to be manifest, this would depend on a community of researchers responding to anomalies (Morgan, 2005).

Originally Kuhn (1962) used the concept of incommensurability to describe a situation where two paradigms have their own structures of meaning and rules of justification. When a paradigm changes, the language and justification strategy associated with that paradigm changes too. Therefore Kuhn argued that if two theories are to be commensurable they must share an overlapping

Alan Bryman* is a professor of organisational and social research at the University of Leicester in the School of Management. He has written extensively on the topic of research methods, paying particular attention to resolving some of the tensions that exist in the mixed method debate.

Bryman's perspective is that the focus on epistemological incongruence between quantitative and qualitative approaches exaggerates the differences and exacerbates the conflict (Bryman, 2008b). He argues that the divergence between the two paradigms has a tendency to confuse philosophical and technical issues by often oscillating between the two, making it difficult to ascertain where one begins and the other ends (Bryman, 1982). As an alternative Bryman promotes a pragmatist position which, in the interest of exploring research questions, favours the focus on compatible technical approaches rather than being concerned with paradigmatic differences (Bryman, 2008b).

Bryman argues that research methods are more 'free floating' in terms of their epistemology than is usually supposed (Bryman, 2008a). This viewpoint therefore gives more flexibility for researchers to engage in mixed methods research, without having to resolve language within which both theories could be translated without losing meaning (Kuhn, 1962). In essence, the notion of incommensurability is metaphorical in that there can be no language into which both theories can be translated without residue or loss (Kuhn, 1982).

Ultimately there is no way in which two scientific theories can be stated in a single language and therefore they cannot be compared (Kuhn, 1982).

epistemological dilemmas. The commitment to pragmatism, which is frequently favoured by more applied disciplines, has promoted a reduction in hostilities within the mixed methods debate (Bryman, 2008b).

This leads to consideration of whether the paradigm divergences matter as much as has been emphasised. For some the lack of resolution is still problematic, whereas for others the diversity of opinion provides an opportunity to examine the social world through some different lenses (Bryman, 2008b). Following Bryman's lead, this more recent emphasis on compatibility has thus fostered a more accommodating climate for 'paradigm peace' (Bryman, 2006, 2008b).

*We thank Professor Bryman for taking the time to read an earlier draft of this chapter.

An essential question that arose, therefore, was how the two paradigms could communicate with one another (Morgan, 2007). For Kuhn (1962), the insurmountable issue was that translation across paradigms was impossible. A suggestion put forward was that scientists from both paradigms would need to become 'lexically bilingual' to address this problem (Tadajewski, 2009). However, this would not necessarily resolve the issue as translation from one 'language' to another involves a degree of interpretation, resulting in some distortion (Kuhn, 1962). Therefore the mixed methods community began to develop a discourse of their own in order to transcend this divide (Freshwater, 2007). Notably, central to this debate, 'paradigms were being reconfigured to fit methodological presuppositions' (Denzin, 2010: 422). Indeed, Kuhn (1996) himself argued that paradigms are a product of a community of researchers and can be redefined by that community over a period of time to reflect developments. This is possible if a paradigm remains flexible, multi-layered and permeable (Denscombe, 2008). The resolution to the 'paradigm wars', therefore, is only possible when a new paradigm emerges which is more sophisticated and informed than the existing ones (Guba and Lincoln, 1994), and pragmatism presents as one possible solution for paradigm peace (Bryman, 2008b).

————————————————— Reflective space —————————————————

What is your personal view on whether it is possible for researchers to be fluent in the languages of both qualitative and quantitative inquiry?

Towards paradigm harmony

The third phase was characterised by a promotion of paradigm peace. The rationale for pragmatists is that combining methods provides a more holistic picture of the phenomenon under investigation. The combination of methods is proposed on the basis that it can help to cancel out the weaknesses of the single approaches (Hammersley, 1996) or to improve the accuracy of the data (Denscombe, 2008).

In order to navigate the 'top-down' epistemological concerns presented by the metaphysical paradigm, pragmatists argue that it is necessary to reconceptualise the discussion at a more technical level. This refocuses attention on more practical concerns promoting congruence at the level of methods. On the technical level, the inter-paradigm debate attends to the merits and limitations of the approaches and the methods associated with them which are critical for resolution (Bryman, 2008b). This allows researchers to choose the best combination of methods which work to answer the research question (Johnson and Onwuegbuzie, 2004).

As mixed method designs have become more acceptable, therefore, it becomes necessary for researchers to engage further with considering this assumption that mixed approaches automatically provide better answers to research questions (Bergman, 2005). One perspective argues for 'paradigmatic ecumenicalism' in order to supersede the polarity of the approaches (Johnson and Onwuegbuzie, 2004). In order for this to be effective there is a reliance on finding a way to engage in shared and meaningful communication (Morgan, 2007). Alternatively, it is arguable that there is a need for multiple investigators with competencies in more than one paradigm or method, and potentially this dual competency issue can be solved with a team approach (Denzin, 2008).

Despite a drive towards paradigm peace, the claim of compatibility and synthesis may be seen by some as a premature attempt to close the debate (Smith and Heshusius, 1986). Additionally, the premise that the whole will be greater than the sum of its parts is questionable; we would suggest that this viewpoint is only valid where there is rigour both within each methodological part and in the process of combining the two. Ultimately it is essential to attend to the theoretical level of methods. If a method was not based on assumptions it would not possess the unique characteristics required to study phenomena, as methods cannot be extricated from theoretical concerns (Yancher and Williams, 2006).

---------------------------------- Reflective space ----------------------------------

This is a good opportunity to stop and consider methodological rigour in both aspects of a mixed methods research project. Think about the consequences of one or both parts of a study lacking rigour and the overall impact this may have on the knowledge produced.

Hierarchies of research evidence

Notwithstanding potential criticisms of pragmatism and the arguments for paradigm peace, more contemporary research arguments are inevitably embedded in the evidence-based movement, which initially emerged from the discipline of health. The term 'evidence-based' was introduced by the scholar David Eddy in his article laying out the principles of evidence-based guidelines (Eddy, 1990), and later the notion of evidence-based medicine was used in the practice of teaching medicine (Guyatt et al., 1992). Sacket et al. (1996) developed this notion further to encourage better and more objective decision-making by encouraging the health profession to reflect on evidence from research.

Notably, this drive to promote research-based practice has created hierarchies of evidence, reinvoking the notion of superiority in methods and approaches and re-establishing a claim for purity. Importantly, a number of hierarchies of evidence have been developed, but most of these have focused on evaluation of the effectiveness of interventions, placing the randomised controlled trial at the top (Evans, 2003). This 'science-based research' movement has enacted a further attempt to return to modernist ways of considering knowledge and potentially re-engages the notion of the paradigm wars (Hatch, 2006). Although many of these developments occurred in parallel with mixed methods debates, it is more recently that the evidence-based movement and arguments regarding the quality of mixed methods design have begun to merge and influence social science research.

While discourses of evidence-based practices have become a cornerstone of healthcare, the question of what constitutes good evidence remains (Rolfe, 2010). The evidence-based movement privileges quantitative research evidence that positions randomised controlled trials as the 'gold standard', an idea that has received extensive criticisms (Grossman and Mackenzie, 2005). Nonetheless the UK National Institute of Clinical Excellence, in the discipline of health, developed guidelines which prescribed the value of different levels of evidence, placing randomised controlled trials at the top of the hierarchy (Marks, 2002). This hierarchy of evidence has been represented in tabular and pyramid form in different ways by many and there is some disagreement as to the order of the methodologies, but typically randomised controlled trials are considered the superior form of evidence (Turner, 2013). This is a view that seems to be pertinent across many countries. We present our own version of this pyramid in Figure 5.2, using information outlined in Marks (2002).

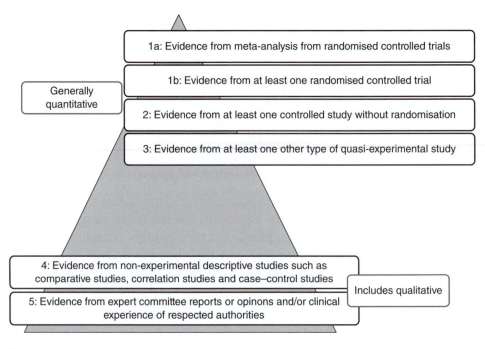

Figure 5.2   Hierarchies of evidence

The hierarchy-of-evidence model determines how research is rated in funding applications – it has relegated qualitative research to a secondary position (Freshwater et al., 2010) and potentially poses a threat to the progress made by the qualitative community (Lester and O'Reilly, 2015). This rhetoric is now having some influence in other disciplines such as the social sciences and education, and the notion of hierarchies of evidence has broader implications for the place, acceptance and promotion of qualitative research. Notably, qualitative evidence is positioned towards the bottom of the hierarchy, as part of the final two levels of evidence (Morse, 2006a). It is therefore an inevitable development for mixed methods researchers that there is a need to address the issues highlighted by the evidence-based movement because of the powerful discourses associated with it and the practical impact that it has had. Potentially, mixed methods approaches are a solution to the challenges faced by qualitative researchers in gaining funding and informing policy to secure a practical place for qualitative research, but this may lead to a compromise in the researchers' principles, epistemology and view of mixed methods (see Lester and O'Reilly, 2015, for a full critical discussion).

Assuming that this way of thinking about research is 'here to stay' (Morse, 2006a: 396), the obvious question is where in the current hierarchy of evidence mixed methods research falls and whether there are different levels of superiority of different types of mixed methods evidence. Thus the emergent arguments within the fourth chronological phase of the mixed methods debate are related to the value of qualitative evidence, driving a renewed interest in revisiting its epistemological underpinnings, particularly given that the epistemology of evidence-based practice is predominantly positivist (Marks, 2002). Notably, it was the struggle for a place for qualitative evidence that drove the elevation of the metaphysical paradigm during the second phase, and with the return to hierarchies these problems have potential to re-emerge. The fact that evidence within certain paradigms is privileged over others perpetuates the notion of paradigm superiority that was characteristic of the second phase. Thus, understanding paradigm development as a relational activity allows us to explore the processes and discourses by which this is achieved (Freshwater et al., 2010).

In the context of this potential devaluation of the qualitative approach, researchers have sought to reconceptualise qualitative evidence in terms of a hierarchy. The rationale for this differentiation has been to identify which types of qualitative studies provide better evidence for practice (Daly et al., 2007). Daly et al. argue that there are four levels of qualitative evidence: at the top, level one evidence is generalisable studies; level two is conceptual studies; level three is descriptive studies; and the lowest level is the single case study. Nonetheless, historically cautions have been expressed against dividing qualitative work up in this way. Arguably the epistemological diversity within the approach renders any single qualitative hierarchy of evidence inappropriate (Mays et al., 2001). The logical progression of this argument is to theorise about where different combinations of levels of quantitative and qualitative research would feature within the overall evidence-based hierarchy. This is because there is an inherent assumption that combining quantitative and qualitative approaches produces superior research when appropriate to the research problem (Bryman, 1992). The other assumption made is that there is greater value in the accumulation of knowledge, as indicated in the fact that the highest level in the evidence-based practice hierarchy is a synthesis of knowledge.

 Would a quantitative randomised controlled study combined with any level of qualitative evidence be superior to randomised controlled studies alone?

Would a quasi-experimental study and a qualitative single case study be superior to any single qualitative study?

The mixed methods community is only just starting to grapple with these complex questions, transcending different disciplines. While mixing methods can be viewed as a positive contribution to evidence, some argue that this is not inevitable by definition (Mason, 2006). Change, therefore, is not necessarily an improvement and mixing methods may not be the *best* approach, but simply the most *politically correct* one (Freshwater, 2005), or potentially the most pragmatic to continue to promote qualitative methods (particularly in practical fields such as health, education, social work and so forth) and to maintain their presence in an evidence-based world (Lester and O'Reilly, 2015).

THE THEORETICAL CHALLENGES OF COMBINING QUALITATIVE APPROACHES

The debates regarding the combination of methods have focused predominantly on the incommensurability versus compatibility of quantitative and qualitative elements within a single research study. However, there has been little work than considers the implications of combining multiple qualitative research methods or methodologies (Lambert and Loiselle, 2008). This may be due to the misconception that combining methods within the same paradigm is less problematic than mixing across approaches (Barbour, 1998). This focus on inter-paradigm differences has overshadowed a more subtle debate about intra-paradigm differences. Within the qualitative approach there are more intra-paradigmatic differences than within quantitative (Denzin and Lincoln, 2005). This is confounded further by the multiplicity of terms used to refer to this combining within the approach. There are various different labels used in the literature, including 'qualitative mixed methods design' (Morse, 2009), 'multiple method design' (Morse, 2009), 'generic qualitative research' (Caelli et al., 2003), 'combined qualitative methodology' (Swanson-Kauffman, 1986), and 'pluralism' (Nolas, 2011). Often these terms are used interchangeably, despite some authors arguing that there are distinctions between them (Morse, 2010).

This raises the question whether the design is 'mixed qualitative methods' or 'multiple qualitative methods', depending upon the stage at which the data are combined or synthesised (Morse, 2009). Resolution of the debates within the qualitative paradigm seems to hinge predominantly on whether we are referring to mixing *methods* or mixing *methodologies*.

 Mixing interviews with focus groups is an example of mixing qualitative methods.

 Mixing grounded theory with narrative analysis is an example of mixing qualitative methodologies.

In the traditional quantitative-qualitative mixed methods debate, there has been a tension between the pragmatist focus on methods and the purist focus on methodology and related epistemology. This parallels the intra-paradigm dichotomy between qualitative researchers who on one end of the spectrum view methods as 'relatively atheoretical' (Carter and Little, 2007) and those who believe that methodological incongruence prohibits the combination of qualitative methods (Lal et al., 2012).

─────────────────── Reflective space ───────────────────

Take some time to consider the potential extent of intra-paradigm differences compared to inter-paradigm differences.

To clarify the potential compatibility of two methods or methodologies, we propose that there are two possible ways of considering the research process. The first is the *mixed qualitative methods* approach. This is characterised by three phases, the first two being the concurrent or sequential collection of data using two separate methods. These are followed by the third phase, which is an integration of both sets of data using the same analytic approach. This approach maintains epistemological integrity by adhering to one subsuming methodology. The second way is the *synthesised methodologies* approach, which is characterised by five discrete phases. Within the first methodological frame, the initial two phases are that data are collected using a compatible method and analysed according to that approach. The second two phases are additional data collection and analysis within the second methodological frame. Notably, these first four phases could also occur in parallel rather than sequentially. The final phase constitutes a synthesis of the two sets of analysis and findings. The difference between mixing qualitative methods and synthesising methodology is outlined in Table 5.3.

Table 5.3 Mixing methods or synthesising methodologies?

Mixed qualitative methods	Synthesised methodologies
Two different methods of data collection are used. Combining of findings happens at the analytical stage of the research.	Two different methodologies of data analysis are applied to the data collected. Combining analysed findings happens at the post-analysis stage of the research.

The term 'mixed qualitative methods' refers to a single qualitative study operating within a singular methodology but using more than one method of data collection. In this case the researcher may require both data sets to provide a more holistic interpretation of the phenomenon of interest. Although the data have been collected by different methods they can be analysed through the same analytic framework dictated by the methodology, and are thus epistemologically congruent.

(e.g.) Example of mixed qualitative methods: A researcher using the methodology of interpretative phenomenological analysis may collect data through interviews and focus groups. In this example the same analytic approach is used to inform data collection and examine both data sets which were obtained using two different methods. Integration therefore occurs at the analytical stage of the research process.

The term 'synthesised methodologies' applies to a research study which employs two separate methodological approaches. This may or may not use the same methods throughout, but the crucial issue is that the methodology will dictate the way that the data collected are analysed. Integration therefore cannot occur at an analytic stage and must necessarily happen during the synthesis of the two separate studies.

(e.g.) Example of synthesised methodologies: A researcher collecting interview data may seek to examine the same data using two different methodologies such as grounded theory and critical discourse analysis. In this situation, although at a methods level the study may appear compatible, at a theoretical level they are incommensurable. Because analysis has to happen separately to conform to methodological rigour, integration of findings can only occur at synthesis.

Similarly, if there were two different methodologies employed using two different methods the same would apply, in that analysis would necessarily have to occur independently before synthesis of findings. Notably, in terms of dissemination, a mixed qualitative methods study is far more straightforward to disseminate in the sense that the way the findings are presented and the potential audience will be more homogeneous. Conversely, for synthesised methodological studies, it is argued that it is more challenging to find a common language to disseminate findings in a meaningful way to different audiences.

The issue of finding a shared language becomes even more challenging for pluralistic combined qualitative studies. This approach utilises a singular data set, which is analysed from a number of different approaches, after data collection. This is neither a mixed qualitative methods approach nor a synthesised methodology approach. Rather each analytic perspective encapsulates different epistemological perspectives which are employed by the different analysts working on the same project.

(e.g.) Frost et al. (2011) describe an example of the pluralistic approach to qualitative data analysis in their study of the transcripts of semi-structured interviews around the issue of second-time motherhood. The analysts took four different perspectives of grounded theory, IPA, narrative analysis, and Foucauldian discourse analysis. They argue that this provides a more holistic multi-layered understanding of the data.

Within different paradigms there are discourse practices which characterise the epistemological concerns operating within those communities. The qualitative rubric is underpinned by a broad range of different theoretical assumptions (Denzin, 2010), and yet for methodological rigour, consideration must be given to these epistemological assumptions and their compatibility (Lambert and Loiselle, 2008). Different qualitative epistemological frameworks have different interests and concerns, with some interested in developing theory and others concerned with better understanding a phenomenon (Nolas, 2011). However, some researchers mix their methods with little acknowledgement of the methodological approach or underpinning theoretical framework (Wimpenny and Gass, 2000). Often studies using a combined approach are poorly anchored within an identifiable theoretical or epistemological perspective (Caelli et al., 2003). Nonetheless, it is well accepted within qualitative work that methodological prescriptions guide data collection and should be consistent (Baker et al., 1992).

Arguments about the compatibility of mixing qualitative methods or methodologies also rest on ontological concerns. The qualitative researcher will have a view of the world which should be acknowledged and is important in terms of what is regarded as reality (Frost, 2011). At the ontological level there is a contrast between the belief that there is a social reality that exists externally to the social actor which can be uncovered by the social researcher, against the belief in a domain that is in a continuous process of creation and recreation by social actors (Bryman, 2008b). Thus if two approaches arise from the same ontological foundation, there is a greater likelihood of epistemological congruence, but if the two approaches are not founded on the same ontology the study is likely to suffer a loss of integrity (Annells, 2006).

Theoretical considerations of combining methods or methodologies

There are a variety of reasons why a researcher may choose to combine multiple qualitative methods or methodologies which invoke different issues for debate. Different methods may be used at different stages in a project, with one informing the other (Barbour, 1998). One qualitative method can be used, therefore, to supplement another in a mixed qualitative methods design project (Morse, 2010). The aim of this is often to seek greater completeness, based on the assumption that the data collected through each method reveal different aspects of the phenomena of interest (Lambert and Loiselle, 2008). However, some argue that this simply produces a more complex view of the topic rather than improving validity (Richardson, 1994). Advocates of the mixed qualitative approach argue that it can provide a more comprehensive understanding in breadth and depth of findings (Nolas, 2011). Often when two qualitative approaches are combined there will be a 'core' or primary component and a 'supplementary' component (Morse, 2010). The supplementary component is intended to add a new perspective, which is possible provided that the two methods are within the same methodological framework.

However, if the supplementary method is incompatible with the main methodological approach then this creates intra-paradigmatic incompatibility which causes problems not dissimilar to the traditional (quantitative/qualitative) mixed methods debate (Morse, 2010). An important way in which qualitative methodologies are differentiated relates to their intended purposes (Lal et al., 2012) and their underpinning epistemologies, with some methodologies being incongruent with certain methods.

> **e.g.** Example of compatibility: Although there are some differences, the epistemological similarities between grounded theory and narrative inquiry suggest that they can be combined within a mixed qualitative study as they are theoretically commensurable and methodologically complementary (Lal et al., 2012). So, for example, the methods of interviewing and focus groups would suit both approaches.

> **e.g.** Example of incommensurability: For a primarily conversation-analytic study, the addition of a supplementary thematic interview component would mean that an integrated analysis is impossible due to the incommensurability of paradigmatic differences (Morse, 2010).

Where there is methodological incongruence, therefore, this necessitates the researcher conducting two discrete phases of the research project (Wilson and Hutchinson, 1991) which can be synthesised after analysis. The value of differentiating between a mixed qualitative methods approach and a synthesised methodologies approach (refer back to Table 5.3) is that the separate components within both approaches can be appraised separately according to their relevant methodological quality criteria. Quality criteria are essential in the current climate of evidence and standardisation, but there are risks that the standardised assessment criteria may be inappropriate for evaluating qualitative work (Barbour, 2001; Carter and Little, 2007).

The different approaches have different quality criteria for judging the 'goodness' or quality of the inquiry (Guba and Lincoln, 1994), and although there is some controversy regarding universality of criteria (see Chapter 2), this has implications for the combining of multiple qualitative methods or methodologies. At one level the general indicators of quality within qualitative research apply to mixed qualitative methods designs in terms of the fact that broad issues such as transferability, trustworthiness, transparency and reflexivity can all be assessed. Nonetheless there are also specific quality criteria inherent in each particular methodology; these particular indicators are important when considering the particular merits of each component of the mixed qualitative methods design. In a synthesised methodologies design each methodology is assessed for quality separately, and additionally the synthesis is appraised according to standardised protocol. However, in a mixed qualitative methods design, while the individual components can be assessed separately, any epistemological incongruence also needs to be critically evaluated, in terms of the overall research design, its ability to meet the research objectives and overall rigour.

One of the most fundamental general quality criteria for qualitative research is reflexivity. Reflexivity is the practice of situating oneself in the context of the research, showing an awareness of and sensitivity to engagement with the cultural and social embeddedness of methods, theories and research questions, as well as checking and critiquing one's own assumptions (Nolas, 2011). Qualitative research differs from quantitative, which tends to strip away context which is an important component of reflexivity, in that context becomes inherent to the understanding and analysis of the data (Guba and Lincoln, 1994). However, it becomes necessary to establish what constitutes the relevant social context and whose orientation to context is consequential (Schegloff, 1997). In some approaches researchers have relied on a priori definitions of context and explore how context mediates or moderates outcomes; others have treated context as emergent through the meanings ascribed by individuals during interaction (Nolas, 2011). One of the difficulties therefore with combining qualitative approaches is that competing understandings of what constitutes context mean that it can be difficult to identify what elements of context are 'imposed' by the researcher and what is 'emergent'. For example, what may appear to be the benign task of identifying participants in an extract of data could be perceived as an act of imposing categories. This unilateral allocation of social labels onto others could be seen by some researchers as 'theoretical imperialism' (Billig, 1999). In some qualitative approaches context refers to the act of reflexivity, whereas in others it refers to transparency regarding the demographics of participants. Those combining multiple qualitative approaches must therefore reconcile these disparate viewpoints in a meaningful way in order to adequately fulfil one of the fundamental quality criteria of qualitative research. This may include an additional layer of reflexivity regarding one's own experience of the process of working in a mixed qualitative methods way. A new approach for which reflexivity is particularly important is facet methodology. This approach differs from mixed methods approaches in that it does not seek to triangulate or integrate methods and data, but emphasises the researcher's use of imagination and interpretation across facets of inquiry (Mason, 2011). While this approach offers the possibility of experimenting with perspectives in an adventurous way, because it is a particularly interpretative approach which encourages creative engagement across epistemologies (Mason, 2011), transparency and reflexivity are essential.

The value of the research team

In order to safeguard the quality of each of the components of combined qualitative methods/methodology studies, consideration needs to be given to whether this necessitates a team rather than an individual researcher approach. Most qualitative researchers tend to have research strengths or interests in a relatively narrow field, aligning with a favoured methodological approach. Due to the complexity of research design implementation and analysis within the qualitative paradigm, this facilitates both a familiarity with and an adherence to the quality frameworks of that approach. For many of the primary methodological approaches researchers require specialist training to develop the skills required for competency in undertaking research within that particular methodology. Therefore an individual researcher working within a particular methodological framework could apply their expertise appropriately within a mixed qualitative methods design. In this approach one methodology would dictate the process of sampling, data collection and analysis, even though two separate methods are utilised. However, in a synthesised methodological approach it may be beneficial to collaborate with other researchers who have expertise in other methodological approaches in order to maintain methodological integrity and assure quality.

Within the quantitative/qualitative mixed methods designs there is a danger of executing neither adequately (Chen, 1997), and therefore some have argued that it may be beneficial to engage qualitative and quantitative experts by using a team approach (Teddlie and Tashakkori, 2003). Arguably working in a mixed methods way lends itself to group working and may be useful for combined qualitative designs (Nolas, 2011). While this has particular benefits of combined expertise and different perspectives on the research problem, team working has a number of challenges. Most notably, the issue of a shared language with which to communicate values, beliefs and interpretations has been raised as the most significant obstacle to effective team working. Indeed, this was initially considered by Kuhn in his early writing on the topic of paradigms (Kuhn, 1962).

Team members may have philosophical differences (Barbour, 1998) and different world-views about the topic being researched (Barry et al., 1999) or even different values about aspects of the research, including issues of academic dissemination (Massey et al., 2006). Researchers coming from different epistemological and ontological positions are likely to have very different perspectives when analysing and interpreting data. These can affect both communication between team members during the research process and the difficulty of developing a shared language for dissemination. A possible solution suggested in the quantitative–qualitative debate was that team members have at least minimum competencies in both methodologies to enable communication (Teddlie and Tashakkori, 2003). Thus a minimum competency in both qualitative methodologies might also have the potential to facilitate their synthesis or combination. Some advocates of combining qualitative methods believe that a solution to the difficulties is to take an 'epistemologically agnostic stance', although currently there are no guidelines on how to engage in pluralistic interpretation (Frost, 2011: 152). Communication is a difficulty not only for dissemination, but also for the interpretation of data and in terms of how the audience will engage with the text. Therefore, in the discourse of mixed methodology it becomes necessary for researchers to include indicators of how the text should be read (Freshwater, 2005).

SUMMARY AND FINAL THOUGHTS

What concerns me is mixing paradigms, or metaphysical models, or, worse yet, simply declaring that one's philosophical belief system associated with research and inquiry are meaningless or irrelevant, or that one has tired of the discussion and withdraws from it, under the guise of being 'pragmatic'. Pragmatism is the new virtue, purism is the new doctrinal error, the paradigmatic sin.

(Lincoln, 2010: 7)

By reviewing the historical development of the inter-paradigm debate we have shown that the concept of a paradigm is both iterative and evolutionary. This has important consequences for the future trajectory of our theoretical understanding and practical applicability of mixing methods. Our presentation of the paradigm wars chronology as having been developed over four overlapping phases demonstrates the evolutionary aspect of how the debate has advanced. Notably, the current evidence-based fourth movement revisits some of the core themes pertinent within the second movement, thus reflecting the iterative and organic nature of paradigm progress. This is consistent with Kuhn's original proposition that paradigms are shaped and developed by the communities that inhabit and promote them.

The incommensurability/pragmatism dichotomy is a consistent theme emergent and perpetuated throughout the four phases of the inter-paradigm mixed methods debate. It is this same theme which characterises the intra-paradigm challenges, particularly in light of the broader range of diversity within the qualitative approach. While the complexities of mixing qualitative approaches have been largely overlooked by the academic community, it is nonetheless a very important topic to consider, given the rise in popularity of traditional mixed methods approaches. Our critical engagement with the advanced theoretical issues surrounding this particular debate has led us to surmise that the most helpful way of conceptualising the core argument is to consider whether the 'mixing' can occur at a methodological or methods level. This solution takes into consideration the ontological and epistemological underpinnings of particular qualitative designs and functions to retain the dialectic of both the incommensurability and pragmatist positions.

In effect, the pragmatist position has always been one which focuses on compatibility at a methods level, and by utilising our terminology, a design which has compatible epistemologies could still be referred to as a mixed qualitative methods design. However, where epistemologies prohibit merger at that technical level it is still possible to conduct a design incorporating two separate qualitative methodologies, the findings from which can be synthesised after analysis. This approach offers an acceptable theoretical and practical solution to the incommensurability argument and retains analytical integrity. Technically, therefore, this approach would not constitute a strictly mixed methods design, but, as we suggest, would nonetheless be a valid alternative.

———————— Case study and reflective questions ————————

Charlie is a PhD student in the School of Business and Management and has collected a data set of audio recordings of several policy development management meetings. The purpose of these meetings was to reach final decisions regarding new regulations on lone working. Charlie is keen to use conversation analysis to explore the sequential nature of the decision-making process. However, Charlie is concerned that the small data set is insufficient and may limit dissemination options. In order to supplement the findings, Charlie decides to conduct some follow-up interviews with those professionals present at the meetings. The aim of these interviews for Charlie is to find out what they were really thinking when they expressed their opinions.

Q: Do you think that Charlie should use a mixed methods qualitative design or a synthesised methodologies approach, and why?

Q: What is the incommensurability problem here?

Suggestions for answering these questions are available at the end of the book.

FURTHER READING

Barbour, R. (1998) Mixing qualitative methods: Quality assurance or qualitative quagmire? *Qualitative Health Research*, 8(3): 352–361.

This early article was one of the first to consider that there are critical issues in mixing or combining two different qualitative methods or methodologies in a single project. The author argues that analytical rigour is important and that there are potentially contradictory assumptions when a researcher seeks to combine qualitative methods.

Bryman, A. (2008b) The end of the paradigm wars? In P. Alasuutari, L. Bickman, and J. Brannen (eds), *The SAGE Handbook of Social Research Methods*. London: Sage. pp. 13–25.

This important book chapter presents a debate about whether the research community has resolved its epistemological issues that promoted the 'paradigm wars'. The author illustrates some of the core debates related to the topic and raises important questions about resolution to the challenges of mixing quantitative and qualitative methods.

Morgan, D. (2007). Paradigms lost and pragmatism regained: Methodological implications of combining qualitative and quantitative methods. *Journal of Mixed Methods Research*, 1(1): 48–76.

This article also considers the issues that are associated with mixing quantitative and qualitative research methods and utilises the original theories proposed by Kuhn to consider the idea of paradigm shifts. The author contextualises the renewed interest in qualitative research and promotes ways of working that allow for a mixed methods approach.

Morse, J. (2010). Simultaneous and sequential qualitative mixed method designs. *Qualitative Inquiry*, 16(6): 483–491.

In this article the author defines mixed methods and considers the different ways in which methods might be combined. She raises important questions about the specific issues that are raised by research that seeks to combine or mix two different qualitative methods or methodologies, and she considers the problem of incompatibility. Importantly, she presents different ways of combining qualitative methods.

Nolas, S.-M. (2011) Pragmatics of pluralistic qualitative research, in N. Frost (ed.), *Qualitative Research Methods in Psychology: Combining Core Approaches*. Maidenhead: Open University Press. pp. 121–144.

In this chapter the author promotes the possibilities for pluralistic research within the qualitative field. Indeed, this chapter is part of a book which considers the practical challenges for combining two or more qualitative approaches. This is a useful resource for planning a mixed qualitative methods approach.

SIX

Recording and transcription

CHAPTER CONTENTS

INTRODUCTION

In contemporary society there has been an evolution of digital technology. In this chapter we present central debates that have evolved alongside this development by considering the relationship between technology and qualitative research. Undoubtedly the depth and richness of data have been promoted through the rise of audio equipment, capable of capturing the details of people's lives beyond the researcher's notes. However, the speed with which technology has moved now means that we have new ways to record visual as well as audio data, and with the rise of the smartphone, the computer and the internet, the options available to researchers have significantly extended. In this chapter we provide a critical discussion of how this has enabled researchers to record participants both through researcher-generated and naturally occurring means, and consider the issues that arise with regard to the potential influence of the recording device, issues raised by using the internet or smartphones for data collection, and modern implications for data storage and protection.

The rise of technology also has implications for transcription, and in this chapter we illustrate some of the arguments that relate to this important qualitative practice. The globalisation of research means that there are important debates about the translation of data from other languages, and we offer some suggestions for how this might be managed in practice. In conclusion, we consider some of the issues and concerns that may be inherent in paying a professional transcriptionist. We outline some of the arguments relating to the impact on the quality of both transcription and analysis, as well as considering some of the concerns for transcriptionist safety.

RECORDING ISSUES

A salient issue for researchers is that of how best to capture data. For several decades researchers have been attempting to capture social life through various recording modalities, from simple field notes, to more sophisticated contemporary digital means. This is in no way a neutral objective process but has evoked many different theoretical and practical debates.

THE EVOLUTION OF DIGITAL TECHNOLOGY

Qualitative research uses and relies on direct observations to explore the human experience in numerous settings and contexts (Grant and Luxford, 2009). Historically the method for capturing data in qualitative work was observation and note-taking in the field. While these field notes were useful, the availability of recording data meant that recordings were less open to interpretation than field notes (Speer and Hutchby, 2003), as the recording provides a record of the actions that is independent of the analysis (Suchman, 1987). Using recordings allowed for improved data management and analysis (Halcomb and Davidson, 2006), providing a rich source of data that allowed for a more detailed analysis of behaviour than traditional observation methods (Bottorff, 1994).

Previously, researchers relied on analogue recordings of their data which gradually eroded over time and reduced in quality when copied (Shrum et al., 2005). However, the rise of digital technology in contemporary times allows for ultra-sharp images and high-quality sound which facilitates the recording of social life (Murthy, 2008). Many modern devices have a large storage capacity, and recordings can be easily and directly transferred onto a computer (Paulus et al., 2013). Thus the commercialisation of technology has made it a more viable and cost-effective option (Gibbs et al., 2002), and has extended the ways in which we are able to collect data (Brown, 2002). Embedded within this rise of digital technology was the development of mobile technology which has facilitated communication and meant that researchers no longer gather data in fixed environments (Hagen et al., 2005). In addition, the development of the internet has allowed for connections that cut across time and space, and barriers to interaction are no longer geographically constrained (Hinchcliffe and Gavin, 2009).

It is important to recognise that the rise of digital technology offers the opportunity for new methods of data collection and analysis, rather than simply a medium for recording social behaviour (Shrum et al., 2005), and researchers should consider how digitisation can enhance the idiographic nature of qualitative work (Brown, 2002). New technologies inevitably interact with the social context (Shrum et al., 2005), resulting in an opening up of the social worlds of many would-be participants who may previously have been difficult to access. One of the implications of the widespread influence and utility of digital media is that there has been a level of erosion of the distinction between formal and informal environments (Heath, 2011). This means that researchers are required to consider and negotiate access to private and public spaces in different ways, balancing the privacy of participants and researcher access to data (Hagen et al., 2005). Consider, for example, the rise of the smartphone. These small devices typically include recording devices, and this can be sufficient for some qualitative projects as some even have video capability (Paulus et al., 2013). Thus the possibilities for researchers in the digital age are immense and social researchers cannot afford to sidestep digital methods (Murthy, 2008).

CHOOSING VIDEO OR AUDIO

While we acknowledge that a growing popular mode of data collection is through text-based means (email, instant messaging, diaries), the concern for this chapter is with recording data and translating them into a text (transcribed) document. This means that researchers generally have two choices: to record in audio or visual format. For non-local contact, particularly in interview research, the modality of interaction would typically either be over the telephone or via Skype, which can be recorded via audio or audio-visually respectively. For geographically local contact, recording options are similarly audio or audio-visual. While the technicalities in local or non-local contexts may differ, the underlying issues for consideration are similar.

Audio recording has always been a default modality, partially due to the lack of or cost of other technologies, conflated with practical and ethical difficulties. However, as video data have become more accessible and widely culturally embedded, video recording has become a more popular research tool, particularly as it allows the analysis of non-verbal interactions.

e.g.

Robins et al. (2004) presented a case study of robot–human interaction between a robot and three children diagnosed with autism, to analyse the importance of joint attention in human development and social understanding. A meaningful understanding of these interactions could not be yielded with only audio recordings as a great deal of attention was paid to the non-verbal aspects of the interaction.

When considering whether to choose video recording as a preferable modality for data collection there are several issues to bear in mind. First, it raises issues relating to both participant and researcher reflexivity. Second, related to this, there has been an evolution and blurring of the boundaries between naturally occurring and researcher-generated data. Third, it invokes additional ethical sensitivities, including the production of more data than necessary, which need to be considered in a balanced way. Finally, using video to record data requires some technical and practical preparations that need careful planning.

There are a number of professions that have found that video recording their practice can be helpful as a tool for reflection in order to promote good practice and professional development. Video provides a medium whereby individuals can observe and constructively criticise their own encounters (Grant and Luxford, 2009). Video thus provides the mechanism through which professionals can be reflexive in a way that is emergent, immediate and embodied (Iedema et al., 2007). Reflexivity is a central practice for the qualitative researcher, not only in analysis but also during data collection, and audio or video recordings can provide the mechanism to facilitate this reflexive practice. However, video recording is often done in research with an absence of reflexive methodological discussion (Sparrman, 2005). We propose that whether using audio or video, it is necessary to remember that this is the primary data, and the transcript merely supports this. Researchers should remain reflexively mindful that the interaction is mutually constituted and the participants' responses are contextually generated. By reviewing the recordings in a reflexive manner it becomes possible to increase one's awareness of the impact of the researcher on the research.

—————————— Reflective space ——————————

We would encourage you to make notes in your research diary about what you have learned about relative benefits of audio and video recordings.

An alternative to manufacturing a setting where a participant can be interviewed for research purposes is to analyse data recorded for other purposes. In Chapter 4 we differentiated researcher-generated from naturally occurring data, and the development and accessibility of digital technology have led to a growth of interest in naturalistic analysis of social interaction (Heath, 2004). Historically researchers had limited choices for recording observations of natural settings or generating interviews/focus groups. However, contemporary qualitative research has a much wider spectrum of modalities to draw from, which has potentially blurred the boundaries of what constitutes naturally occurring data.

> (e.g.) The proliferation of webcams allows participants to capture 'natural' or 'researcher-generated' data and upload them for researchers (Murthy, 2008), and the internet means that modalities such as Skype can be harnessed for research purposes by recording conversations which to a greater or lesser degree may have been instigated by the researcher.

The use of recording through the internet can create specific ethical sensitivities as the boundaries between public and private tend to overlap in cyberspace (Watson et al., 2007). One example of this is the increase in the number of videos on YouTube, which illustrates that users are becoming more comfortable with presenting themselves online (Murthy, 2008). This familiarity with being recorded transcends cyberspace, and extends to all aspects of society. The ethical issue for researchers using audio or audio-visual material is therefore that both have density and permanence (Grimshaw, 1982). For video in particular there are greater risks of identification which participants may need to be reminded of. Specifically, in the context of participants' familiarity with surveillance and recording in many other areas of life, the issue of whether their comments are made 'on or off the record' is particularly pertinent (O'Reilly et al., 2011). Additionally, there is an ethical issue in terms of the quantity of data generated. Due to the rich nature of the material collected, researchers need to make rational decisions about the necessity for collecting video data (Luff and Heath, 2012).

Most pertinently, using recordings creates ethical sensitivities in relation to data storage and data protection. This is because data storage and retrieval are at the forefront of digitisation (Brown, 2002). Qualitative research generates large amounts of recorded data which can take up significant amounts of physical or computer space. An alternative to this is to store the files virtually on the internet through storage centres such as iCloud or Dropbox. However, this raises ethical dilemmas for researchers as it opens the risk of hacking or file corruption. Alternatively, when the files are stored on mobile devices such as external hard drives or smartphones there is a risk of the device being stolen or lost. Despite developments in encryption software, ultimately there is a different type of risk to data protection in its digital form.

Aside from the ethical considerations, researchers must also pay attention to the practical issues that arise from recording participants. One of the most obvious issues to consider is the nature of the environment. For example, there are inherent difficulties in capturing video data in noisy or crowded environments as things cannot be recaptured if missed (Plowman and Stephen, 2008). As qualitative researchers move to relying heavily on the recordings, there is less impetus to make detailed field notes and therefore any technical problems with the recording quality may mean that data are lost. It is therefore important to endeavour to ameliorate any technical difficulties in advance. For example, to maximise picture and/or sound quality it is preferable to have the recording device in a fixed position and to test the recording quality beforehand (Heath, 2011). There may be more specific issues for researchers who choose modern devices such as smartphones, including battery life, extracting the data from the phone, and generating backup files of the data (Raento et al., 2009).

DEBATES ABOUT ALTERED BEHAVIOUR IN THE PRESENCE OF RECORDING DEVICES

The evolution of digital technology has also influenced debates about how people behave when being recorded. In the 1980s and 1990s when the use of video was fairly new both in general culture as well as in the research field, a pervasive viewpoint was that the introduction of recording equipment would invoke anxiety in participants, causing them to alter their behaviour (Blaxter et al., 1996: Martin and Martin, 1984). The focus therefore was on reducing the visibility of the device and facilitating the acclimatisation of the participants to its presence (Bottorff, 1994). At that time research indicated that participants tended to feel less anxious about audio recording than video (Bain and Mackay, 1995). However, in modern times there has been a routinisation of surveillance and a normalisation of the social practice of recording, leading to an increased familiarisation of recording presence (Shrum et al., 2005).

 Usually when making a telephone call to service providers an automated message will warn callers that the conversation will be recorded for training and quality purposes.

Nonetheless, the issue of influencing the participant with the presence of a recording device is something that is still considered by contemporary researchers. The concern has been to put effort into making the recording equipment as unobtrusive as possible in order to reduce discomfort and anxiety, thus potentially limiting any effects on behaviour. The premise behind this was to maintain the 'naturalness' of the behaviour while maintaining the ethicality of the study (Themessl-Huber et al., 2008). This idea is based on the notion that there is an objective reality that is open to contamination from the recording device. An alternative perspective challenged this idea, arguing that the distinction between natural and non-natural is unnecessary and that each interaction is constructed and situated (Speer and Hutchby, 2003). From this perspective the recording device is not simply a neutral entity but an interlocutor in the interaction and a portal to those behind the machine (O'Reilly et al., 2011). Thus the device becomes an actor in the social situation and the idea that it is possible for it to be non-present is an illusion (Shrum et al., 2005). But there are still those who argue that the presence of video can be perceived as threatening and thus efforts are made by researchers to minimise the impact of technology (Iedema et al., 2006). This has been facilitated by the development of smaller and more discrete devices. We discuss the value of technology further in Box 6.1.

influential **voices**

────────── Box 6.1   The value of technology ──────────

Christian Heath, Jon Hindmarsh, Paul Luff and Dirk vom Lehn

Christian Heath* is a professor of work and organisation, Jon Hindmarsh* is a professor of work and interaction, Paul Luff is a professor of organisations and technology, and Dirk vom Lehn is a lecturer in marketing, interaction and technology. They developed the Work, Interaction and Technology Research Centre at King's College London and have written extensively in the area of video-based studies of social interaction, with a particular interest in the use of tools and technologies. Their work has made a significant and influential impact on our understandings of both the theoretical and practical issues of using video. This has been particularly noteworthy in health and public settings.

In their recent book *Video in Qualitative Research*, they demonstrate the practical application of video-based research in a number of everyday and institutional settings (Heath et al., 2010). Here they argue that video is a central means of observing and understanding human behaviour. Because of advances in technology there has been a rise in studies of social interaction in both formal and informal environments (Heath, 2011). It is therefore necessary to consider the visual features of interaction because the physical environment in which activities take place is not a stable influence on the interaction (Heath, 2004). Heath and Hindmarsh (2002) argue that the accomplishment of talk as a social activity is inextricably embedded within the material environment. Additionally, verbal and non-verbal behaviours are not discrete and both are used by participants integratively (Heath, 2004); the range of actions arising in interaction are not available to the analyst through the inspection of talk alone, as talk is accompanied by visible and material actions (Heath and Luff, 2008).

The rise in the use of video in qualitative research has coincided with the introduction of cheap and reliable technology (Heath et al., 2007). Video cameras are now fairly commonplace in society and the availability of video-editing systems has allowed for the manipulation of video for research (Luff and Heath, 2012). This has provided a technology through which researchers are able to capture human behaviour in many

(Continued)

(Continued)

contexts, and facilitates opportunity for repeated scrutiny through the use of slow-motion facilities (Vom Lehn et al., 2002), as video has the advantage of capturing a version of an event as it happens (Hindmarsh, 2008). This allows access to the finer details of conduct such as tracking, gestures, and their significance within the inter-action (Heath and Hindmarsh, 2002). An advantage of this is that it allows researchers to share the raw data with colleagues, which promotes collaborative analysis and facili-tates the development of research groups (Fraser et al., 2006). Video recordings also allow an opportunity to develop a database that can be subjected to a range of analytic interests and concerns (Heath and Hindmarsh, 2002).

While there are numerous analytic benefits to the collection of a corpus of video data, there are inherent challenges that require attention. This includes decisions regarding where, what and when to film, how to categorise and transcribe the data, and how to select fragments to analyse (Luff and Heath, 2012). At the planning stage of the research the ethical considerations relating to consent and distribution of data need to be addressed, particularly if the data are of a sensitive nature (Fraser et al., 2006). The ethical issues do, however, differ depending on the nature of the record-ings, and problematically there is a relative lack of guidance on the use of video in ethical parlance (Hindmarsh, 2008). There are a number of pragmatic decisions that need to be made regarding the number of cameras and their positions in the setting (Heath, 2011). A particular practical difficulty for researchers relates to the problem of selecting an angle and framing of the recordings (Luff and Heath, 2012). It is important to maximise the picture and sound quality (Heath, 2011) as the quality of the recordings of the data will have a direct impact on the analysis possible (Luff and Heath, 2012). Heath (2011) argues that the video itself is the principal tool for analysis, but this can be enhanced with fieldwork, including interviews, observations, and discussions with participants. Conventional fieldwork thus enriches and helps make sense of the video recordings (Heath and Hindmarsh, 2002), and field notes can facilitate the analysis (Vom Lehn et al., 2002). A wider understanding of the specific jargon used by partici-pants and familiarity with the particular setting in which the interactions take place can help the researcher to understand the cultural ethos of the environment (Heath and Hindmarsh, 2002).

*We thank Professor Heath and Professor Hindmarsh for taking the time to read an earlier draft of this chapter.

TRANSCRIPTION

While the audio or video data remain the primary source for analysis, for conveni-ence and the practicalities of dissemination it is usually necessary to translate this medium into written text. The purpose of this translation is to produce a transcript.

The main rationale for producing these transcripts is that they represent a highly detailed and accessible version of the data (Peräkylä, 1997). The transcripts therefore are the primary source of evidence for the analytic claims made (Roberts and Robinson, 2004). However, this process is neither neutral nor straightforward, and there are a number of debates which are important for all qualitative researchers to engage with.

Active versus passive transcription

It has been recognised in the qualitative field that early qualitative research transcription was inappropriately viewed as a technical and mundane process and as such was considered unproblematic (Lapadat and Lindsay, 1999). This meant that transcription received little attention as it was believed to be neutral and objective (Green et al., 1997). The lack of concern regarding transcription was largely due to assumptions that transcription is transparent (Lapadat, 2000). However, there is now greater agreement that there cannot be a 'neutral' transcription system as the transformation from audio/video into a written format represents a selection process (Psathas and Anderson, 1990) and is reflexively tied to the context of its production (Mondada, 2007). Researchers make choices regarding their transcription process, and this tends to reflect their theoretical position (Lapadat and Lindsay, 1999) and their discipline's conventions (Green et al., 1997). For example, for linguistic anthropologists transcription is viewed as a cultural activity (Duranti, 2007), for sociolinguists transcription is seen as a political act (Green et al., 1997), and for conversation analysts transcription is considered a situated practice (Mondada, 2007). Thus it is now fairly well established that transcription is an active rather than passive process, and requires the analyst to make rational and informed transcription decisions.

Until fairly recently, despite its central role in qualitative research, the practice of transcription has only been superficially examined (Oliver et al., 2005). To facilitate a more open understanding of these practices, it is argued therefore that researchers ought to disclose the rationale for their transcription decisions (Skukauskaite, 2012). This is because various different theoretical and methodological perspectives of researchers mean that they develop transcripts that differ from others (Davidson, 2010; Lapadat, 2000). This reflects two different, albeit potentially overlapping, types of concern: epistemological and practical (Hepburn and Bolden, 2013). Some consider transcripts to be theory (Ochs, 1979) in the sense that transcripts are an embodiment of the theoretical orientation of the researcher (Mondada, 2007). This is also reflected in the process of the research. Researchers should organise and analyse their data by accommodating the iterative nature of the research process (McLellan et al., 2003). While the transcript itself becomes a static feature of the process, the researcher has a responsibility to revisit the actual recorded data to maintain an iterative position. As Lapadat (2000: 204) puts it: 'Verbatim transcription serves the purpose of taking speech, which is fleeting, aural, performative and heavily contextualized within its situational and social context of use, and freezing it into a static, permanent, and manipulable form.'

─────────────── Reflective space ───────────────

Consider the various active decisions made about the format and style of transcription extracts you have seen published in various journal articles and how they helped or limited your reading of the data.

Transcription annotation

Having established the active process of transcription that requires a number of decisions to be made, it is necessary for the researcher to reflect upon how their chosen methodological approach will influence the nature and detail of the transcript.

 Some approaches such as conversation analysis require extremely detailed prosodic notation, whereas other approaches such as thematic analysis would find this level of complexity in representation unwieldy.

When researchers begin the process of transcription they have a range of decisions to make, from the practical issues of page layout, margin width and typeface to more sophisticated decisions about the inclusion or exclusion of pauses, intonation and paralinguistic features (Lapadat, 2000). Hammersley (2010a) argues that there are nine core decisions to make regarding what should be included in a transcript, and we represent these in Figure 6.1.

At a practical level the process of transforming speech into written text becomes challenging when there is background noise, poor recording quality, incomplete speech, or lack of clarity (McLellan et al., 2003). Added to this, researchers need to make a reasoned decision about whether to transcribe verbatim, representing the data word for word (Poland, 1995), or whether to 'tidy up' the data by transcribing them according to grammatical convention. This can be particularly difficult when speakers convey noises (for example, laughter, sneezing, coughing) or onomatopoeia in their talk, as there is no orthography for transcribing such 'active noises' (O'Reilly, 2005). Transcription could be considered as a 'spectrum', a continuum of detail from the tidied-up, grammatically correct version to the highly detailed verbatim, Jefferson version which demands absolute detail.

The difficulty for transcription is that different researchers collect different types of data for different purposes and the transcription system used should reflect this purpose (Lapadat, 2000). This variation has led to debate regarding the nature of

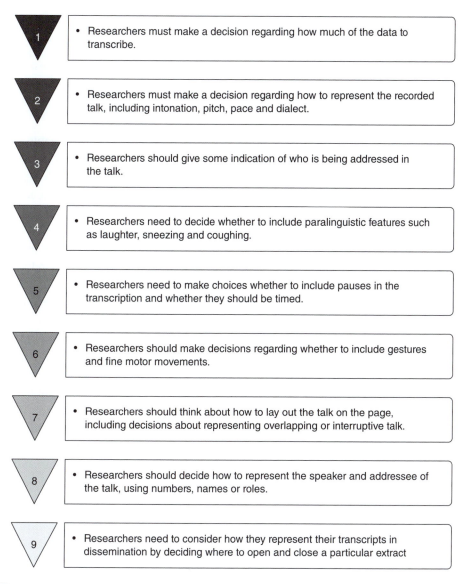

Figure 6.1 Hammersley's nine core features of transcription

transcription conventions. It can be argued that overcrowded detail is distracting, and researchers should employ notation that is accessible and easy to read. Alternatively, there is the argument that the transcript should be as close a representation as possible to the audio version in order to minimise misrepresentation. This kind of detail is essential for some forms of analysis such as linguistic analysis. These different arguments have led to calls for more standardised conventions for particular approaches in order to facilitate the comparison between transcription methods (Lapadat, 2000).

———————————————— Reflective space ————————————————

Consider your own research and think about what level of detail would be most appropriate for your data.

Lapadat noted, however, that a single exhaustive system is not attainable, but that different approaches should develop their own standardised transcription protocols. The best example of this is conversation analysis, which as a discipline has put considerable effort into defining and developing a uniform approach to transcription.

Notably the developments in the conversation analysis approach have had considerable influence on a wider qualitative audience (Duranti, 2007). The aim of conversation-analytic transcripts is to preserve as much as possible of relevant vocal, verbal and multimodal details of the interactional event (Jefferson, 2004). Jefferson developed an evolving system incorporating symbols to represent non-vocal activities and capture the characteristics of speech delivery (Atkinson and Heritage, 1999). Thus those practising conversation analysis use this wide range of orthographic and typographic conventions to represent the prosodic, phonetic and other vocalic details as well as for utterance alignment, temporal features (like pauses) and suprasegmental properties (like speech rate) (Roberts and Robinson, 2004). The reason why this high level of detail is considered necessary and intrinsic to a good transcript is that it is deemed that removal of the detail will have a detrimental effect on the analysis (Potter, 1996). As conversation analysis has moved away from purely audio recordings of mundane conversations into audiovisual material there has been some new discussion regarding whether and how to transcribe visual information such as gaze, pointing and body posture. We consider the issue of transcription further in Box 6.2.

influential **voices**

———————————— Box 6.2   Detail in transcription ————————————

Gail Jefferson

Gail Jefferson* greatly influenced the sociological study of interaction but held no concrete university position. She unfortunately passed away in 2008. In 1963 she was hired as a clerk typist at the University of California, Los Angeles, during which time she developed a more structured and detailed approach to transcription. She worked alongside Harvey Sacks during his pioneering work in conversation analysis, as well as Emanuel Schegloff, developing analysis and contributing to the literature using this method, including synthesising Sacks's lectures into a two-volume book. The system of transcription that Jefferson developed is still widely used by conversation analysts and other disciplines today, with some extensions being undertaken by scholars such as Alexa Hepburn and Galina Bolden.

Until Jefferson brought the importance of transcription conventions to the awareness of qualitative researchers it had not been considered to be a topic but rather something that researchers did to prepare materials for analysis (Jefferson, 2004). However, now this method of transcription is established as being an important part of the analytic process (Atkinson and Heritage, 1984). This Jefferson system (as it is now known) was specifically designed for use by conversation analysts and its notation reflects this analytic stance (Psathas and Anderson, 1990). It is perhaps unsurprising that the transcription conventions build intuitively on familiar forms of literary notation (Hepburn and Bolden, 2013). Nonetheless, readers of Jefferson transcriptions need to be familiar with these conventions (Mazeland, 2006). As Hutchby and Woofitt (2008) point out, transcription notation encompasses two concerns, that of the dynamics of turn-taking and that of the characteristics of speech delivery. These characteristics are represented symbolically. Some examples appear below (for a more comprehensive guide, see Jefferson, 2004):

↑ upward intonation

↓ downward intonation

o spoken more quietly

> speeded up speech <

< slowed down speech >

.hhh in-breath

hhh out-breath

Conversation analytic transcripts are designed to capture the relevant vocal, verbal, and multimodal details (Jefferson, 2004) and are designed for transcribing speakers of languages that use a conventional alphabet (Jefferson, 1996). However, contemporary researchers are applying the system to incorporate other languages, such as Russian, using the Roman alphabet, while being sensitive to the sound system of the Russian language (Bolden, 2003). One of the characteristic features of this system is that it captures and times pauses so that silences may be understood relative to the tempo of the talk (Hepburn and Bolden, 2013). This is because conversation analysis distinguishes between gaps that are silences between speakers' turns and pauses that are silences within a continuing turn; thus silence is analytically relevant (Sacks et al., 1974) and these gaps often function in analytically different ways.

One of the significant contributions of Jefferson's work has been in relation to how to capture the interactional significance of laughter. Through the processes of

(Continued)

(Continued)

transcribing laughter Jefferson made some important analytical observations about these interactions. Jefferson (1979) distinguished between voluntary laughter and invited laughter, where invited laughter related to incidences where the speaker began laughing themselves, thus warranting laughter from the recipient. In transcription notation the researcher may choose to represent the laughter in double parentheses ((laughs)). However, following Jefferson, some scholars argue it is more appropriate to capture the detail of its delivery and represent it with tokens such as 'hah', 'heh', 'hih', or 'huh' (Hepburn and Bolden, 2013).

In reality, participants speak in a range of ways, and may produce words which are not grammatically or phonetically correct, such as 'wutche doin'?', or produce words that are acoustically distinct ('yeah' or 'yes'), which may be analytically relevant (Jefferson, 1983: 3). Additionally, marking overlapping talk of two or more speakers may be analytically relevant and therefore important to capture in transcription, as may be acknowledgement tokens such as 'uhum' or 'mm' (Jefferson, 1984). In this system of transcription, therefore, the words are typed as they are sounded and not corrected for grammar or pronunciation (Jefferson, 2004).

Hepburn and Bolden point out that the Jefferson transcription system has received some criticism from scholars who prefer a more standard English orthography, as this system is argued to be difficult to read. Additional criticism from participants tends to relate to the very literal nature of the way in which talk is represented. Jefferson (1983: 2) herself recognised some of the criticisms of the system with arguments that it risks 'caricaturing' the speakers by representing exactly what was said, making participants look 'stupid', but counters this by claiming that standardising orthography obscures the interactional features of the data.

*In her lifetime Gail Jefferson made a huge contribution to our understanding of transcription, and we thank Dr Alexa Hepburn (who is recognised as an expert in Jeffersonian annotation) for taking the time to check through this box.

Deciding who undertakes transcription

A decision regarding who actually does the transcribing is not only a practical but also a theoretical consideration. While it is fairly common and understandable for researchers to employ professional transcriptionists to transcribe data (Tilley, 2003), it is important to consider the rationale for doing so. This is also a decision that should be made at the design stage (Tilley and Powick, 2002) and may be required by ethics committees or funding bodies. It is well documented that transcription is very costly in terms of time and physical and human resources (Halcomb and Davidson, 2006), and this is a key reason why qualitative researchers often make use of paid transcriptionist services (Davidson, 2009).

Because transcription is considered to be an interpretative and subjective process it is arguable that it is more ethical and prudent for qualitative researchers to complete the task of transcription themselves (Lucas, 2010). It may therefore be logical for researchers to transcribe their own data as they have the knowledge and expertise of the data collection (Halcomb and Davidson, 2006). Additionally, transcription can be a useful mechanism to help researchers gain some distance from the participants' worlds and provide some physical distance as well as emotional distance as the discourse is transformed into text (Hamo et al., 2004). While it may feel preferable to save time by paying a transcriptionist, two transcriptionists are likely to transcribe the same segment in different ways (O'Connell and Kowal, 1995) and therefore the researcher will need to be active in supervising transcriptionists and in reviewing and editing the transcripts, thus not necessarily saving time (Lucas, 2010). Without such close supervision, research has shown that transcriptionists are likely to make their own decisions regarding how to represent participants in the text (Tilley and Powick, 2002).

Reflective space

We recommend that before making this decision, researchers discuss it with their colleagues or supervisor.

Nonetheless when researchers do choose to employ professional transcriptionists, because of the complexity of the task it is important to engage in regular communication (Tilley and Powick, 2002). This is not only to facilitate the process of transcription, but also to consider the emotional impact that the data may have on their welfare. This is because the transcriptionist becomes a participant in the process and is not 'merely an extension of the tape recorder' (McCosker et al., 2001). While the transcriptionist is often invisible in the process and there have been assumptions that they are unaffected (Gregory et al., 1997), transcribing may have an emotional effect on this party (Dickson-Swift et al., 2008; Kiyimba and O'Reilly, in press), which is supported by research evidence (Lalor et al., 2006; Wilkes et al., 2014). During the recording participants may talk about a range of issues, and express diverse emotions which may resonate deeply with the transcriptionist (Gregory et al., 1997; Kiyimba and O'Reilly, in press). Transcriptionists are after all not immune to the sensitivity and power of the narratives they hear (Warr, 2004). Repeated listening and continued work of this nature may have a cumulative effect. This may even lead to vicarious traumatisation, particularly if there is little opportunity for debriefing (Etherington, 2007). This is especially pertinent as transcriptionists are rarely given the opportunity to discuss the emotional effects on them (Warr, 2004). This is compounded by the fact that due to confidentiality, transcriptionists have little opportunity to discuss the emotional impact with anyone outside the research team (McCosker et al., 2001). This is further problematised if there is limited or no established relationship between transcriptionists and researchers, as it can make it difficult for researchers to be involved in their welfare (Etherington, 2007).

ISSUES OF TRANSLATION

Globalisation and changing patterns of migration mean that society has become increasingly diverse (Wong and Poon, 2010). An important issue which has been largely overlooked in the literature relates to the fact that there is an increasing portion of analytic work being performed in languages other than English (Nikander, 2008). Nikander argues that researchers who prefer to analyse their data in their native language face difficult decisions about how to transcribe their data and then translate them into another language for dissemination. There are several different situations where translation may affect data collection, analysis and dissemination (typically English). Additionally, there may be situations where two individuals who are natives of different countries are communicating with each other in English, a third language, and this may add a problematic element to transcription (Jefferson, 1996). However, generally speaking when dealing with translated materials there are two core issues:

- Data collected via an interpreter: This is the case when the participant speaks in their native language but the data are collected in English through the presence of an interpreter. This represents a complex challenge.
- Data collected in languages other than English: This is the case when researchers and participants speak their native language and the data are translated into English for international audiences.

For data analysis these two issues have practical implications for researchers:

- When data have been collected through an interpreter there is the possibility for interpreter bias, loss of fidelity and possible glosses on nuances. The implication for analysis is that researchers need to be clear that they are analysing the interpretation of the participant's talk.
- When data have been collected in languages other than English, researchers need to decide whether to analyse the data in the native language and then translate them into English for the audience, or whether to analyse directly in English. These decisions have implications for quality and transparency.

 Hayashi (2004) transcribed Japanese conversations post-positional particles in a range of interactional contexts. In the article Hayashi included both the original Japanese, the literal translation and the grammatically readable translation for an

English-speaking audience. This inclusion of the original Japanese has the benefit of greater transparency, particularly for bilingual audiences. We cite an example of data from the article taken from page 351:

'Masaki: *ni:*   *tadoritsuite nakattaRA:*

        at arrive not:if

        ((if I)) haven't arrived ((there)) at'

At the point of transcription and dissemination there are broader challenges that researchers may face in light of these two issues:

- When data have been collected through an interpreter there is likely to be an audio/video file of both the participant's and interpreter's talk. Researchers need to make a decision at the transcription stage as to whether to include the participant's utterances in the native language or just the English interpretation.
- When data are collected in languages other than English, there are dissemination issues in relation to the trustworthiness and transparency of analysis. Where researchers have ana-lysed the original non-English data and translated them for dissemination purposes, the audi-ence are unable to validate the accuracy of the interpretations made.

The most common way that the potential obstacle of translating original data into English is addressed in transcription prosody is through the tri-inter-linear method as demonstrated below. In this model the original non-English text is presented first. This is followed by a literal grammatical English translation, and then a final 'cleaned-up' version in which the word order is corrected and some words may be added or modified to secure meaning. An example is presented in Box 6.3.

Box 6.3   Example of Arabic translated by Ejalal Jalal

Arabic

الدورة التدريبية للمهنيين متعددة التخصصات للمتعاملين مع حالات إيذاء الأطفال وإهمال الأطفال هي جزء من سلسلة من الدورات التدريبية الأساسية التي يتم تقديمها سنويا من قبل برنامج الأمان الأسري الوطني بالتعاون مع آخرين.

Literal

Training session for multidisciplinary professionals for clients with cases of child abuse and neglect of children is part of a series of basic training courses that are presented annually by the National Family Safety Program in collaboration with others.

Translation

The multidisciplinary training course is part of a series of basic training courses that are offered annually by the National Family Safety Program in collaboration with others.

(Continued)

(Continued)

Arabic

تهدف هذه الدورة لإكساب المشاركين المهارات الأساسية للتعامل مع حالات إيذاء واهمال الأطفال، والتعرف على آنواعها و أسبابها و مؤشراتها وعواقبها، وبالتالي يتم تزويد المتدربين بالمهارات اللازمة للتقييم والتدخل ووالوقاية وطرق العلاج والتأهيل.

Literal

This course is designed to give participants the basic skills to deal with cases of abuse and neglect of children, and to identify the types and causes and indicators and their consequences, and therefore are provided trainees with the necessary skills for assessment and intervention.

Translation

It provides participants with basic skills in how to deal with child abuse and neglect cases; and identify the types, signs, causes and consequences of child abuse and neglect. It supports participants with skills to evaluate, intervene and protect children, in addition to treatment and rehabilitation techniques.

Arabic

كما تهدف لتعريف المشاركين بكافة التشريعات الدولية والمحلية والإجراءات المتبعة في هذه الحالات، واطلاعهم على أحدث المستجدات و الدراسات العلمية في هذا المجال.

Literal

Also aims to familiarize participants with all international legislation and local procedures in these cases, and informing them the latest developments and scientific studies in this area.

Translation

It also aims to provide participants with knowledge of national and international laws and regulations that govern child protection, and to bring to their attention the latest research evidence on the subject.

While we would argue that this example of translated data accommodates the need for transparency, publications' policies may dictate how data translations are produced and presented, which may hide the original and be counterproductive to transparency (Nikander, 2008). The fundamental issue in relation to translating data is that in cross-cultural qualitative research it may be detrimental where there are taken-for-granted assumptions that the process of translation is objective and neutral (Wong and Poon, 2010). Rather, there are a range of practical and ideological questions in relation to both the detail of the transcription and the way in which it is presented (Nikander, 2008). For example, the omission of a word or phrase in a translated text may have a significant influence on data interpretation, meaning construction and the final representation of the participant's reality (Wong and Poon, 2010).

SUMMARY AND FINAL THOUGHTS

In this chapter we have focused on two important theoretical issues. First, we explored the debates about choice of recording options. The primary divide has been focused on whether to collect audio or video recordings of data, and we have explored both the ethical and methodological tenets relating to how researchers make informed decisions. These decisions have been influenced by the debate about the extent to which the presence of a recording device might alter the behaviour of participants. In summary, we propose that the benefits of collecting video material outweigh the potential practical and ethical constraints. In particular, we agree with the arguments presented by Hindmarsh and Heath, that in face-to-face interactions it is crucial to observe and analyse the interplay between verbal and non-verbal communication in order to better understand participants' social worlds.

Second, we explored debates related to transcription choices. We presented an argument that transcription is actually an active process about which methodological and analytical decisions need to be made. Furthermore, we explicated the issues relating to pragmatics of transcription annotation and demonstrated that the process of transcription is inevitably an integral part of the analytical process. We concluded this chapter by outlining some of the challenges related to working with data in other languages and contentions around translation for analysis and dissemination. In summary, we contend that transcriptionists should not be perceived as merely technical conduits for transforming data into text but are integral components influencing the way in which data are understood and therefore the knowledge that is gained from them. We support the benefits of performing transcription oneself, but recognise the practical constraints in doing so. This in part is related to our preference for using highly detailed Jefferson transcription systems. This is because it promotes transparency, trustworthiness and collaboration and also provides a mechanism for close scrutiny of participants' interactions.

Case study and reflective questions

Sabine is a professor of social anthropology and works for a French research institute. She is interested in researching teenage café culture. There is a particular group of teenagers who are students at the local high school who are in the process of organising a local fashion show. Sabine is interested in how the teenagers go about this task and their group culture. The teenagers frequently use their mobile phones to make video recordings of one another to upload onto social media sites, and some of the teenagers bring their laptops to the café to Skype with friends.

Q: What factors will Sabine need to consider in her decision whether to use audio or audio-visual recordings of the teenage behaviour?

Q: Sabine wishes to present her findings at an international conference which will use English as the main language. What issues does she face in translating the data?

Suggestions for answering these questions are available at the end of the book.

FURTHER READING

Heath, C., Hindmarsh, J. and Luff, P. (2010) *Video in Qualitative Research: Analysing Social Interaction in Everyday Life*. London: Sage.

This is a useful and practical book that considers a wide range of issues in using video to record data for qualitative research. The authors provide useful information on the ethical and practical issues that arise in data collection and consider the ways in which video provides new ways of presenting qualitative insights to a different audiences. Helpfully, the authors draw upon their own research experiences to provide clear examples and to situate the guidance they offer.

Hepburn, A. and Bolden, G. (2013) The conversation analytic approach to transcription, in T. Stivers and J. Sidnell (eds), *The Blackwell Handbook of Conversation Analysis*. Oxford: Blackwell. pp. 57–76.

In this chapter the authors provide specific guidance on the Jefferson approach to transcription as favoured by the methodology of conversation analysis. The authors also provide some useful detail regarding the symbols used in such transcripts.

Hindmarsh, J. (2008) Distributed video analysis in social research, in N. Fielding, R. Lee and G. Blank (eds), *The SAGE Handbook of Internet and Online Research Methods*. London: Sage. pp. 343–361.

The focus for this book chapter is on digital tools and their usage in qualitative research. The chapter considers how research teams can share and utilise digital data, as well as considering the value and possibilities of e-tools. Additionally, some of the ethical and practical issues raised by internet-based technologies and sharing data are critically discussed.

Jefferson, G. (2004) Glossary of transcript symbols with an introduction, in G. H. Lerner (ed.), *Conversation Analysis: Studies from the First Generation*. Amsterdam: John Benjamins. pp. 13–31.

This book chapter provides a useful summary of the transcription system devised by Gail Jefferson which is used by conversation analysis and some discourse analytical approaches.

Paulus, T., Lester, J. N. and Dempster, P. (2013) *Digital Tools for Qualitative Research*. London: Sage.

This is a useful and practical textbook that considers qualitative research in the contemporary age of digital technology. It is a practical guide for researchers that considers how technology can aid reflexivity, promote collaboration, and help researchers manage their data sets. It also considers the ethical issues associated with technology and includes a companion website with additional resources.

Speer, S. and Hutchby, I. (2003) From ethics to analytics: Aspects of participants' orientations to the presence and relevance of recording devices. *Sociology*, 37(2): 315–337.

In this article the authors consider the debates about the presence of recording devices having an effect on the behaviour of research participants. They propose an alternative approach seeking to analyse and explore participants' orientations to the recording device. To develop their argument they draw upon empirical data and illustrate how the relevance of a recording device is negotiated in situ.

SEVEN

Primary and secondary data analysis

CHAPTER CONTENTS

INTRODUCTION

In this chapter we examine the distinction between primary and secondary data, a distinction that we regard as overly simplistic and misleading. In order to clarify this particular aspect of the debate we differentiate the different kinds of data as they relate to qualitative research. From this platform a critical discussion of the parameters of secondary analysis is given. Within this discussion we consider the potential differences between reuse of one's own data and secondary analysis. This requires us to investigate the fundamental issues of context, quality and ethics. The chapter concludes with consideration of the costs and benefits of archiving qualitative data for the purposes of secondary analysis.

THE DIFFERENCE BETWEEN DATA AND RESEARCH DATA

In common parlance, the word *datum* is a singular piece of information or fact, and the plural of this is *data* (http://www.yourdictionary.com/datum). However, for the purposes of research this generic definition is insufficient. Generally speaking, collections of information do not become research data until they have been assembled intentionally by the researcher for the purposes of answering a particular research question. However, we acknowledge that the term 'data' is often used by researchers in different ways.

> **e.g.** A newspaper article may be data in the sense that it is a collection of 'facts', but it only becomes research data when a researcher specifically assembles a number of articles together with the intention of addressing a research question and undertaking analysis. Similarly, a series of Facebook posts are simply an example of social media, but become identifiable as research data when printed as a data corpus for the purposes of research.

A common differentiation between different types of research data has been to categorise them as 'primary data' or 'secondary data'. These have been understood differently within different disciplines. For example, there is a discrepancy between what historians mean by primary versus secondary sources and how social scientists employ the concepts. While the literature on this distinction has been rather sparse, primary data are generally understood to be the initial data specifically collected by the original researcher for their research purposes, whereas secondary data are understood to be collected by someone other than the researcher. In other words, primary data have been considered to be the face-to-face collection (such as interviews and focus groups), whereas secondary data have been understood to be existing available sources. It is important to make a distinction at this point between secondary data and secondary data analysis, which is the reanalysing of data collected by another researcher, a point we return to later in the chapter.

We see this distinction between primary and secondary data as problematic for qualitative research. The reasons for this are that this differentiation fails to account for the arguments related to 'researcher-generated' and 'naturally occurring' data (as discussed in Chapter 4). It also fails to account for the defining parameters that distinguish the particular characteristics of 'research data' from general information which is colloquially referred to as 'data'.

> **e.g.** A set of recordings of telephone calls to a customer services helpline exists as data in the sense that they are recorded information. However, it becomes a naturally occurring research data set if, having met ethical criteria, it becomes a corpus of research data for the purpose of analysis in order to address a research question.

While we acknowledge that there are several ways in which data might be differentiated, we also propose one particularly useful distinction between privately solicited research data and publicly available data which could form part of a research data corpus. In the example above, pre-existing data were privately secured by the researcher through negotiations and ethical procedures with the organisation. In this sense they are privately solicited research data. In contrast, some naturally occurring research data are publicly available, such as television documentaries and newspaper and magazine articles. The reason we offer this distinction between privately solicited and publicly available, naturally occurring data is that the former data corpus would solely be available to that individual researcher whereas publicly available data could potentially be simultaneously collected by numerous researchers. This has implications for ways in which secondary data *analysis* may be defined, an argument we address shortly.

e.g.
In the case of analysing YouTube video clips of pedagogical guides to craft activities, these naturally occurring data are publicly available to potentially become research data. However, a researcher may post an advert on the internet requesting permission to record the activities of a specific 'knitting circle'. This would then be naturally occurring, privately solicited research data.

Furthermore, in the case of audio-visual data, some qualitative research traditions in particular argue that the actual recording is the primary data and the transcription is a representation of that recording. The transcript therefore would not in and of itself be considered to be data; rather the original recording would be viewed as actual data. In other words, the transcript itself does not constitute research data; rather it is seen as a tool to enable the practical task of analysis and dissemination. From a pragmatic perspective, however, some researchers argue contrary to this, that the recording and the transcript can be considered and treated as data.

In summary, within the field of qualitative research we argue that the distinction between primary and secondary research data is misleading. We propose instead that more useful ways of differentiating research data are to consider:

- Data and research data – the difference between information and information specifically collected together for the purposes of addressing a research question.
- Naturally occurring and researcher-generated research data – the difference between data that are used for research but would have existed anyway, and data created through interviews or focus groups etc. by a researcher.
- Publicly available research data and privately solicited research data – the difference between data available to anyone which can be used for research purposes, and data which are deliberately collected from a sample for research.
- Research data and representations thereof – the difference between original audio or visual data and written, transcribed representations of those data used for the purposes of convenient analysis and dissemination.

We recognise that these categories are not discrete and are likely to overlap. For example, data may be both privately solicited and naturally occurring, such as video recordings of counselling sessions that are recorded as standard practice which may be privately collected for research. We have now established what we propose are theoretically and pragmatically more appropriate and sensible ways of differentiating between types of data and research data. This offers us the foundation to now move on to the second issue, which is the importance of distinguishing primary and secondary data *analysis*.

PRIMARY AND SECONDARY DATA ANALYSIS

There has been a well-established tradition of reanalysing quantitative data, but in qualitative research there has not been a research culture of secondary analysis (Corti and Thompson, 2004), with limited progress of secondary analysis in this field (Fielding, 2004). Traditionally secondary data analysis has been understood as analysis of data gathered for a previous study by another researcher (Heron, 1989), requiring the use of pre-existing qualitative data (Heaton, 2008). Heaton (2008) argued that secondary data analysis in qualitative research can be approached in three modalities as listed in Table 7.1.

Table 7.1 Modalities of secondary analysis (Heaton, 2008)

Modality	Description
Formal data sharing from publicly available data	The researcher accesses data sets that have been deposited in public archives by other researchers. These are then subjected to secondary analysis. These data were likely to have been well documented for archiving purposes and are likely to have met the necessary ethical and legal requirements for being shared with others.
Informal data sharing between researchers	For this type there are different possibilities. The primary researcher may give their data to another researcher and then have no subsequent involvement in the secondary analysis, or two or more researchers may pool their data sets and work independently in carrying out the secondary analysis.
Reuse of one's own data	The researcher may reuse their own self-collected data as a way of investigating new or additional questions that were not explored in the primary research, or they may use secondary analysis to verify their previous findings. The researcher may also team up with others to combine their respective data sets.

There are a number of proposed benefits for the secondary analysis of qualitative data. Far more than for quantitative data, qualitative research generates significant amounts of material which is rich in detail; this can often mean that much of it remains unanalysed (Äkerström et al., 2004). From an ethical perspective, therefore, it is respectful to participants to make the best use of data that are collected (O'Reilly and Parker, 2014). Furthermore, for potentially 'overresearched' groups or hard-to-reach participant groups, secondary analysis allows for a wider use of the data (Heaton, 1998). In addition, from a very practical point of view, secondary data analysis is a cost-effective, convenient approach and is arguably a credible method for generating knowledge (Heron, 1989). Thus secondary analysis can be used to investigate additional or new research questions and arguably can be used to verify the findings of previous research (Heaton, 2008). It has also been suggested that secondary analysis allows the researcher an opportunity to view the data with some detachment, which arguably is more challenging for the researcher who originally collected the data (Szasbo and Strang, 1997).

Thorne et al. (2001) conducted a secondary analysis of a large primary data set of interviews with a wide range of participants on the topic of oral health in long-term care. In this study Thorne et al. reanalysed an existing database to address a new research question.

Some of the key benefits and limitations of secondary analysis have been discussed in the literature, and Hammersley (1997, 2010b) has summarised some of these key debates as illustrated in Box 7.1.

influential **voices**

———— Box 7.1   Contentions in secondary data analysis ————

Martyn Hammersley

Martyn Hammersley* is a professor of educational and social research at the Open University, UK. He has written extensively on qualitative methodological issues in relation to theory and practice and has raised some questions about secondary data analysis. Hammersley wrote two seminal articles on this topic in which a number of salient issues were raised. We distil the main points raised by these two articles in order to illustrate the contribution to the debates that have been made.

Hammersley (1997) predicted that data archiving for the purposes of secondary analysis was likely to become much more common in the future. To some extent this prediction has been borne out and there has been a greater drive towards archiving data. However, Hammersley (1997) drew attention to a number of problems for both the archiving process and for secondary analysis, and indeed these have hindered the culture of archiving in contemporary practice. In this article there were several issues raised, and we summarise the three core points here:

- As data are socially constructed through the process of data collection and through the interaction of researchers and their participants, the findings are not *found* in the data but rather are created through those interactions in particular locations and at particular times.

(Continued)

(Continued)

- Even where contextual information is available to secondary analysts there is still considerable scope for different views regarding what types of data are required in order to establish the credibility and validity of the claims.
- As secondary analysts are likely to have different concepts and frames of reference from the original researcher, there are likely to be problems of 'fit' causing gaps in information about the data.

Overall, therefore, Hammersley (1997) argued that the archiving of qualitative data had potential for assessing the validity of particular studies and increasing the scope for secondary analysis, but the problems and challenges may limit the contribution that it is able to make.

In a later article, Hammersley (2010b) debated the benefits and limitations of secondary analysis of qualitative data. He noted that there have been conflicting views about the benefits and practical challenges. Within those broad debates Hammersley focused on the challenge of the data not fitting the research questions, that relevant contextual information was mostly absent in secondary analysis; this was a problem which he also argued was found in some primary analysis. While by no means a comprehensive overview of the article, we explicate the key points that he makes in this piece:

- Arguably there is some ambiguity in the meaning of various terms used when talking about secondary analysis, including the word 'data' which is routinely used but rarely defined. Hammersley suggested that we should use these labels in consistent ways in order to avoid confusion.
- It is argued that it is necessary to differentiate between research employing data that have been produced by another researcher and one's own data – in other words, between reanalysing data produced by another researcher and reanalysing one's own data.
- It is important to recognise that what counts as data is determined functionally within the research process. As data cannot exist independently of the research process, they are formed by the process in which they are given meaning. Thus a process is involved within which data are collected and selected in order to provide evidence relevant to candidate answers to the research question.
- The research question is essential to the process and guides the researcher's selection and interpretation of what constitutes appropriate data, and is pertinent to decisions regarding what can be legitimately inferred from that data.
- It is argued that there is a legitimate differentiation between reuse (by a researcher of her or his own data) and secondary analysis of data (produced by others), advocating that both can be of value when employed appropriately.
- In research teams where researchers analyse data collected by another member of the team, this should not be considered either reuse or secondary analysis, but as still constituting primary analysis.

Overall Hammersley (2010b) argued that the effect of the difficulties of secondary qualitative analysis are in reality much less severe if researchers are able to take into account that all data are constituted and reconstituted within the research process, but concludes that there is little that can completely eliminate the difficulties of 'context' and 'fit'.

*We thank Professor Hammersley for taking the time to read an earlier draft of this chapter.

Debates about reuse of data as a form of secondary analysis

From reading the contribution of Hammersley, it should be clear that there is some contention regarding definitions and terms. Some researchers consider the reuse of data to be a form of secondary analysis. However, this perspective has been debated with different views represented in the qualitative field. We argue that there is a logical rationale for differentiating between reuse of one's own data at a later stage with the generation of a new research question, and the secondary analysis of data collected by another researcher for different purposes.

Fielding (2004) argued that qualitative researchers need to engage with the debate over secondary analysis by making a clear distinction between what they define as 'reuse of archived data' and what they define as 'secondary analysis'. A difficulty for qualitative research has been in relation to terminology, and specifically to whether the reuse of data from a previous project is sufficiently distinctive to require its own label such as 'secondary analysis' (Hammersley, 2010b).

However, the problem which arises when trying to create a distinction between primary and secondary analysis is that qualitative work by nature tends to be driven by open broad research questions. Several papers may be produced over an extended period of time in attempting to address the general research question. Nevertheless, the mere fact that material has been written up does not mean that it cannot be revisited and reanalysed by the same researcher (Åkerström et al., 2004). This flexibility to return to data sets also compounds the issue that there is a lack of a clear distinction between the terms 'use' and 'reuse' (Hammersley, 2010b). Therefore, distinguishing between primary analysis and the reuse of one's own data for secondary analysis poses challenges in determining whether a new research question is being addressed. We argue that what distinguishes reuse or reanalysis from primary analysis is the generation of a new research question relating to the same data set. We also argue that reuse in a technical sense is not a form of secondary analysis. Furthermore, it is plausible that available data may be simultaneously analysed by different researchers addressing different research questions.

> **e.g.** Two unconnected researchers may both access the same publicly available data from the internet without being aware that the other is engaging in analysis of those data. In this case both the researchers are engaging in simultaneous primary analysis.

We propose, then, that there are four forms of analysis: primary analysis, reuse/reanalysis, secondary analysis and simultaneous analysis (as illustrated in Table 7.2). The differentiation between these four types of analysis is an important clarification as the simple polemic of either primary or secondary analysis does not truly reflect the subtleties of actual research practice. Such a definition of terms is important, as previously indicated when we argued for a more sophisticated understanding of the issues related to types of data.

Table 7.2 Modes of analysis

Mode of analysis	Description
Primary analysis	The initial analysis of the data collected by the researcher to address the main research question.
Reuse or reanalysis	Subsequent analysis of the initial data set by the same researcher to address a new research question.
Secondary analysis	The analysis of data collected by a different researcher for the purposes of answering a different research question.
Simultaneous analysis	Analysis of the same data set by different researchers concurrently, either in the same research team or independently. This type of analysis can be either simultaneous primary analysis or simultaneous secondary analysis.

We now turn our attention to consideration of the general criticisms aimed at secondary analysis. There are three main arguments that call into question the credibility of what has been broadly referred to as 'secondary analysis' which has historically also included reuse of one's own data. We argue that the arguments put forward against secondary analysis represent legitimate concerns in relation to our now more specifically defined understanding of secondary analysis, but are of less concern (although still potentially relevant) when applied to the reuse or reanalysis of data or to primary data analysis. This is therefore an important reason for making the distinction that we do between reuse of one's own data and secondary analysis of another researcher's data.

Reflective space

Consider and discuss the distinctions between data and research data.

At this point we invite the reader to review the distinctive types of analysis presented in Table 7.2 and think about why these distinctions in terminology are important.

DEBATES ABOUT SECONDARY ANALYSIS

There are three main areas causing contention in relation to secondary analysis. First, there is the problem that a researcher analysing data they did not collect is at the disadvantage of not having the full details of context relating to how and where the data were collected. Second, there is the problem of quality in relation to qualitative research, which is mainly focused on issues of transparency, reflexivity and trustworthiness. Third, there is the problem of ethics, in the sense that participants may not have been fully informed about the secondary analysis of data at a later date and may not have consented to have their responses used in that way. Each of these issues is considered in turn.

Context

We acknowledge that the notion of context encompasses a broad range of issues and that the term is used in different ways. In relation to the criticisms put forward regarding the deficiencies of secondary analysis, there are three key arguments. First, questions are raised in terms of the difficulties of having limited access to information about the situated nature of the data collection such as the historical, political or cultural setting. Second, there is concern that data generated for the purposes of answering a particular research question may not be a good 'fit' with the purpose of the secondary analysis. Third, related to fit, the usual research trajectory begins with an epistemology which informs methodological choices. The secondary analyst may not have access to complete information about the original researcher's epistemological position from which the data were collected. Therefore, secondary analysts should exercise caution and question their assumptions about the assumed congruence between their own epistemological positions and that from which the data were collected.

Depending upon where the data were accessed, the researcher who is performing the secondary analysis has a greater or lesser degree of information relating to the specific contextual detail of the original research project for which those data were collected (Hammersley, 2010b). Access to this information is important as the situated nature of the data collection, its cultural, institutional and interactional context, have a significant bearing on the way the data are interpreted (Bishop, 2007). Thus there is a risk that the influence of the particular features of the original data set may not be obvious to the secondary analyst (Thorne, 1994). Secondary analysis therefore raises risks regarding potential misrepresentation of data due to selective interpretation (Corti and Thompson, 2004).

Within the broad spectrum of qualitative research there is significant variability in depth and breadth of topics addressed and relative flexibility in the nature of the research design (Heaton, 2008). The problem of limited access to the original context in which the data were collected means there may be a lack of 'fit' between the data available and the requirements of secondary analysis, which can lead to potential difficulties in interpretation and unintentional errors (Gillies and Edwards, 2005). Thus the compatibility of data depends on the closeness of 'fit' between the purpose of the secondary analysis and the nature of the original data (Thorne, 1994). The purpose of any data collected will be tailored to address a particular research question and therefore it is likely that there will be a gap between the projects (Hammersley, 2010b). The secondary analyst will need to account for the relationship between the original and secondary research questions but they will also have to think about the implications of explicit and implicit methodological variations between the original pieces of research (Thorne, 1994).

As there is such diversity in relation to epistemology and methodology within the qualitative approach, the methods employed for data collection are varied and ultimately informed by the theoretical stance of the researcher.

A researcher employing phenomenology is likely to conduct interviews which seek to gather detailed information on the lived experience of participants. This shapes the trajectory of the interview and influences the style and content of questioning.

It is important for any would-be secondary analyst to be aware of this framework within which the data were collected as the secondary analyst may be attempting to employ a form of analysis that is incongruent with the way in which data were collected. We argue, therefore, that data collected are not necessarily interchangeable across methodologies (refer back to Chapter 5).

In grounded theory there is a successive process of collection, coding and analysis which is an organic process led by the interest in developing a theory, and cannot be replicated in secondary analysis (Szabo and Strang, 1997).

Mauthner et al. (1998) caution researchers engaged in secondary analysis to make their epistemological position explicit and to openly address the difficulties related to any potential mismatch between their position and that of the original researcher. Some researchers argue that these epistemological concerns need not negate the pragmatic application of secondary analysis (Fielding, 2004). We would contend, however, that while taking a pragmatist position is in many ways attractive, the quality of the secondary analysis may be compromised. In order to defend against this possible criticism we propose that the secondary analyst is transparent in their reflexive consideration of matters of methodological fit.

Quality issues

Another of the key concerns about secondary analysis in qualitative research relates to issues of quality. It is important that secondary analysts attend to issues of quality as a mechanism for ensuring methodological rigour (Szabo and Strang, 1997). Notwithstanding debates about universal markers of quality, these concerns relate primarily to the main quality criteria of transparency, reflexivity, transferability, ethicality and integrity, as outlined in Chapter 2. In relation to the overall credibility of the research project, the broader issue of trustworthiness in secondary analysis is brought into question due to limitations in the way that transparency can be managed. With regard to transparency the secondary analyst faces a twofold challenge. First, they must report openly and clearly about issues and events in which they were directly involved. Second, they have the difficulty of being limited in illustrating details relating to the collection of data in which they were not privileged to be involved in the first instance. Similarly, secondary analysts face obstacles in trying to communicate reflexivity in the dissemination of their findings because they were not present during the data collection phase of the research.

The trustworthiness and credibility of qualitative secondary data analysis are brought into question when limited information about the process of data collection is available. While it is possible to assess the credibility of new secondary findings by recourse to archived information (Hammersley, 1997), it is more challenging and relies on considerable knowledge about the original project. Problematically, the secondary analyst has a lack of control regarding how the original data set were conceived, generated and recorded which may restrict the quality of the analysis (Szabo and Strang, 1997). The reason for this is that the data were not originally collected for the specific purposes of the secondary analyst's research question.

(e.g.) Regarding the issue of transcription (which is an active process; see Chapter 6), the secondary analyst is limited in the information they may be able to access about the rationale behind decisions related to transcription, such as who transcribed the data and how (Bishop, 2007).

These are important factors which should be reported by original researchers in the interest of transparency in a way that may facilitate the possibility of secondary analysis later. Additionally, it is necessary for the secondary analyst to recognise the complexity of the work and account for any limitations of access which may impact upon their interpretations in regard to the design, methods and issues (Heaton, 1998).

An essential aspect of qualitative work is that it requires the monitoring of the effects of the research process through reflexivity. A fundamental methodological issue in qualitative research is the intersubjective relationship between the researcher and the participants, and there is concern that there will be a significant deterioration in the quality of reflexive insight in secondary analysis (Heaton, 1998). Arguably, however, because data are in effect reflexively constructed, some researchers believe that the loss of original context is less of a problem (Moore, 2007).

Some researchers position this issue of quality as a practical matter which is argued to be more easily overcome (Fielding, 2004). However, our stance is that issues of quality in qualitative research are inherently tied to the epistemological position of the researcher. While there are some overarching quality criteria which arguably can be usefully applied to any methodology, the specificity of particular qualitative approaches dictates that additional measures of quality within that discipline are attended to.

Argument of ethics

The argument of ethics is twofold. On the one hand, it is ethically advantageous to perform secondary analysis as it negates the need to recruit additional participants and expose them to potential risks and burdens (Heaton, 1998). On the other hand, however, it is often the case that original researchers do not recruit participants with future secondary analysis in mind and therefore fail to weave this into the informed consent procedures. Nonetheless, if the original researcher has made provision for the possibility of later secondary analysis then it resolves the ethical issue in a straightforward way (Szabo and Strang, 1997). An alternative option available in some cases is for the researcher to seek additional consent from participants for secondary analysis, but this may not be feasible and is generally not typically done (Hinds et al., 1997).

In cases where explicit written consent for secondary analysis cannot be or has not been obtained (whereby obtaining consent is preferred), judgements about the ethicality of reuse or secondary analysis of data for a different purpose need to be grounded in assessments of risk to participants (Bishop, 2007). However, in qualitative research the use of sensitive data is common (Heaton, 1998). This raises three issues. First, the nature of the sensitive data is more likely to raise concerns from the participants' perspective in terms of how the data are to be stored and used. Second, with sensitive data there are likely to be tighter parameters imposed by ethics committees with regard to a definitive date for data destruction. Third, there is a greater risk of harm to participants in relation to breaches of confidentiality, failures of anonymity and the potential for distress.

e.g. In our own work on family therapy there was no intention of later use of data for secondary analysis by new researchers. This was due to the sensitive nature of the video recordings of naturally occurring family therapy sessions. The topic and setting were sensitive by definition. Had we asked the families for consent to store the data for other research teams to view, this probably would have resulted in a low or zero response rate as we could not have given assurances as to how the data would be treated. It is unlikely that the ethics committee would have allowed an indefinite time-frame for the storage of such sensitive material. Furthermore, if the data had been stored and accessed by new research teams, there would have been a greater risk of breach of anonymity and confidentiality, with the potential to distress the families involved. Thus neither the data nor the transcripts were ever made available for secondary analysis.

Archiving

Despite the issues that we have discussed so far in this chapter, it is worth noting that in contemporary research practice there has been a drive towards archiving data for secondary analysis. Much of this has been driven by funding organisations. For example, in the UK, the Economic and Social Research Council (ESRC) commissioned a survey which revealed that 90 per cent of data were lost or at risk and that the 10 per cent archived failed to meet the requirements of an archive such as public access or security (Thompson, 1991). Thus, in 1994 the Qualidata qualitative archiving project was launched with the support of the ESRC; this was not an archive in itself but an action unit with a remit to locate and evaluate research data sets, organise their transfer to suitable archives and catalogue them (Corti and Thompson, 2004). However, there are many countries that have not yet put such infrastructures in place.

The drive towards archiving qualitative data for later secondary analysis has been motivated by consideration of the benefits of both archiving and secondary analysis itself. Fielding (2004) argued that there are three core benefits:

- The process of archiving a data set in itself ensures that the data corpus is kept in an organised and accessible way.
- The requirements of the archiving process dictate that data need to meet minimum standards whereby recordings have to be audible, documents have to be legible and there are no significant gaps in the material.
- A necessary aspect of archiving is that original researchers are constrained to ensure that appropriate informed consent from participants is obtained and that legal standards are met.

One of the benefits of a data archive is that researchers are able to conduct comparative analysis of historical and contemporary materials, events and issues (Corti and Thompson, 2004). This enables the exploitation of older data which can be a rich source of material regarding historical attributes and behaviours of individuals, groups, societies and organisations (see http://bit.ly/1tQwvgE). It has been argued that an additional benefit of using archived data for secondary analysis is that original research might be verified through the process, in a similar way to quantitative research (Heaton, 2008). However, the use of data for the purpose of verification through secondary analysis is controversial (Heaton, 2004), and there is little evidence to suggest that archived data are being used in this way (Corti and Thompson, 2004).

There have been a number of further criticisms put forward in relation to the shortfalls inherent in archiving. First, researchers may be reluctant to archive their data until their own analysis has been exhausted (Mauthner et al., 1998), which may be difficult to judge. Second, researchers may feel vulnerable in terms of others viewing their data and being made accountable and open to criticism (Corti and Thompson, 2004). Third, there are issues of ownership of the data, and complex legal and copyright matters (Mauthner et al., 1998). Finally, there are questions regarding the cost-effectiveness of archiving material as it is a time-consuming process and researchers typically have pressing administrative and teaching responsibilities placing demands on their time available for such matters (Mauthner et al., 1998).

SUMMARY AND FINAL THOUGHTS

In this chapter we have explained how the typical discourses of primary and secondary data have created an unnecessary dichotomy. In reality, what has been regarded as 'secondary data' is actually the same data as primary data and therefore the distinction is misleading. Rather we have clarified the distinctions between different types of data in a more sensible way. By recognising the broader qualitative literature on researcher-generated and naturally occurring data, solicited and unsolicited mechanisms for collecting data and the possibility of simultaneous data collection, we have provided clarity as to why the notion of secondary data is a misleading concept.

While negating the logic of primary and secondary data concepts, we acknowledge and recognise the necessity of differentiating primary and secondary data analysis. Within the broad topic of secondary analysis we have argued that there is a distinct and qualitative difference between reuse of one's own data and secondary analysis of data collected by another. However, we recognise that qualitative analysis, whether of one's own data or data collected by someone else, should always be rigorous and of a high standard and we recommend engagement with textbooks which explicate the process (see, for example, Bryman, 2008a). We argue that clearly defining what constitutes reuse of one's own data and distinguishing it from secondary analysis of another's data facilitates the attendance to issues of quality.

In relation to issues of quality assurance in secondary analysis, we have discussed the three main arguments that have caused contention for its credibility. These were problems of context and data 'fit', transparency and reflexivity, and ethics. Each of these was addressed in turn and illustrated some of the complexities and difficulties of conducting secondary analysis while maintaining the quality criteria for qualitative research. Expounding the rationale for these quality arguments demonstrates the distinctive differences between reuse and secondary analysis.

As a consequence of the arguments we have presented in this chapter, we propose that the issue is more complex than may have previously been presumed. Particular issues related to qualitative research, which are problematic in a way that does not apply to the analysis of quantitative data, relate to two broad issues: the fact that qualitative research is an iterative and reflexive process, and that epistemology needs to be taken into account during all phases of the process.

With regard to the non-linear process of qualitative research, the use of data for secondary analysis can restrict the iterative process and confines the availability of the reflexive aspect of the original researcher. However, the benefits of making data available for secondary analysis by others are that there is potential for a different kind of transparency which embraces the possibility of new insights from researchers or research teams. The promotion of such archiving of data has the potential to foster a culture among qualitative researchers which is more open, collaborative and supportive. Ideally, original researchers could make themselves available to secondary analysts for consultation to contextualise the material where needed (Heaton, 1998). Within this environment students are likely to benefit from this culture in a more tangible way, making them part of a broader research community with opportunities for managing their research time constraints.

As archived data sets continue to grow there will be a greater requirement for systematic cataloguing which is meaningful to would-be secondary analysts. In order to facilitate the methodological, epistemological and quality issues that are pertinent in qualitative research we propose a number of suggestions. First, in relation to the potential paucity of contextual information, we advocate that the original researchers supply as much detail as possible about context alongside their data set. Supply of original documentation such as field notes (where they exist) may help to recover a degree of context and may also enhance the secondary analysis (Corti and Thompson, 2004). Second, with regard to ethical considerations, we suggest that where practical, consent from participants is obtained for later use of the data. Third, bearing in mind the epistemological variance within qualitative research, we propose that it would be useful to catalogue data sets in accordance with their epistemological positions, or have a cross-referencing system in place. While this places a greater onus on the original researcher, we argue that the benefits for knowledge and research community culture are worth the effort. These benefits are threefold. First, the original researcher is more likely to take greater care with these important issues in order to meet criteria for archiving, resulting in better-quality information for reuse or secondary analysis. Second, the stipulations would ensure that if sensitive data were being collected, there would be more stringent procedures in place to manage and protect the data. Third, if the necessity for all researchers to approach a primary source is mitigated, there is potential to protect vulnerable and overly researched groups from further exposure to risk.

——————— Case study and reflective questions ———————

Group discussion activity

Stephanie is a criminology graduate and is interested in hoax calls requesting assistance from police services. She has been employed as an independent researcher by the police commission as the number of hoax calls has increased, causing significant costs to already stretched budgets. Stephanie has identified five research papers spanning 20 years which have used small-scale data sets of such calls. She intends to look at general themes and trends in the calls, as well as the demographics of hoax callers. In order to do so she plans to contact each of the five researchers to request access to their data sets for secondary analysis.

Q: What will the benefits be of using existing data for secondary analysis?
Q: What difficulties is Stephanie likely to encounter?

Suggestions for answering these questions are available at the end of the book.

FURTHER READING

Corti, L. and Thompson, P. (2004) Secondary analysis of archived data, in C. Seale, G. Gobo, J. Gubrium and D. Silverman (eds), *Qualitative Research Practice*. London: Sage. pp. 327–343.

In this book chapter the authors provide some context and history for archiving qualitative data and illustrate some of the modern methods for utilising archived data. They discuss some of the challenges that analysts face when undertaking secondary analysis of qualitative data and some of the issues related to ownership.

Hammersley, M. (2010) Can we re-use qualitative data via secondary analysis? Notes on some terminological and substantive issues. *Sociological Research Online*, 15(1): 5. doi: 10.5153/sro.2076.

In this article the author considers some of the benefits and challenges of undertaking secondary analysis in qualitative research and considers some of the key arguments in the literature. More specifically, he examines the problems of 'fit' and 'context' and the argument that there are difficulties in attempting to resolve such challenges.

Heaton, J. (2008) Secondary analysis of qualitative data: An overview. *Historical Social Research*, 33(3): 33–45.

This is a useful article as it provides an overview of secondary analysis in social research. The author provides definitions of secondary analysis and looks at the history of this in the qualitative field. She provides examples of how secondary analysis has been used and looks at some of the challenges that researchers face.

Thorne, S. (1994) Secondary analysis in qualitative research: Issues and implications, in J. Morse (ed.), *Critical Issues in Qualitative Research Methods*. Thousand Oaks, CA: Sage. pp. 263–279.

Although over 20 years old, this book chapter still provides some useful information about the issues inherent in secondary analysis. The author provides a critical discussion of the possibilities and implications of secondary analysis and considers some of the opportunities that this provides for the academic community.

EIGHT

Dissemination practice in qualitative research

CHAPTER CONTENTS

INTRODUCTION

Although this chapter is positioned near the end of the book, we acknowledge that qualitative research is an iterative process, and dissemination is not necessarily the end point and may be part of an ongoing process. Dissemination is an important issue for qualitative research, and in this chapter we begin by briefly attending to the wide variety of potential verbal and written modalities for dissemination, including peer review, internal organisational reports, journal articles, conference presentations, information leaflets, media web pages, posters, and participant feedback. This leads onto discussions about the style of language used in dissemination for different audiences. The debate focuses on the polemic between ensuring accessibility to certain audiences and the potential dilution of important theoretical concepts. Second, we discuss the arguable benefits of collaborative working with key stakeholders from both a pragmatic and ethical standpoint. This includes debates about sharing transcripts with participants, representing their talk in quotations, and negotiating analytic interpretations. We encourage the reader to reflect on decisions regarding representations of their participants, through respondent numbers, pseudonyms, or role categories. This is not a neutral decision and requires considerable thought. Participants themselves may have opinions on how they are represented in the dissemination phase. The chapter concludes with a consideration of the purpose and ethicality of dissemination choices as a way of highlighting the importance of the links between research and practice.

MODALITIES OF DISSEMINATION

It is not our intention to provide detail about how to use the particular modalities of dissemination as this is well covered in practical textbooks. Instead we introduce the range of modalities to critically consider the theoretical debates that exist. Dissemination is a core activity of academic life (Barnes et al., 2003) and is the means for conveying the research findings to particular audiences. Modalities of dissemination are for some research activities predefined by the context of the research project; for example, an educational dissertation or commissioned piece of research. Other modalities are more fluid and flexible and are determined by the active choices, epistemological positions and perceived purpose of the research, by the researcher. There are therefore a number of factors which influence decisions of dissemination and outputs. These include the rationale and purpose of the research, the audience being addressed, the obligations imposed by those involved in the project, and the resources available (White et al., 2014). Due to this diversity of possible dissemination practices there is considerable variety in reporting styles of qualitative research (Sandelowski, 1998).

These forums have typically included journal articles, books, posters, conference presentations, internal reports, workshops, leaflets and dissertations. Importantly, these modalities have remained the most common ways in which research is disseminated (Blaxter et al., 1996). Less common interpretations of data include painting, poetry, videos/DVDs, photographs, animation, dance, song, and drama (Keen and Todres, 2007). The choice of which mode of dissemination is preferable is largely determined by the intended audience and the resources available. An important contemporary resource which has facilitated broader and more sophisticated opportunities for the dissemination of research is the rise of the internet and technological advances. Internet services including email, web pages, newsgroups and blogs have provided powerful ways of disseminating and collecting information (Koo and Skinner, 2005). Furthermore, advances in technology have provided new possibilities for the presentation of research. Researchers are now able to present their work with photos, movie clips, internet graphics and colour in a creative way (Cleary and Walter, 2004), and digital video provides the scope for the creation of clips, still frames and transcribed text (Miles, 2006). These advances in technology have resulted in the possibility of greater access to research findings for a broader audience, including the general public (Cleary et al., 2007).

Nonetheless, despite advances in technology and a broadening of modalities for disseminating work, there remain a number of clear challenges for the researcher in writing up their work for various audiences. White et al. (2014) outlined five of these core challenges, listed in Table 8.1.

Table 8.1 Challenges of writing up qualitative research (White et al., 2014)

Challenge	Description
Telling the story	When preparing a written account it requires considerable thought to effectively convey the depth and richness of the data. It can be a challenge to tell the story in a way that is coherent and intelligible while simultaneously doing justice to the layered complexity.
Displaying an evidential base	In qualitative work there is a need for integrity in the reporting and this requires a demonstration that the interpretations and conclusions are generated from and grounded in the data. It can be difficult for researchers to condense the raw data and thus there should be a balance between displaying the subtlety and detail from the original data and the explanation and interpretation that have taken place.
Need to display diversity	The power of qualitative research stems from the ability to identify the diversity associated with the topic being studied. By relying solely on the dominant message this can be misleading as it only provides a partial map of the evidence.
Determining the length of the written account	A choice may need to be made by researchers as to which findings to leave out of the piece, which can conflict with the need to provide rich detail. In many areas of dissemination there are restrictions on word counts that can make reporting qualitative research more difficult.
Need to explain the boundaries of qualitative research	Not all audiences are familiar with qualitative research, the methods the approach employs or the type of evidence it produces. For some, therefore, it will be necessary to ensure that the audience understands what qualitative research can and cannot do.

Audiences and accessibility

Considerations about dissemination should not be post-hoc decisions upon completion of data collection and analysis, but rather be integral to the research process as a whole. Ideally, reflection about the purpose of the research and possible modalities of dissemination would be addressed during planning. This is promoted by many funding bodies that require a clear impact strategy which includes a dissemination plan. This dissemination plan should be determined by the target audience(s) (Cleary and Walter, 2004) and the most appropriate recipient of the research message. Importantly, dissemination is an active task of applying research in practice (Keen and Todres, 2007). Very broadly speaking, target audiences fall into two categories, academic/practitioner peers and stakeholders/participants. The intended audience will inform both the forum in which the research findings are communicated and the language/medium utilised to express those findings. We illustrate this in Figure 8.1.

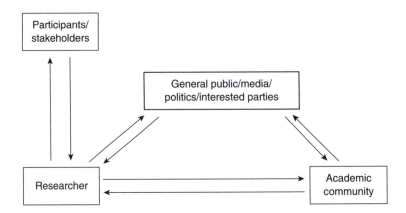

Figure 8.1 Audiences and the connection to research

This diagram illustrates how dissemination is bidirectional in that it is both informed by and informs different audiences. So although dissemination is typically viewed as the end point of a linear research design, arguably the literature-reviewing practice is also part of the process by which the design is informed (Barnes et al., 2003). Decisions about the mode of dissemination, the forum for dissemination and the type of language used in expressing the findings will be determined by this bidirectional relationship. For example, journal articles are typically written by academic scholars for their academic peers, but the research will also have been informed by a literature review using such modalities of information.

──────────────── Reflective space ────────────────

Consider how prior knowledge of your participant influenced the research question design, and what mode of dissemination might be most appropriate for your research project.

SHARING FINDINGS WITH COLLEAGUES, PRACTITIONERS AND THE ACADEMIC COMMUNITY

Arguably the main reason why researchers write is that writing is an academic currency (although the term 'currency' has a pejorative slant) and a tool that enables the sharing of knowledge and research (Colyar, 2009). Publishing is an institutional requirement, and universities expect and demand the production of research. This forms part of the quality and research assessment which determines the hierarchical ranking of those institutions in the public eye. Notably, the fundamental way in which research quality is recognised is through publication in high-impact, peer-reviewed journals. This influences the ways in which research is disseminated and the types of research produced. This can create some dilemmas for qualitative researchers who have historically competed on the academic stage for recognition in high-impact journals, confounded further by the contemporary call for evidence-based work with a scientific appeal.

The notion of impact and what constitutes impact is arguably contentious. While journals have a wide academic circulation and tend to reach national and international audiences, other forms of dissemination may have more immediate or local impact (Cleary and Walter, 2004), and particular forms of dissemination may be more likely to reach the audiences who may benefit most from the findings. Thus the researcher may make a real difference in practice by publishing in journals or through other forms of dissemination that are not as well recognised as important by academic institutions. This is particularly pertinent given that there are limited institutional incentives to disseminate beyond scientific journals as these are most influential in securing further research funding (Cleary et al., 2007). Some researchers thus find a balance by publishing in a range of forums, but with increased pressure in terms of time and resources there is a temptation to prioritise the high-impact journals. This may mean that the potential benefits of the research become compromised.

Nonetheless journals and academic papers play an essential role in the dissemination and sharing of knowledge within and beyond the academic community. To ensure quality within these publications, journal editors require that the work is peer-reviewed. The advantage of the peer-review process is that reviewers give feedback to editors and writers about the strengths and weaknesses of the manuscript (Craswell, 2005), which facilitates the credibility and quality of the research published. Notably, many journal articles are rejected (Marvasti, 2011). However, this does not mean that such articles are of poor quality. While some work is substandard and is appropriately rejected, other manuscripts are rejected for their poor fit with the aims of the journal, and on some occasions because the journal, the editor or the reviewers fail to appreciate the theory, value and process of qualitative methodology and/or particular analytic techniques.

SHARING FINDINGS WITH STAKEHOLDERS, SERVICE USERS AND PARTICIPANTS

While writing for academic audiences is seen as an important aspect of dissemination, it is also often necessary to write for non-academic audiences, especially stakeholders who may have been involved in commissioning the research (Robson, 2011). This is especially pertinent as commissioners often expect the research to have some application to an area of practice.

> (e.g.) In the field of health it is hoped that research will facilitate prevention, early detection and treatment of a range of conditions (Kerner et al., 2005). Additionally, the goals and needs of stakeholders can affect the dissemination process (Chen et al., 2010).

In recent decades, the notion of a 'stakeholder' has gained popularity and has been defined as an individual or organisation that has a legitimate interest in a project (O'Reilly et al., 2013). These are individuals or groups that contribute on a voluntary basis to a wealth-creating capacity or activity (Post et al., 2002). It is generally argued that having stakeholder involvement in a project gives that project more credibility as it helps the researcher to plan and design their research (O'Reilly et al., 2013). For research, a best-practice model advocates that stakeholder groups contain a number of adults who have an interest in the research and that this group should be regularly consulted through various decision-making processes (O'Reilly and Parker, 2014). However, service user and/or stakeholder involvement in the research process is complicated as those individuals may not be well equipped to understand the complexity of the research (Koski, 2007). This is important when the dissemination phase is thought through, because if this group has been engaged effectively they will have been instrumental to the process and researchers have an obligation to feed key findings back to them in a way that is comprehensible. This is equally important when disseminating to those individuals who participated in the project.

> (e.g.) In action research and participatory research there is an emphasis on building partnerships with participant and stakeholder groups. This has the intention of effectively translating research into practice (Cargo and Mercer, 2008).

One of the fundamental reasons why participants agree to take part in a research project is that they believe that their participation will lead to some level of benefit for other people in a similar situation (Fry and Dwyer, 2001). Thus their concern with research impact is more focused towards practical and more immediate outcomes. This can create a potential tension between the participants' and researchers' expectations of research outcomes. One of the ways in which researchers can attempt to bridge this gap is argued to be by sharing findings with participant groups during the process of dissemination or as part of their dissemination plan. In other words, researchers may choose to involve participants to facilitate dissemination to academic audiences by actively involving them in the interpretation of data, or by engaging them as one of the audiences communicated with.

Reflective point

Consider whether it is more valuable to disseminate to participants and stakeholders or to academic colleagues in peer-reviewed journals, and reflect on the reasons for your choices.

Typically, sharing research findings with participants to facilitate methodological goals is referred to as 'member checking' (Goldblatt et al., 2011). As noted in Chapter 2, this is a process whereby researchers go back to the participants and check whether the categories, explanations, interpretations and constructs resonate with the participants in some way (Merriam, 2002). Some methodologies approaches favour this approach, whereas others may see it as an inappropriate part of the process. For those qualitative methodologies that favour member checking as a valuable part of their work this process forms a bridge between analysis and dissemination. Nonetheless member checking is a contentious process and there are some documented problems with this practice. Goldblatt et al. (2011) identify several of these criticisms which are outlined in Table 8.2.

Table 8.2 Problems with member checking (Goldblatt et al., 2011)

Problem	Description
Invasion of privacy	The researcher needs to balance the potential of enhancing credibility against invading the privacy of the participants. Involving participants post-analysis may leave them feeling vulnerable as this process may lead them to relive their narratives.
Participants' perspectives may change over time	In the time period between data collection and member checking the participants' views and perceptions may alter, leading them to question the findings and interpretations presented to them by the researcher.
Increased risk of deductive disclosure	Qualitative research designs typically use small sample sizes and therefore exposure of the narratives for discussion runs a risk that participants may identify each other.
May have iatrogenic consequences	Participants may find it difficult to challenge the interpretations made by a perceived knowledgeable expert, which may lead them to feel disempowered. In practice, member checking may cause more harm to participants, despite being well intentioned.

Importantly, member checking is only a partial aspect of dissemination, and for some approaches it is not utilised at all. Thus, dissemination for participants is a much broader practice and is not one that is always performed by researchers. In the field of qualitative research there has been some controversy about giving feedback or disseminating research back to the participant group (Dixon-Woods et al., 2011), with some conflicting research regarding whether participants actually want feedback or not (Fernandez et al., 2009). However, despite reluctance by some scholars in the academic community to engage in this practice, there is evidence that generally participants favour receiving feedback regarding the main findings or results of a project that they have participated in (Dixon-Woods et al., 2006a). Furthermore, some participants may actually benefit from hearing about the main project findings (Cleary et al., 2007). Nonetheless, disseminating for participants or other general public groups is a complex process and one to which the researcher should pay particular attention. When drafting a report, information website or leaflet, the researcher needs to keep their audience in mind and be heedful of technical jargon (Robson, 2011). Furthermore, there are potentially negative implications of returning findings back to participants as it may cause them some emotional distress (Markham, 2006). Unfortunately, there has been little guidance for qualitative researchers as to how best to give feedback to participants, service users or members of the general public (Partridge and Winer, 2009).

LANGUAGE AND ACCESSIBILITY

Disseminating to a variety of different audiences requires careful consideration about the interests and needs of the audience and how the findings of the research may be tailored appropriately.

> (e.g.) One of the key arguments relating to disseminating to non-academic audiences, and particularly participants and the general public, has been how to write the findings in a way that is accessible to audiences unfamiliar with the particular methodology without losing the robustness or credibility of the approach.

This is also an important issue when writing for professional audiences or academic colleagues from different disciplines, less familiar with the approach taken. This is particularly pertinent for qualitative work due to the heterogeneity of different methodologies. Where there is a certain level of consistency in the way in which quantitative research is reported, a challenge for qualitative research is to find more creative ways of ensuring accessibility for different audiences (Sandelowski and Leeman, 2012).

When writing for audiences less familiar with the technical aspects of a particular methodology it is essential that the messages are comprehensible and that the language used is either non-technical or appropriately clarified. Thus it is arguably the responsibility of the researcher to make sense of the data and make it accessible to the particular audience (Reason, 2010). The aims of disseminating qualitative research are to both satisfy the research objectives and engage the target audiences (White et al., 2014). In order to achieve this engagement it is necessary to carefully consider the interests of that targeted audience, their levels of technical knowledge and their familiarity with particular types of research language. We have highlighted some of these considerations in Table 8.3 for the most common audiences.

Table 8.3 Modification and different audiences

Audience	Emphasis	Language and accessibility
Academic qualitative	The rigour of the methodology and adherence to quality markers	This ought to be technical and methodological in scope.
Academic non-qualitative	The validity of the methodology and the value of the findings	Technical language is included with clarification of key terminology.
Practising professionals	Practical implications and applications for their area of practice	Technical language is modified and key concepts explained.
Stakeholders involved in the project	The immediate and potential long-term benefits for their organisation or group	Technical language is modified and key concepts explained.
Participants	The core messages and how their contribution may have helped inform the field	Lay discourse is adopted to explain findings, and technical language is avoided.
General public	Applicability and relevance to their own personal circumstances.	Lay discourse is adopted to explain findings, and technical language is avoided.

It is clear from this table that the style of writing and emphasis of the message require careful consideration of the needs of the intended audience and that some methodological details may need to be modified or omitted. This does not affect the rigour of the research process and analysis; it is merely a pragmatic decision at the dissemination stage. In other words, it is important not to mistake simplified writing for oversimplification of the complexity of the experiences and events targeted in the study (Sandelowski and Leeman, 2012). Each of the qualitative methodologies is loaded with its own concepts, technical processes and style of language, which may be confusing for particular audiences or even impenetrable.

e.g. Within conversation analysis it is regarded as very important to annotate transcripts in a very detailed manner. For an academic qualitative audience familiar with conversation analysis, this practice is essential to the quality of the analysis. However, to audiences unfamiliar with interpreting the transcription notation the level of detail may make it difficult to read the excerpts of data.

e.g. Within interpretative phenomenological analysis it is regarded as very important to the methodology to utilise concepts such as intersubjectivity and embodiment to make sense of the life-worlds of the participants. For an academic audience familiar with IPA, this practice would be easily comprehensible. However, to audiences unfamiliar with these concepts the language may be inaccessible.

We argue that it is important for researchers of all types to play an active role in decision-making processes about not only where to disseminate their findings but also how to tailor the core messages for a particular audience in a way that is conceptually and linguistically comprehensible. If researchers fail to appropriately consider who they are writing for they may hinder the utility of their research (Sandelowski, 1998).

REPRESENTATION OF PARTICIPANTS

It is generally taken for granted that qualitative researchers represent their data in the form of direct quotations from the participant group (Corden and Sainsbury, 2006) in order to emphasise the evidentiary power and establish credibility (Beck, 1993). This promotes the validity of the analysis, and quotations capture the richness of the narrative in a powerful way that showcases the voices of the participants. Verbatim quotations also play an important role in 'grounding' potentially complex analyses in the participants' own accounts (White et al., 2014). There are a number of issues in relation to how quotations are used and how participants are represented. The first is how participants are labelled for the sake of the extract (for example, respondent number, pseudonym, title or role). The second, within the quotations, is how participants' names are anonymised and whether participants are given a say (for example, culturally sensitive or age-appropriate names). The third is the extent to which the quotation is grammatically or otherwise 'tidied up'.

A practical consideration for all qualitative researchers representing their data in the form of extracts is to consider how to label those extracts. We argue that this is not a neutral process but that active decisions are interpretative and may be tied to their methodological positioning. The same participant may be labelled or represented in different ways as demonstrated in the example below.

(e.g.)

Extract 1: Respondent/participant 1

Extract 1: Mother

Extract 1: Susan

Extract 1: Female 1

Extract 1: Japanese female

Extract 1: 58-year-old participant/woman

Decisions regarding how extracts are labelled may be influenced by two main factors: the researcher's methodological stance and the participants' personal preferences. In relation to methodological stance, for example, it may be more appropriate for a phenomenological study to use pseudonyms rather than representational numbers as this would be more in keeping with the perspective of the approach. However, for those approaches which value consultation with participants about how they are represented, researchers may discover that participants have strong views about how they are labelled.

(e.g.)

In the study conducted by Corden and Sainsbury (2006) they reported that many of their participants preferred gender and age categorisation to pseudonyms and they found that participants held quite strong opinions on how they are represented by qualitative researchers in the dissemination process.

Similarly, participants may have views on which pseudonyms are used to replace their real names in the data segment. Researchers need to make decisions whether to utilise a name that is culturally equivalent, is age appropriate, or has the same number of syllables and initials. Note that, in the example above the pseudonym 'Susan' is clearly not a traditional Japanese name and thus misrepresents potentially important information about the participant.

(e.g.)

In the study by O'Reilly et al. (2012) they reported that some of their child participants preferred not to be represented by a pseudonym, but preferred to be identified by their real name instead. They also found that some children disliked the idea of being given an alternative name and preferred other techniques of anonymisation. The study showed diversity in the opinions of parents and children on the ethics of anonymity in dissemination practice.

An equally important consideration in relation to representation of participants is the matter of whether quotations are strictly verbatim or whether grammatical imperfections, regional dialect and swear words are edited. In the qualitative field there is a difference of opinion as to how quotations are represented and whether they should be tidied up or not (Corden and Sainsbury, 2006). In some cases researchers may prefer to make minor alterations for the sake of improving the readability of the text, such as replacing 'ave' with 'have', or 'winda' with 'window'. While for some methodological approaches this type of editorial intervention may not affect the analysis, in other approaches it would be seen to be crucially important to maintain the integrity of the exact verbatim dialect. From a participant perspective individuals are often surprised at seeing their own words written down verbatim and may be uncomfortable or embarrassed at how their contributions are represented, even though strictly speaking the transcript is more 'accurate' (Corden and Sainsbury, 2006).

THE VOICE OF THE RESEARCHER

A further consideration that the qualitative researcher faces when disseminating their work is how to represent their own voice. Qualitative research dissemination involves creating a narrative which expresses both process and outcomes, and the positioning of the author's voice is an essential part of this form of writing (Blaxter et al., 1996). This decision is bound up with concerns of authorial presence and power, and it is argued that participants' voices may be overridden by that of the researcher (Sandelowski, 1998). This relates to debates about reflexivity in the dissemination process as researchers make decisions whether to use the active or passive voice, whether to use the present or past tense (White et al., 2014) and whether to write in a detached third-person voice or to use a first-person approach (Gilgun, 2005). By attending to these processes the researcher is acknowledging that writing is a generative process in the sense that it is self-witnessing and a self-knowledge act (Colyar, 2009). Additionally, writing for dissemination is necessarily a rhetorical practice and therefore is not simply a case of passively reporting findings (Bryman, 2008a). A decision to write in a detached, third-person voice, for example, may both contradict the ethos of the methodological approach and potentially mute the voices of the participants and the author (Gilgun, 2005).

SHARING FINDINGS WITH THE GENERAL PUBLIC, MEDIA AND OTHER INTERESTED PARTIES

It is clear that in the world of academia the practice of dissemination has tended to be narrowly defined as publishing in peer-reviewed journals (Chen et al., 2010). The rigour of the peer-review process facilitates a degree of trustworthiness in the validity of the claims made. Additionally, the advantage of knowledgeable colleagues giving constructive feedback on draft versions of articles strengthens and enhances the quality of the final version produced. It is often the case that publication through this medium is essential for the success of academics in terms of promoting their work and in building a profile (Chen et al., 2010). Unfortunately, academic journals are often not read by the general public, as shown earlier in the chapter. This in turn can mean a significant delay in the core messages reaching the general public as the information proceeds through several professional channels first (Wilkes, 1997).

However, there are several ways in which researchers can reach wider audiences, including the general public, such as television, radio or newspapers (Robson, 2011), and all researchers can now use the internet to promote their research findings (Thelwall, 2002). Importantly, it is arguable that researchers are ethically obliged to disseminate more widely to include the general public and media (Emanuel et al., 2000), and some researchers contend that ethics committees should play an active role in encouraging public dissemination, particularly where results may have direct public benefits (Mann, 2002). Additionally, over time the general public has taken an increased interest in research (particularly in the field of health) (Wilkes, 1997).

--- Reflective point ---

In your research diary make a note of your own personal view on this issue. Question whether it is the academic's responsibility to disseminate to the general public or not.

Notably, there are a range of different media outlets for research, including television, radio and newspapers. The role of the media is both to make important information available to the general public and to enable people to communicate with one another regarding those issues (Moe, 2008). This is typically received positively by the research community for a number of reasons as identified through a questionnaire conducted by Wilkes and Kravitz (1992):

- It helps researchers to achieve their professional goals.
- It has the potential to improve the image of the profession.
- It informs the professional community of the research.
- It allows the public to understand the topic better.

However, there are a number of concerns that researchers often have with regard to disseminating their findings through the media:

- Researchers perceive that it takes considerable time to consult with and disseminate through the media (Wilkes and Kravitz, 1992).
- They may have little control over what is written (Robson, 2011).
- In some fields there is a regulation referred to as the 'Ingelfinger rule' which states that research cannot be published in a journal if it has already received publicity (Wilkes, 1997).
- The media may display the research findings in a negative way (Wilkes and Kravitz, 1992).
- There are issues regarding the credibility and legitimacy of any message mediated by the media (Moe, 2008).

Although it is clear that there are several benefits of using the media as a way of disseminating research to the general public, and arguably it is important to reach this audience, the obstacles to doing so can preclude dissemination in this format. A popular alternative or additional approach that is now available to researchers who do not wish to directly engage with the media is to upload research findings or journal articles that have been published, directly to the internet. However, caution must be exercised in directly uploading published work to the internet without checking the publisher's or journal's copyright guidelines.

The internet is therefore a widely used format for disseminating research, particularly through digital libraries and electronic documents (Harter and Ford, 2000). There are a range of audiences who may use the web to look at research, including customers of research, the general public, journalists and educators (Thelwall, 2002). The internet allows the general public to access reports, articles, presentations and so forth online, which is especially important if the research was publicly funded (Duffy, 2000). This is particularly useful for qualitative researchers as it provides the opportunity to supplement the text with visual or audio-visual material (ethics permitting). This modality allows research reports and articles to be multi-layered, cross-referenced and with the integration of additional links to other resources (Duffy, 2000). This facilitates the accessibility to the general public and allows a forum through which they may communicate with the researcher or each other through a discussion forum or blog, should they choose to. Furthermore, the use of the internet promotes a reduction in asymmetry by this enablement of active public contribution (Moe, 2008).

ETHICS AND DISSEMINATION

There are a range of ethical issues in relation to the practice of dissemination, many of which we have already discussed in relation to dissemination for academic peers, participants, stakeholders and the general public. Broadly speaking, there are three core theoretical ethical issues in relation to the dissemination of qualitative research. The first is the institutional requirement and moral obligation of researchers to disseminate their findings. The second relates to disseminating beyond the academic community and the ways in which research findings are made accessible. The third relates to the ethics of giving feedback to the participants, if the data are sensitive, the findings are potentially upsetting, or if unexpected findings occur.

In adhering to the obligation to disseminate, whichever medium the researcher chooses will involve an inevitable degree of structured discourse designed to clearly elucidate the argument and to convince the audience of the legitimacy of the findings. It is important, therefore, to acknowledge the power of well-written academic writing in shaping thought about the world (Reason, 2010). The objective of research, which is to extend knowledge, is achieved in this way and public perceptions about what is known are shaped by research messages. It is important for researchers to acknowledge that rhetoric is an essential aspect of dissemination with an aim to convince others of the credibility of the claims made (Bryman, 2008a). Part of this rhetoric is the use of data in the form of direct quotations, and particularly the process of choosing quotes to enhance a particular argument (White et al., 2014). One of the dangers in qualitative work is that quotations can be misused to support misinterpretations rather than to inform (Sandelowski and Leeman, 2012). The ethical dilemma, therefore, in disseminating qualitative research is to balance the necessity of presenting a convincing argument with the awareness of the power that rhetorical writing carries with it.

In adhering to the obligation to make research findings accessible to a range of different audiences, researchers are faced with ethical questions regarding who the most important audience is for their work. As noted earlier in the chapter, there are pressures on researchers to fulfil their academic obligations to their professional institutions, while ensuring that the core messages reach those persons who will benefit most from the findings. Where time and resources are limited, these decisions become more complex and ideals may become compromised. Additionally, researchers may feel that the methodological integrity and robustness of their design may be diluted by efforts to simplify research findings for non-expert audiences. The ethical dilemma in situations where researchers desire to disseminate their work to non-expert audiences is to find a balance between rigorously abiding by the methodological quality criteria and practical considerations about the competency of the audience to comprehend potentially complex messages.

In adhering to the possible obligation of disseminating to those who participated in the study, there is a risk in sensitive qualitative research that the participants may become distressed by this process. Although their own contribution to the research will have been familiar to them, reading extracts of transcripts from other participants with similar experiences may produce a particularly empathetic response due to the affiliative nature of their common participation. Additionally, the researcher may generate findings that were unexpected, and this poses an ethical dilemma whether to and how these should be fed back to participants.

(e.g.) A study of biomarkers for cancer unexpectedly discovered potentially problematic results that may have had clinical significance for the child participants and their families (Hernick et al., 2011). The team of researchers faced the difficult decision whether or how to communicate these results to the young participants. Ultimately they decided to report back through a community-based communication plan and family meetings.

SUMMARY AND FINAL THOUGHTS

In this chapter we have covered a topic that is often not addressed in theoretical textbooks. We acknowledge that dissemination is an integral part of the research process and not simply a necessary adjunct at the end of a project. As such there are several important decisions that need to be made about the process and ethical considerations of the practice of dissemination. We have demonstrated that there are particular issues pertinent to qualitative writing that are not central to quantitative work. Specifically, much qualitative dissemination requires the usage of direct quotations from participants. This raises issues about how participants are represented and whether they should be consulted both on their opinion on how they are represented and on their views about the analytic interpretations. One of the main reasons why careful consideration needs to be given to the issues of representation and anonymisation in qualitative writing is the risk of deductive disclosure.

Furthermore, we have addressed the theoretical debates about how researchers disseminate, through what modality, and to which audiences. With regard to how research is disseminated, we have critically discussed the various modalities available, considering the benefits and limitations of the different options. This was contextualised against debates about the ethical and practical issues when writing for different types of audiences. In particular, we have highlighted the ethical dilemmas and concerns that researchers face when balancing ethical ideals in relation to good dissemination practice and practical constraints of institutional requirements. It has been argued by some researchers that academic institutions restrict the freedoms of researchers to reach out and thus limit the achievement of greater impact (Vannini, 2012). We note that the process of dissemination is one of co-construction of meaning and extends beyond the writer. Audiences are not merely passive recipients of disseminated knowledge but are active agents making active choices about what information they choose to access and how they interpret it.

Case study and reflective questions

Group discussion activity

Yeo-Jeong is a research associate near the end of her project in education, looking at teachers' opinions of working longer hours. She has six weeks remaining before the end of her contract. Her immediate line manager has expressed a preference that she writes a report for the website so that it may be widely acknowledged. However, Yeo-Jeong is currently looking for further employment and is aware that a journal article would be impressive on her limited CV.

Q: Is it ethical not to disseminate to her participants or the general public?
Q: How can Yeo-Jeong balance her commitment to broader dissemination with developing her own career profile?

Suggestions for answering these questions are available at the end of the book.

FURTHER READING

Goldblatt, H., Karnieli-Miller, O. and Neumann, M. (2011) Sharing qualitative research findings with participants: Study experiences of methodological and ethical dilemmas. *Patient Education and Counseling*, 82: 389–395.

In this article the authors consider the usefulness of member checking as an aid to quality of dissemination and to promote participant involvement. They explore the benefits and risks of using member checking in a healthcare context and use examples from three different studies. They illustrate the methodological and ethical difficulties that can arise and consider the harm that may be caused to participants.

Sandelowski, M. and Leeman, J. (2012) Writing usable qualitative health research findings. *Qualitative Health Research*, 22(10): 1404–1413.

In the article the authors discuss the fact that little attention has been paid to the ways in which qualitative findings are reported and issues of accessibility for different audiences. The focus of the article is on the issue of accessibility and the translation of qualitative language for non-qualitative readers.

White, C., Woodfield, K., Ritchie, J. and Ormston, R. (2014) Writing up qualitative research, in J. Ritchie, J. Lewis, C. McNaughton Nicholls and R. Ormston (eds), *Qualitative Research Practice: A Guide for Social Science Students and Researchers*. London: Sage. pp. 367–400.

In this book chapter the authors acknowledge the diversity in reporting practices for qualitative findings and discuss the different modes of dissemination that are available for qualitative researchers. The authors address these different outputs and discuss the benefits and limitations of their usage. Overall the chapter is designed to be practical and advisory and includes a range of useful information about the dissemination process.

NINE

Applying qualitative research in practice

CHAPTER CONTENTS

INTRODUCTION

In this chapter we draw together all of the issues discussed throughout the book by considering the practical application of qualitative research to the 'real world'. We present an ideological discussion about the value of research as a mechanism for generating new knowledge and theory versus a growing emphasis on evidence-based practice which demands practical application of research findings. In this age of austerity, funding bodies are placing pressure on researchers to indicate the potential applicability of their projects at the conception stage. This can be challenging for some qualitative researchers as it is contrary to the fundamental epistemic understanding of knowledge generation that is central to some approaches. Some academics would argue for the value of theoretical knowledge generation without the need for 'real-world' applicability, whereas others would strongly disagree with this viewpoint. We explore both sides of this argument, highlighting the pertinent issues, and argue that theoretical and applied knowledge are both valuable and can in many ways inform each other.

REVISITING THE THEORETICAL ISSUES

In this book we have not attempted to rehearse the inter-paradigm differences between quantitative and qualitative research. Instead we have focused on intra-paradigm considerations and have sought to promote greater quality in qualitative work. The core argument in seeking to promote rigorous qualitative research has been to encourage qualitative researchers to maintain an integrity which priori-tises congruence between ontology, epistemology, methodology, axiology and methods. Furthermore, we have sought to honour the traditions of each of the different methodologies, respecting the different qualitative traditions and encouraging the fostering of a qualitative community, despite the underlying differences between its members.

A thread throughout this book has been a concern that, just as qualitative researchers have baulked at the imposition of quality criteria from quantitative work, ill-fitting and often inappropriate as these are, qualitative researchers working within different methodological streams with different underpinning epistemological traditions should resist the temptation to judge other qualitative approaches against their own quality criteria. Instead we have advocated that researchers within each qualitative tradition collaborate to clarify and promote the particular philosophical underpinnings and methodological values out of which particular nuances of familiar methods are applied.

We have recognised that qualitative approaches are treated as unitary in the general academic space, whereas there is a great heterogeneity within the rubric. We have advocated an acknowledgement that qualitative researchers are part of the same species, but within it there are different breeds; '"Birds of a feather should flock together" – but there are different breeds; let the ducks be ducks and the penguins be penguins.' While qualitative researchers may all fall under one broad grouping (birds), the differences between them should be acknowledged and celebrated (ducks and penguins). There are two common goals of the qualitative community which unite the different approaches. The first is to maintain a presence within pedagogical undergraduate and postgraduate curricula. The second is to promote the value and acceptability of qualitative forms of evidence in practice. Thus while it is essential to maintain the integrity of individual methodological approaches, and useful to specialise within a particular type of qualitative research, we advocate that as a community of qualitative researchers it is important to promote the overall rubric of qualitative methods and unite to illustrate the value of the approach, to policy-makers, practitioners, commissioners, funding bodies, journal editors, academics, students and so on.

QUALITATIVE EVIDENCE IN AN EVIDENCE-BASED ERA

The premise of the evidence-based practice movement is that research is a specialist activity which should be carried out by skilful researchers who then pass on their findings to practitioners who can put their work into practice (Rolfe, 1998). This modern movement towards evidence-based practice is founded on the presupposition that the best way to improve outcomes in a range of applied settings is to identify empirical evidence that illustrates which practices are most effective. Although the theoretical and empirical discussions about evidence-based practice have in large part been generated in the field of health, it has become a significant contemporary issue in many other disciplines. It is often claimed that adoption of these particular practices as standardised protocols will lead to greater consistency of positive outcomes across a wide range of settings. While we support the premise of identifying practical ways to ensure positive outcomes in applied settings and the broader population, there are a number of limitations within the model of evidence-based practice, which tends to marginalise the value of qualitative evidence. This issue was considered in relation to the challenges of mixing qualitative approaches. This marginalisation of qualitative evidence occurs despite acknowledgement that different types of knowledge are needed, which have been broadly grouped into three categories:

1. Descriptive knowledge so that assessments may be performed.
2. Explanatory knowledge in order that linkages between an individual's problems and the broader social and environmental factors that contribute to them are understood.
3. Control knowledge in relation to the success of particular interventions in practice.

(Rosen et al., 1999)

Evidence-based practice has become dominant across many fields, and because qualitative research has tended to be relegated to the lower end of the evidence hierarchy pyramid (see Chapter 5) there is the risk of less qualitative evidence being produced by the qualitative community. If qualitative evidence is not well valued it means that potentially there is less qualitative evidence to inform practice, which perpetuates the myth that it is less useful. This is further compounded by the priorities of funding bodies in their decisions not to promote this type of evidence. This creates an oppressive movement in the 'politics of evidence' which impedes how, when and to whom qualitative methods are taught, funded, published, read and implemented (Morse, 2006a). Problematically, this lack of focus on qualitative evidence could actually impede advances in practice (Morse, 2006b). There is a need to ask questions from multiple epistemological perspectives, as a richness of knowledge is better served by a variety of approaches rather than relying on one preferred perspective, and in social sciences or where there is a focus on human behaviour this is essential: 'If the goal is generalisability then quantitative methods are accepted to be superior, but if the goal is a rich understanding of a particular phenomenon, then qualitative methods are indispensable' (McNeill, 2006: 151). Clearly, therefore, process research (as opposed to outcomes-driven research) is essential in the advancement of knowledge and understanding in a range of disciplines (Rhodes, 2011; Strong et al., 2008).

As a practice, the evidence-based movement has received extensive criticisms, particularly in relation to implementation, in (among others) the fields of health-care (Berenholtz and Pronovost, 2003), mental health (Waddell and Godderis, 2005), psychology (American Psychological Association, 2006), social work (Webb, 2001), probation (Trinder, 2000), education (Biesta, 2007), criminal behaviour (Welsh and Farrington, 2001) and social policy (Boaz and Nutley, 2003), in terms of how effectively research evidence may be translated or utilised in practice. In the academic community the application of research in practice is sometimes considered unproblematic, as something that simply flows from the conclusions of the research, and yet the reality is that the uptake of research in professional arenas is patchy (Fox, 2003). Applying evidence to practice requires more than simply identifying relevant evidence; also important is consideration of organi-sational fit and congruence with the particular context (Rycroft-Malone et al., 2004). A key difficulty with a system within which experts in one field are pro-ducing knowledge, which is then passed on to experts in an applied context, is that of differences in language, meaning and interpretation. Research and practice have differing world-views on the same subject, and research data must be trans-lated from the research world-view to the practice world-view so that it may be recognised as relevant by practitioners (Fox, 2003). Therefore, there is a need for translation of research evidence from academic to applied language (Rychetnik et al., 2012). This raises the question of whose responsibility it is to translate empirical evidence from an academic format which can be disseminated in an applied setting. Arguably this also poses an ethical question about whether it is acceptable to undertake research that employs the time and resources of partici-pants but does not have any applied benefit.

─────────────── Reflective space ───────────────

Having read this chapter so far, we would encourage you to reflect on your opinions about whose responsibility it is to translate empirical evidence into a format that can be used in applied settings.

Some would argue that it is the responsibility of researchers to engage with discussions about applicability as part of the process of dissemination. However, some researchers, particularly those who are more theoretically oriented, do not necessarily have the expertise to comment on how the findings may be translated into practice, nor in some ways should they be expected to. Similarly, profes-sionals who have expertise in the delivery of practice cannot also be expected to be well rehearsed in the language of research or have the time to do so. Thus it is sensible that evidence is developed into standardised guidelines which are a mechanism for translation and also provide professionals with more accessible versions of research findings. Problematically, the 'gatekeepers' who provide the service of translating academic findings into practice-based guidelines may limit the scope of their synthesis of what they regard as appropriate evidence to the higher levels of the hierarchy of evidence, which can exclude much qualitative research. Qualitative evidence is not ranked highly in the hierarchy and thus tends to be dismissed as 'mere opinion' (Morse, 2006a) by those who are in the powerful position of translating research evidence into practice-based guidelines. We therefore strongly encourage qualitative researchers to continue to engage in rigorous and relevant qualitative work. We recommend that they define their work in its own terms, as it has been common for researchers to lead their arguments by pitching them against quantitative evidence (Burnard and Hannigan, 2000). Additionally, qualitative researchers may need to be mindful of the need to find ways to demonstrate the applicability of their research in practice so as to narrow the research–practice gap. This has the potential benefit of making scientific products more palatable to wider audiences (Green, 2008).

PRACTICE-BASED EVIDENCE

One of the major solutions proposed relating to the gap between research and practice, and between researchers and practitioners, has been a focus on translation and dissemination (Green, 2008). This has been necessitated by the significant difference in the conceptualisation and language of academically oriented empirical research and the requirements of professionals working in different fields of practice. The pragmatic question that many practitioners ask of empirical research is how it can actually inform areas of their daily work and make a difference to them. The question of relevance of research findings is therefore paramount for all practitioners. Problematically, however, concerns have been raised that the drive for evidence-based practice may not be the most appropriate or relevant way of informing practice (Barkham and Mellor-Clark, 2000). There have therefore been a number of proposed remedies to the problem of the evidence–practice gap as outlined by Green (2008):

- Bring research closer to practice in the form of action and participatory research so that findings are more relevant, actionable and tailored to specific populations.
- Offer incentives to practitioners to pursue evidence-based practice guidelines (although practitioners' concerns are that the evidence may not be applicable to their particular setting).
- Give greater attention to external validity in the way that research evidence is assessed. Problematically, the emphasis on internal validity within some academic research practice occurs at the expense of external validity.

Thus there is a need for practice-based evidence (Barkham and Mellor-Clark, 2000), which has the benefit of greater external validity and therefore has more real-world authority for professionals (Fox, 2003). As we have noted, traditionally the evidence base of evidence-based practice has been developed by giving particular credence to highly controlled trials (Green, 2006), which generate statistical information about which interventions or approaches are most effective. In turn this is presented as 'evidence' which dictates which practices are employed in various fields. On the other hand, practice-based evidence gives more credence to observation and analysis of the nuances of the actual activities of practitioners' work. The advantage of this is that practitioners become more directly involved in the generation of evidence, and research questions are developed with applicability in mind (Fox, 2003). Thus Fox (2003) advocated that there are three key propositions upon which practice-based evidence rests and in terms of how knowledge of the world is sought. These are outlined in Tables 9.1–9.3.

These three propositions suggest that not only is practice-based evidence contingent upon how knowledge of the world is sought, but also knowledge is a local and contingent process, therefore knowledge of the local setting does not

Table 9.1　Proposition 1: The pursuit of knowledge is a local and contingent process, and understanding the local will not mean it will inform other settings (Fox, 2003)

Research process	Description
In terms of the research question	In traditional research it has been emphasised that the research should not proceed until a clear research question is developed. However, this is based on the principle that research is linear and results in an answer to the question. However, from a practice-based perspective because knowledge is local and contingent it is impossible to establish the most appropriate questions to ask until the researcher has a better understanding of the characteristics of the setting.
Research design: the validity of the study and the instruments are tied with questions	As knowledge is local and contingent, we should not make assumptions regarding the methodological approach or instruments used to uncover this knowledge. It is important not to assume that one research design or instrument will be sufficient to answer a question.
For data collection	The reliability of the data would be compromised in a practice-based evidence approach, and thus there is a requirement for reflexivity to manage this; however, such 'bias' is a virtue as it guarantees that the research is relevant and adequate to address the research question. This is especially pertinent for social sciences and also for some aspects of health.
For data analysis	Traditionally this is viewed as completing the cycle of research. However, the practice-based evidence model is more cyclical and analysis is part of ongoing evaluation and reflection. Thus if knowledge is local then the analysis of the data is linked with reflections on the research process by both participants and researchers. In terms of action being constitutive of difference, it requires that the analysis is constituted within the ethical and political commitments of participants.

Table 9.2 Proposition 2: Research is a political activity, and a political engagement with the world has the potential to legitimate or repress certain aspects of the world that it observes, including for example the irrationality of practice. All action is constitutive of difference (Fox, 2003)

Research process	Description
In terms of the research question	The research question should be constitutive of difference and should not close down or limit the ways in which participants in the research conceive themselves. Thus the 'subjects' become 'participants' and are not subjected to the will of the researchers.
In terms of research design	The second presupposition of practice-based evidence is also relevant in the sense that participants should be fully involved in the research process, which fits with qualitative approaches that enable participants.
For data collection	The instruments of social research may actually be the participants themselves, and research situations may involve direct interaction with the participants; thus the questions asked will depend upon the identity or characteristics of the participants. Furthermore, participants may be assisted in challenging the established social and political order.
For data analysis	Data analysis is constituted within the ethical and political commitments of the participants.

Table 9.3 Proposition 3: Theory building is a necessary aspect of understanding, and the value of theory is in its applicability to the practical settings in which it has been developed (Fox, 2003)

Research process	Description
In terms of the research question	Theory should be related to practice and thus research questions should be developed in ways whereby the theoretical consequences are directly relevant in practice.
In terms of the research design	Theory should be closely linked to the practical concerns of participants instead of the concerns of the disinterested research community.
For data collection	The development of theory is made relevant through the process of data collection that is relevant to those involved in the study and in ways that are related to their practical concerns.
For data analysis	In terms of theory being related to practice, the data analysis should inform the practical concerns of participants and researchers through recommendations for change.

necessarily allow generalisation to other settings (Fox, 2003). Additionally, Fox argued that all research should be considered a political activity in the sense that some of the 'messiness' of daily practice is usually omitted or glossed over, which not only sanitises the findings but also abstracts them from their context. Furthermore, practice-based evidence seeks to integrate theory building in research with applicability to the practical settings within which it was developed. Importantly, practice-based research acknowledges the circularity of the research process, as question development, theory building and findings are iterative and reflexive.

ACTION RESEARCH AND PARTICIPATORY RESEARCH

A contemporary model of research which engages the interests of both the academic community and participant community, combining both theory and practice, is action research (see the description in Chapter 4). This is a particularly versatile approach that potentially combines the strengths of both evidence-based practice and practice-based evidence. It is a research approach in which there is a synergistic relationship, with research informing practice and practice informing research (Avison et al., 1999). Action research is inherently an iterative process which engages researchers and practitioners or participants together throughout the research project (Avison et al., 1999). The fundamental tenet of this approach is that all knowledge is socially constructed and that research is inevitably influenced by systems and values (Brydon-Miller et al., 2003). Action research is essentially a participatory process which advocates a democratic approach to developing practical knowledge by seeking to offer solutions to issues of concern to the participant community (Reason and Bradbury, 2001). Thus the purpose of action research is to solve particular problems and to produce guidelines for best practice (Denscombe, 2010).

(e.g.) Young and Barrett (2001) conducted a participatory action research project with street children in Kampala, Uganda, to develop an understanding of their socio-spatial geographies and survival mechanisms. Due to language difficulties they employed four visual action research methods, which were mental maps, thematic drawing, daily time-lines and photo diaries. This successfully elicited important knowledge about this population.

Although there are different types of action research, they share a fundamental underlying driver that emphasises social justice and favours an explicitly political and democratic practice, actively engaging with the theoretical frameworks of critical theory and feminism (Brydon-Miller et al., 2003). Within the field of action research it has been argued that qualitative research has tended to be 'about practice, not with practitioners', thus losing much of the local knowledge and context of the research (Huang, 2010: 94). We argue that qualitative research can effectively engage with issues of context and subjectivity, without necessarily engaging with the socio-political ideology of action research. It is has been our perspective in this chapter that building partnerships between academics and practitioners has the potential to facilitate the relevance, practical implementation and application of qualitative research. We believe that action researchers make an important point in recognising the value of involving stakeholders, particularly practitioners, in the qualitative research process, but argue that this can be achieved successfully without the strong political agenda of feminism or critical theory, and using a range of different methods or methodologies, underpinned by different epistemological and ontological positions.

> **e.g.** In our research we do not hold a critical, political ideology but we advocate the value and importance of seeking to work collaboratively 'with' practitioners, stakeholders and participant groups. These include academic–psychology, academic–psychiatry and academic–stakeholder autism group partnerships to promote practical relevance in particular fields.

While we respect the potential usefulness of action research as both a political and apolitical approach that utilises qualitative methods, we acknowledge that there are some limitations. Most obviously, by the specific nature of the approach, research is undertaken largely on a case-by-case basis within a local situation and therefore may not extend beyond the local context (Brydon-Miller et al., 2003).

An approach that has many similarities with action research and in some cases draws upon an action research framework is participatory research. 'Participatory research' is a general term for a school of approaches which share a philosophy of inclusivity and integrate research and non-academic persons' knowledge and experience into partnerships that are meaningful (Cargo and Mercer, 2008). Participatory research tends to emphasise a bottom-up approach and focuses largely on locally defined priorities and local perspectives (Rahman and Fals-Borda, 1991). These partnerships thus build on local strengths and resources and facilitate the progress of the research (Cargo and Mercer, 2008). One of the advantages of the participatory approach is its innovation and flexibility to adapt conventional research methods for use in local contexts, with and by local people (Cornwall and Jewkes, 1995). By involving the people who are directly affected by the research topic this approach offers the possibility of integrating academic knowledge with local knowledge to offer practical solutions (Cargo and Mercer, 2008).

While the intentions behind participatory approaches are noble, the pragmatic application of these principles is sometimes challenging. One of the difficulties in attempting to develop working partnerships between community stakeholders and researchers is the difference in common terminology which potentially hinders the ways in which participants can be most effectively engaged (Lasker et al., 2001). Additionally, partnerships of this kind require time and patience to build shared objectives and practices (Metzler et al., 2003), and it is not unusual for tension and conflict to be part of the process (Wallerstein et al., 2008). This is particularly important given that members of the partnership may have different social, economic, ethnic, cultural or academic backgrounds (Chávez et al., 2008). However, with time and effort equal participation can be achieved, and the community and research outcomes may be richer (Cargo and Mercer, 2008).

REFLEXIVITY IN THE RESEARCH PROCESS

As knowledge is not a static objective entity, but a fluid co-constructed phenomenon, the process of knowledge production is inherently an interpretative endeavour. Therefore, it is essential as a qualitative researcher that reflexivity is an integral part of the work. This means that qualitative researchers should be reflexive from the inception of the research until and including any knowledge translation or application.

Reflexivity is an iterative process, and in its basic form means that researchers make visible their impact on the research process and the impact of the research process on them. In quantitative research this impact is often considered to be a bias which preferably needs to be controlled for, but for qualitative researchers it is considered an enriching and informative part of the work (Gough, 2003). As Mauthner and Doucet (2003: 414) state, 'most methods continue to be presented as a series of neutral, mechanical and decontextualized procedures that are applied to the data and that take place in a social vacuum', despite this not being the case. Any research that is undertaken inevitably occurs within a particular social, cultural and economic climate with a particular group of participants, and this contextual information cannot be artificially extracted from the knowledge claims made. Meanings are ultimately a product of a negotiated interaction between the researcher and participant (Finlay, 2002). Thus all claims to new knowledge need to be acknowledged as reflexively situated.

Some researchers have proposed a range of different types of reflexivity (see, for example, Finlay, 2003), and Willig (2008) broadly conceptualised reflexivity into two main types, personal and epistemological, for researchers engaging in qualitative work. She proposed personal reflexivity to involve reflecting on the ways in which the attitudes, values, beliefs, experiences, political commitments and social identities shape the research in terms of how the research is affected and changed by the researcher. Epistemological reflexivity was described as requiring the researcher to consider how the research question is defined and limited and how the design of the study constructs the data, encouraging the researcher to reflect on their assumptions for the research and its subsequent findings.

(e.g.) Researcher reflexivity is a mechanism for evaluating the process, which in turn manifests itself as a way of learning, which will inform future decisions. As such, reflexivity enables the research process to be cyclical and iterative as well as developmental.

Evidently reflexivity is central to qualitative research, and the process of reflecting on how one's own views and values may have influenced the production of findings adds credibility to the research (Jootun et al., 2009). It is important to recognise that social researchers are an integral part of the social world which is being studied (Mauthner and Doucet, 2003), and therefore the researcher's construction of meaning must be acknowledged as having inevitably being influenced by this (Willig, 2008). In order to be reflexive, researchers need to be prepared to take a critical perspective in relation to themselves and their work (Finlay, 2003). Essentially the attitude and behaviour of the researcher will ultimately affect both how participants respond and the nature of the findings produced (Finlay, 2002). This is a continuous process which enables implicit agendas to be made explicit (Gough, 2003). Without this critical reflexivity there is the risk of iatrogenic difficulties whereby there may be an unintended harmful impact as a result of claims to neutrality, objectivity or non-interpretation, which are essentially misnomers. Thus the importance of reflexivity becomes an ethical issue as well as a quality one.

Reflective practice is considered to be the cornerstone of many applied disciplines. As such there is a symbiosis between the practical application of reflective work as a practitioner and the reflexive process of the academic researcher. Importantly, reflexivity and reflection are concepts that are on a continuum, with reflection tending to occur post hoc and reflexivity being more immediate, dynamic and continuous (Finlay, 2002). Although these two terms have sometimes been confused, both are important for research and knowledge translation. Thus, whether knowledge production is generated via evidence-based practice or practice-based evidence, reflection and reflexivity are the essential components which ensure that knowledge claims are transparent in how they are generated and therefore more trustworthy.

───────────────── **Reflective space** ─────────────────

Take this opportunity to consider why reflexivity might be important for you in your own work.

SUMMARY AND FINAL THOUGHTS

In this chapter we have considered a number of issues related to the difficulty of applying research in practice. One of the arguments presented has been that it need not be an incumbent concern that is placed upon predominantly academic theory- or philosophy-based researchers. We have argued both for the need to recognise and appreciate the contribution that theorists offer in the development and extension of knowledge, and that this role is essential. Therefore it is justifiable that research is valuable as an end in itself without necessarily having immediate application (Green, 2008). Nonetheless, some academic researchers strongly consider their work to have an applied aspect and strive to consider the applicability of their findings in an area of practice. We advocate that theoretical and empirical research are both needed to advance the academic community and provide a greater contribution to knowledge and philosophy.

The recognition of qualitative research within the broader academic space has been a theme throughout this book, and we have oriented to the challenges that qualitative researchers face in a culture which still favours quantitative work. We note that unfortunately it seems that this preference for the positivist 'scientific' paradigm has been ratified by the drive for evidence-based practice. This drive has explicitly prioritised quantitative work in its hierarchy of preferable evidence. This has had the negative consequence of biasing funding priorities away from qualitative work and limiting promotional opportunities for those not engaging in research which is compliant with the higher levels of the evidence-based practice hierarchy (Green, 2008). While we recognise that internal validity is a crucial component in producing good-quality generalisable findings, our concern is that perhaps this has been at the expense of external validity, which is a more pressing concern for practitioners. Furthermore, we question whether the terminology of validity is appropriate within the context of qualitative research and argue that, as mentioned previously, the quality of different qualitative methodologies needs to be assessed according to relevant and approach-specific criteria.

Although in this chapter we have presented the arguments about evidence-based practice as potentially dichotomous to practice-based evidence, this has simply been to outline the core features of the arguments. It is important to acknowledge that practice-based evidence is complementary to evidence-based practice (Barkham and Mellor-Clark, 2003), and both have an important role to play in epistemic advancement. We support the position that evidence and practice are not binary concepts but that in a very real sense they are intertwined and mutually informing (Fox, 2003).

We strongly advocate the value and importance of qualitative research as a mechanism for both generating knowledge and informing practice. We also take a particular position with regard to promoting the significance and benefits of partnership working where mutually beneficial partnerships between practitioners and researchers are cultivated. This position reflects our own research, clinical and academic partnership working. Our partnership works on the basis that one author is a practice-based clinician seeking to make research links with the academic community (Kiyimba), while the other is an academic-based scholar seeking to ensure applicability of research in practice (O'Reilly). The common link between us is a shared passion for qualitative research, with a particular emphasis on promoting the value of discourse and conversation analysis.

In conclusion, we have been very clear in arguing that while qualitative researchers share a common appreciation of process, there are broad intra-paradigm differences in fundamental, philosophical, methodological and axiological perspectives. In consideration of these intra-paradigm differences we have celebrated the heterogeneity and proposed that each qualitative approach takes responsibility for clear quality criteria against which their particular qualitative approach can be meaningfully judged. In the absence of this there is a risk that there will be a fairly arbitrary assignation of quality criteria from either other qualitative approaches or more quantitative methods. A dominant theme throughout this book has been our proposition that it is imperative for each qualitative domain to retain an integrity and congruence between ontology, epistemology and methodology. This is vital because we have observed that novice qualitative researchers can mistakenly attempt to engage in research by starting with methods and then choosing analytic approaches after the data have been collected. This is problematic because where the parameters of a particular methodology have not been considered from the outset the research product may lack credibility, integrity and trustworthiness, since essential quality criteria for that methodology have not been adhered to.

During the process of writing this book, we have consulted a number of experts in different fields of qualitative work in developing the themes and debates, and have attempted to provide a balanced view of different ideas within the qualitative community, but we do acknowledge that we have presented our particular perspective on the issues covered. We have felt it essential to be transparent about our own personal position within the debates, and recognise that some of our esteemed peers will have different points of view. The purpose of this book has been to stimulate academic discussion, and we hope that the issues raised will become a springboard for further engagement with these important topics.

Case study and reflective questions

Constance is an experienced child-protection social worker with a high caseload who has recently been given a trainee to supervise. A requirement of the social work degree that the trainee is studying for is to show evidence of compliance with evidence-based practice guidelines in her work through a presentation to her peer group. Constance and her trainee are working with a particular client group and have recognised some specific cultural characteristics and ways of making sense of their experiences which mean that the generic evidence-based practice guidelines are not particularly tailored to their needs.

Q: What issues should Constance's trainee pick out for her presentation, and how will she reconcile the practical difficulties?

Suggestions for answering this question are available at the end of the book.

FURTHER READING

Cheek, J. (2007) Qualitative inquiry, ethics, and politics of evidence: Working within these spaces rather than being worked over by them. *Qualitative Inquiry*, 13: 1051–1059.

In this article the author considers the interpretative process of qualitative researchers in terms of how they conceptualise, write and report their research. She provides a useful discussion of how this matters for the politics of evidence and considers the tensions that are inherent within qualitative work.

Finlay, L. (2003) The reflexive journey: Mapping multiple routes, in L. Finlay and B. Gough (eds), *Reflexivity: A Practical Guide for Researchers in Health and Social Sciences*. Oxford: Blackwell Publishing. pp. 3–20.

This is a useful book chapter for readers who wish to gain a better understanding of reflexivity in qualitative research. The author considers how reflexivity is promoted to provide a more transparent account of the research, but argues that this has ties with positivism, which is less useful. She presents an argument for a more radical reflexive approach to embrace the negotiated and socially constructive nature of the research experience.

Fox, N. (2003) Practice-based evidence: Towards collaborative and transgressive research. *Sociology*, 37(1): 81–102.

In this article the author considers the application of research to policy and service delivery, arguing that translating research into practice is not a straightforward endeavour. He presents the conflict between academics and practitioners and considers an alternative practice-based model.

Green, L. (2008) Making research relevant: If it is an evidence-based practice, where's the practice-based evidence? *Family Practice*, 25(1): i20–i24.

In this article the author proposes a difficulty in the typical search for solutions for the research–practice gap and provides a critical discussion for the problems that this creates.

Morse, J. (2006) The politics of evidence. *Qualitative Health Research*, 16(3): 395–404.

In this article the author explores the evidence-based movement in the field of health and considers how and why qualitative methods are often excluded. She provides a critique of the narrow definitions of what constitutes evidence and provides an argument for the value of qualitative evidence, arguing that it is essential that we reframe our definitions of evidence.

Suggested answers to case study questions

CHAPTER 1: RAJESH

Q: How would Rajesh demonstrate an understanding of why epistemology is important in a qualitative project?

We recommend that Rajesh consider Figure 1.1 as the basis for his presentation as this illustrates the iterativeness and circularity inherent in qualitative methods. It also indicates the mutually dependent relationship between ontology, epistemology, axiology, methods, methodology and knowledge. From this diagram Rajesh could demonstrate specifically how his particular project fits coherently with each of these interrelated elements. Additionally, Rajesh might want to consult some of the literature such as Staller (2013), as this explains how and why ontology, epistemology and methodology are related.

It is important that in his presentation Rajesh demonstrates and transparently acknowledges which epistemological position he holds and how that shapes and informs the type of research that he will conduct. He needs to recognise that there are different debates in the field of qualitative research regarding the relevance and importance of epistemology, and he should be clear where he positions himself within that debate. He should also demonstrate an awareness of some of the alternative theoretical views that exist in qualitative approaches, as outlined in the chapter. This will afford the opportunity to demonstrate why those alternative positions are incongruent with his own world-view.

CHAPTER 2: LUKAS

Q: Are there any general qualitative criteria that apply to both grounded theory and IPA studies that Lukas could draw upon to inform his review?

Lukas might find it useful to draw upon the arguments that favour universal criteria for judging quality in qualitative research, as these would arguably apply to both grounded theory and IPA. We recommend therefore that Lukas engages with some of the literature in this area, such as the Spencer et al. (2003) framework and the list produced by Tracy (2010). He does, however, need to recognise that this reflects one particular viewpoint within qualitative work. Lukas will need to be mindful that as yet no universal criteria have been developed and agreed across the different qualitative approaches and that there are a range of different debates about quality as we outlined within the chapter. Nevertheless, in his role as reviewer, and as someone less familiar with the specifics of the methodology used in the paper, these may serve as a useful benchmark for him to make some judgements about quality. For example, as noted in the chapter, Spencer et al. (2003) have suggested that qualitative research should be:

- Contributory
- Defensible
- Rigorous
- Credible

However, other scholars have produced slightly different criteria. For example, as we noted in the chapter, Tracy (2010) suggested eight universal markers:

- Worthy topic
- Rich rigour
- Sincerity
- Credibility
- Resonance
- Significant contribution
- Ethics
- Meaningful coherence

Lukas could cite one of these authors and use their suggested criteria or he could favour fewer key markers that are well respected and used by many in the qualitative field – transparency, reflexivity, trustworthiness and rigour.

Q: Do you think that he needs to take anything else into consideration when assessing the quality of the method and the interpretation of findings?

While Lukas may feel that the universal criteria are sufficient to judge the IPA article that he is reviewing, he may want to familiarise himself with the methodological approach and the more specific quality markers that are indigenous to that methodology. In doing so he may need to reflexively suspend his own judgements that may arise specifically from his own preferred alliance with grounded theory so as not to unfairly disadvantage the authors of the IPA study.

CHAPTER 3: EDUARDO

Q: How might the process of iterative consent be applicable to this research project?

If Eduardo chooses to adhere to the principalist approach to ethical research, his overall approach to gaining informed consent would comply with the principles of respect for autonomy and the need to uphold justice, beneficence and non-maleficence. Eduardo should recognise that internet research carries some specific issues with regard to the public and private sphere and he should engage in some additional reading about consent in internet-based research.

We recommend that his initial consent procedures make a number of important aspects clear to the participants, including the following:

- Eduardo should be clear, when discussing access to social media with the participants, which aspects of the feeds/pages he is allowed access to.
- Eduardo should specify in writing a definite start and end date for accessing the material.
- Eduardo should make it clear to the participants that they have the right to withdraw their consent at any point during the process.
- Eduardo should consider the issue of consent for third parties. Social media typically will involve interactions with parties other than the consenting participants, and thus he should make provision to ensure that these other parties are aware of the research so that they can choose to or not to post their contributions during the period of research.

With regard to the important issue of iterative consent, it would be good ethical practice for Eduardo to revisit the issue of consent at several points during the data collection period to ensure that the participants are still in agreement with the terms and conditions of the informed consent contract.

Q: What might Eduardo need to consider in relation to power and positionality?

This is a challenging issue for Eduardo as he holds a clear position of authority in this context, being the senior lecturer for the students he is trying to recruit. Eduardo must consider the issue of the inherent power differential between him and his students, and as such there is a real risk of unintentional or inadvertent coercion. We discussed these issues in the chapter and showed that role and title in themselves can affect the relationship with participants (see Richards and Emslie, 2000). Eduardo should be circumspect in how he recruits his participants, making it very clear that participation in the study has no bearing on students' grades or success in their course. Likewise, non-participation would not result in failing their course. However, Eduardo should be mindful that even when making this clear in both information sheets and verbally, some students may still have concerns. It may therefore be advisable for Eduardo to recruit students from courses that he is not involved in teaching.

In terms of positionality, there is a risk of violating the boundary between formal and informal relationships, which is all the more problematic given the personal nature of the data that Eduardo is requesting access to. It would therefore be important for Eduardo to remain reflexive throughout the process. One other possible solution for Eduardo is to delegate the responsibility for data collection to a research assistant who could anonymise the data before Eduardo has access to it. This would create an ethical buffer in order to safeguard the professional relationship between Eduardo and his students.

CHAPTER 4: BRUCE AND CAROLINE

Q: What problems may Bruce face in his retrospective decision to use IPA?

The key problem for Bruce is that he did not conduct phenomenological interviews which would have emphasised the personal meanings and life-worlds of the participants. IPA interviews are conducted within the parameters of a particular theoretical framework which is acknowledged and transparent in the research, but Bruce has failed to consider his own epistemological position in relation to the data or thought about how this might have shaped the interview process.

The problem for Bruce at this juncture is that if he attempts IPA it is unlikely to satisfy the specific quality criteria that an IPA study would expect and therefore his finished piece of work is unlikely to be of an acceptable standard. Bruce needs to be more aware of the issues and accept the impracticality of attempting to impose a phenomenological analysis on the data at this stage. Again we recommend that Bruce read some of the debates in this area; for example, he could consult the Wimpenny and Gass (2000) paper that compares two different types of interviewing style. Ultimately, however, Bruce needs to utilise a more epistemologically flexible method of analysis, such as thematic analysis or template analysis.

Q: How will having attended the workshop help Caroline to plan her data collection?

Caroline is at an ideal stage for decision-making about the whole process of data collection and analysis and would be best advised to follow up on any recommended reading from the workshop. This reading would also help Caroline to clarify her own world-view and epistemological position to ensure that it fits with the framework of IPA. This would then help her to consider how to plan her data collection in a manner congruent with the epistemological and methodological tenets of IPA. Approaching her research study with a clear plan regarding how to ensure congruence between her research question, data collection methods and analytic approach will facilitate the process and promote quality in the final piece.

CHAPTER 5: CHARLIE

Q: Do you think that Charlie should use a mixed methods qualitative design or a synthesised methodologies approach, and why?

Charlie could recognise that small sample sizes in conversational analysis are entirely appropriate and can generate a wealth of rich and interesting data. Therefore, Charlie need not be overly anxious about supplementing a good-quality conversational analysis study on the basis of small sample size. We recommend that Charlie consider his own ontological position carefully as this may inform his decision regarding whether he would prefer to do either a conversational analysis study or an interview study.

It is possible that Charlie is simply being pragmatic about his decisions. If it is necessary due to institutional or funding pressure, then we recommend that Charlie take a synthesised methodologies approach as opposed to a mixed methods approach. This would ensure methodological integrity for each of the two separate parts of the study. Importantly, Charlie would need a good understanding of the issues in mixing qualitative methods and the different points of view, so he should also engage in some reading around the issues, such as Barbour (1998) and Morse (2010), as well as the materials in this chapter. Furthermore, Charlie will need to think about how he will analyse his interviews, as it would be inappropriate to use the analytic approach of conversational analysis on researcher-generated data. He would, therefore, need to be clear as to which methodologies he is synthesising, and which methodology the interview methods were part of.

Q: What is the incommensurability problem here?

Conversation analysis is based on the ontological premise that reality is co-created and tends to adopt a relativist stance (see Chapter 4). Charlie's decision to conduct supplementary interviews is based on a world-view that reality can be accessed through particular methods and adopts a realist (or at least a critical realist or similar) ontological position, which is contrary to the position taken by conversation analysis. Due to this fundamental incongruence it is therefore arguably inappropriate for Charlie to attempt a mixed qualitative methods design for this project.

It may be that Charlie's own ontological position is not congruent with conversational analysis and he may wish to find an alternative methodology that fits better, such as critical discourse analysis. If, however, he reflects and feels that his views are congruent with conversational analysis, then he needs to consider why he plans to conduct an interview-based study in addition to the conversational analysis one, given the broadly realist position taken.

CHAPTER 6: SABINE

Q: What factors will Sabine need to consider in her decision whether to use audio or audio-visual recordings of the teenage behaviour?

There are a range of practical issues that Sabine will need to account for when considering how to record the café culture. As the fieldwork will be taking place in a public location there are likely to be several extraneous factors which may impinge upon the quality of data collection, such as other café users, levels of background noise, insufficient lighting, multiple voices on the recording, and participants joining and leaving the conversation. A key concern for Sabine therefore will be where she locates the recording device in order to collect the necessary data. Sabine could consult Heath (2011) to help with some of the important issues.

Practically speaking, it may be advisable for Sabine to utilise a combination of several audio and visual devices in order to capture the interactions in full. This will of course raise some ethical concerns in terms of capturing only the consenting participants and no other visitors to the café. This will be particularly pertinent with the use of video data which carries a greater likelihood of identification. However, using the combination of both audio and video equipment will enhance the data collection process as multiple devices will improve the capturing of voices and non-verbal information. If something is missed on the microphone of the video camera it is possible that the audio recording device will have picked the voice up more clearly. Additionally, as Sabine is interested in the café culture, she will benefit from being able to see the accompanying actions and behaviours of the participants as they interact.

In terms of transcription, one of the most challenging aspects of multi-party conversations is the identification of different speakers from audio material. Therefore, the use of audio-visual devices would facilitate the transcription of talk into text. Additionally, Sabine needs to carefully consider whether and how she chooses to transcribe non-verbal communication as this may be pertinent to her anthropological study.

Q: Sabine wishes to present her findings at an international conference which will use English as the main language. What issues does she face in translating the data?

As the data were both collected and transcribed in French originally, Sabine faces the challenge of translating her transcripts into English for an international audience. Sabine could provide a straightforward translation into English or she could provide an inter-linear transcript which maintains the French original text as well as English literal translation and the grammatically modified English version (similar to the Arabic example we gave in the chapter). Some of the problems she may face in translating her data may be that the English language does not have the exact word or phrase to adequately capture the nuances of the words spoken in French. This can result in the meanings of some of the data being altered or lost.

CHAPTER 7: STEPHANIE

Q: What will the benefits be of using existing data for secondary analysis?

It would be very challenging for Stephanie to conduct a longitudinal study over 20 years, and thus by acquiring data from other researchers across different points in this time-span she would be able to explore trends and patterns. Additionally, conducting secondary analysis on previously collected data has the advantage of being less labour-intensive as Stephanie would not need to actively engage and recruit participants, acquire ethical consent or transcribe the data. This means that secondary analysis may be more time-efficient. Some of these benefits, along with some of the debates, are outlined in Heaton (2008), and Stephanie would benefit from the additional reading when planning her work.

Q: What difficulties is Stephanie likely to encounter?

Stephanie faces several difficulties in both acquiring and analysing the data for her research. Unlike accessing a data archive, Stephanie intends to contact the original researchers directly to request access to their data. This may prove to be problematic in that those original researchers were unlikely to have gained consent from their participants for research beyond the scope of their own study and thus there may be ethical issues with allowing Stephanie access. Furthermore, there are likely to be a number of other inconsistencies between the data sets of the five researchers that Stephanie intends to contact; for example, the data would have been collected from different populations, for different purposes, and may have been transcribed using different transcription conventions. Additionally, as Stephanie was not involved in the original data collection, much of the original context may have been lost. If Stephanie goes ahead with her secondary analysis we recommend that she is transparent and reflexive about these issues in the write-up of her study, and engages with the literature in this area.

CHAPTER 8: YEO-JEONG

Q: Is it ethical not to disseminate to her participants or the general public?

The main ethical consideration for dissemination is balancing the inconvenience and commitment of the participants against the potential benefits for a wider population. Thus we would argue that it is unethical not to disseminate after having conducted a piece of research involving participants. The appropriateness of the route of dissemination, however, is more particular to the specific research project and thus there is not a definitive answer to this question. We therefore encourage the reader to think about:

1. Whether the participants in the study either are expecting or would benefit from dissemination to them personally.
2. Whether it would be unethical in this particular study to withhold the information from the general public.
3. The best dissemination approach to facilitate the most impact in practice.

Typically researchers engage in a range of dissemination strategies, but it is important that the audience is considered carefully and that the purpose of any piece is thought out in a clear way.

Q: How can Yeo-Jeong balance her commitment to broader dissemination with developing her own career profile?

Yeo-Jeong is likely to have an obligation to fulfil the criteria of her employment contract and may need to follow the request of her line manager to fulfil her institutional obligation as a priority. This would mean that the online report for the website would have to be completed before engaging in other dissemination activities. As Yeo-Jeong favours the publication of a journal article for her own personal career advancement, her decision for this form of dissemination is more for personal than public benefit. With this in mind it may be more appropriate for her to consult with her line manager about the possibility of writing this additional publication in her own time with support.

CHAPTER 9: CONSTANCE

Q: What issues should Constance's trainee pick out for her presentation, and how will she reconcile the practical difficulties?

In preparing for her presentation, Constance's trainee should first familiarise herself thoroughly with the current evidence base in this area of social work practice. This should form the basis of her presentation and will demonstrate knowledge and understanding of the current empirical work in the field. Additionally, the trainee should clearly outline the particular characteristics of the cultural group that Constance and she have been working with. In particular, this part of the presentation should include specific details and arguments about why current evidence-based practice might not be fully applicable to this cultural group. In order to make a coherent and valid argument, Constance's trainee would need to offer a constructive and well-grounded rationale for possible alternative approaches for working with this particular group, which may also retain some of the evidence-based suggestions for practice where possible.

References

Academy of Medical Sciences (2011) *A New Pathway for the Regulation of Health Research.* http://www.acmedsci.ac.uk/policy/policy-projects/a-new-pathway-for-the-regulation-and-governance-of-health-research/ (accessed 5 January 2015).

Åkerström, M., Jacobsson, K. and Wästerfors, D. (2004) Reanalysis of previously collected material, in C. Seale, G. Gobo, J. Gubrium and D. Silverman (eds), *Qualitative Research Practice.* London: Sage. pp. 344–357.

Alderson, P. (2007) Governance and ethics in health research, in M. Saks and J. Allsop (eds), *Researching Health: Qualitative, Quantitative and Mixed Methods.* London: Sage. pp. 283–300.

Aluwihare-Samaranayake, D. (2012) Ethics in qualitative research: A view of the participants' and researchers' world from a critical standpoint. *International Journal of Qualitative Methods*, 11(2): 64–81.

American Psychological Association (2006) Evidence-based practice in psychology. *American Psychologist*, 61(4): 271–285.

Anastas, J. (2004) Quality in qualitative evaluation: Issues and possible answers. *Research on Social Work Practice*, 14(1): 57–65.

Angell, E., Jackson, C. J., Ashcroft, R., Bryman, A., Windridge, K. and Dixon-Woods, M. (2007) Is 'inconsistency' in research ethics committee decision-making really a problem? An empirical investigation and reflection. *Clinical Ethics*, 2(2): 92–99.

Angell, E., Biggs, H., Gahleitner, F. and Dixon-Woods, M. (2010) What do research ethics committees say about applications to conduct research involving children? *Archives of Disease in Childhood*, 95(11): 915–917.

Angen, M. (2000) Evaluating interpretive inquiry: Reviewing the validity debate and opening the dialogue. *Qualitative Health Research*, 10(3): 378–395.

Annells, M. (1996) Grounded theory method: Philosophical perspectives, paradigm of research, and postmodernism. *Qualitative Health Research* 6(3): 379–393.

Annells, M. (2006) Triangulation of qualitative approaches: Hermeneutical phenomenology and grounded theory. *Journal of Advanced Nursing*, 56(1): 55–61.

Antaki, C. (2011) Six kinds of applied conversation analysis, in C. Antaki (ed.), *Applied Conversation Analysis: Intervention and Change in Institutional Talk.* Basingstoke: Palgrave Macmillan. pp. 1–14.

Armstrong, D., Gosling, A., Weinman, J. and Marteau, T. (1997) The place of inter-rater reliability in qualitative research: An empirical study. *Sociology*, 31(3): 597–606.

Arneson, P. (2009) Axiology, in S. Littlejohn and K. Foss (eds), *Encyclopaedia of Communication Theory*. Thousand Oaks, CA: Sage. pp. 70–74.

Arsenault, M., Sampson, Z. T. and Fox, J. C. (2014) BC's Irish project leads to the arrest of Gerry Adams. *Boston Globe*, 1 May. http://bit.ly/1n6xoQr (accessed 15 May 2014).

Ashcroft, R. (2003) The ethics and governance of medical research: What does regulation have to do with morality? *New Review of Bioethics*, 1(1): 41–58.

Ashworth, P. (2003) The origins of qualitative psychology, in J. A. Smith (ed.), *Qualitative Psychology: A Practical Guide to Research Methods*. London: Sage. pp. 4–25.

Atkinson, J. M. and Heritage, J. (1984) *Structures of Social Action: Studies in Conversation Analysis*. Cambridge: Cambridge University Press.

Atkinson, J. M. and Heritage, J. (1999) Jefferson's transcript notation, in A. Jaworski and N. Coupland (eds), *The Discourse Reader*. London: Routledge. pp. 158–166.

Attkisson, C., Rosenblatt, A. and Hoagwood, K. (1996) Research ethics and human subjects in child mental health service research and community studies, in K. Hoagwood, P. Jensen and C. Fisher (eds), *Ethical Issues in Mental Health Research with Children and Adolescents*. Mahwah, NJ: Lawrence Erlbaum Associates. pp. 43–58.

Avison, D. E., Lau, F., Myers, M. D. and Nielsen, P. A. (1999) Action research. *Communications of the ACM*, 42(1): 94–97.

Bain, J. and Mackay, N. (1995) Videotaping of general practice consultations. *British Medical Journal*, 311(7010): 952.

Baker, C., Wuest, J. and Stern, P. (1992) Method slurring: The grounded theory/phenomenology example. *Journal of Advanced Nursing*, 17(11): 1355–1360.

Balen, R., Blyth, E., Calabretto, H., Fraser, C., Horrocks, C. and Manby, M. (2006) Involving children in health and social research: 'Human becomings' or 'active beings'? *Childhood*, 13(1): 29–48.

Barbour, R. (1998) Mixing qualitative methods: Quality assurance or qualitative quagmire? *Qualitative Health Research*, 8(3): 352–361.

Barbour, R. (2001) Checklists for improving rigour in qualitative research: A case of the tail wagging the dog? *British Medical Journal*, 322(7294): 1115–1117.

Barker, C. and Pistrang, N. (2005) Quality criteria under methodological plural-ism: Implications for conducting and evaluating research. *American Journal of Community Psychology*, 35(3/4): 201–211.

Barkham, M. and Mellor-Clark, J. (2000) Rigour and relevance practice-based evidence in the psychological based therapies, in N. Rowland and S. Goss (eds), *Evidence-Based Counselling and Psychological Therapies*. London: Routledge. pp 127–144.

Barkham, M. and Mellor-Clark, J. (2003) Bridging evidence-based practice and practice-based evidence: Developing a rigorous and relevant knowledge for the psychological therapies. *Clinical Psychology and Psychotherapy*, 10(6): 319–327.

Barnes, V., Clouder, D., Pritchard, J., Hughes, C. and Purkis, J. (2003) Deconstructing dissemination: Dissemination as qualitative research. *Qualitative Research*, 3(2): 147–164.

Barnett, J. (2007) Seeking an understanding of informed consent. *Professional Psychology: Research and Practice*, 38(2): 179–182.

Barry, C., Britten, N., Barber, N., Bradley, C. and Stevenson, F. (1999) Using reflexivity to optimize teamwork in qualitative research. *Qualitative Health Research*, 9(1): 26–44.

Bass, E. and Davis, L. (2002) *The Courage to Heal: A Guide for Women Survivors of Child Sexual Abuse*. London: Vermilion.

Beauchamp, T. and Childress, J. (2001) *Principles of Biomedical Ethics*. New York: Oxford University Press.

Beck, C. (1993) Qualitative research: The evaluation of its credibility, fittingness, and auditability. *Western Journal of Nursing Research*, 15(2): 263–266.

Beck, U. (1992) *Risk Society*. London: Sage.

Berenholtz, S. and Pronovost, P. (2003) Barriers to translating evidence into practice. *Current Opinion in Critical Care*, 9(4): 321–325.

Bergman, M. (2005) The strawmen from the QL/QN divide and their impact on mixed method designs. Paper presented at Mixed Methods in Health and Social Care, July Conference, Cambridge.

Bernard, H. R. (2011) *Research Methods in Anthropology: Qualitative and Quantitative Methods* (5th edition). Lanham, MD: AltaMira Press.

Biesta, G. (2007) Why 'what works' won't work: Evidence-based practice and the democratic deficit in educational research. *Educational Theory*, 57(1): 1–22.

Biggerstaff, D. (2012) Qualitative research methods in psychology, in G. Rossi (ed.), *Psychology – Selected Papers*. Rijeka: InTech Open Science. pp. 175–206.

Billig, M. (1999) Whose terms? Whose ordinariness? Rhetoric and ideology in conversation analysis. *Discourse and Society*, 10(4): 453–582.

Bishop, L. (2007) A reflexive account of reusing qualitative data: Beyond primary/secondary dualism. *Sociological Research Online*, 12(3): 2.

Blaikie, N. (2007) *Approaches to Social Inquiry* (2nd edition). Cambridge: Polity press.

Blakely, K. (2007) Reflections on the role of emotion in feminist research. *International Journal of Qualitative Methods*, 6(2): 1–7.

Blaxter, L., Hughes, C. and Tight, M. (1996) *How to Research*. Buckingham: Open University Press.

Bloor, M., Fincham, B. and Sampson, H. (2007) *Qualiti (NCRM) Commissioned Inquiry into the Risk to Well-Being of Researchers in Qualitative Research*. Cardiff: School of Social Sciences. http://www.cf.ac.uk/socsi/qualiti/CIReport.pdf (accessed 31 May 2014).

Bloor, M., Fincham, B. and Sampson, H. (2010) Unprepared for the worst: Risks of harm for qualitative researchers. *Methodological Innovations*, 5(1): 45–55.

Blumer, H. (1969) *Symbolic Interactionism: Perspective and Method*. Englewood Cliffs, NJ: Prentice Hall.

Boaz, A. and Nutley, S. (2003) Evidence-based policy and practice, in T. Bovaird and E. Löffler (eds), *Public Management and Governance*. London: Routledge. pp. 225–236.

Bolden, G. (2003) Doing being late: The use of the Russian particle *–to* in personal state inquiries. *Crossroads of Language, Interaction, and Culture*, 5: 3–27.

Bolden, G. and Robinson, J. (2011) Soliciting accounts with *why*-interrogatives in conversation. *Journal of Communication*, 61(1): 94–119.

Bottorff, J. L. (1994) Using videotaped data recordings in qualitative research, in J. M. Morse (ed.), *Critical Issues in Qualitative Research Methods*. London: Sage. pp. 244–261.

Boyatzis, R. (1998) *Transforming Qualitative Information: Thematic Analysis and Code Development*. London: Sage.

Bradley, J. (1993) Methodological issues and practices in qualitative research. *Library Quarterly*, 63(4): 431–449.

Brann, E. (1992). What is postmodernism? *Harvard Review of Philosophy*, Spring, 4–7.

Braun, V. and Clarke, V. (2006) Using thematic analysis in psychology. *Qualitative Research in Psychology*, 3(2): 77–101.

Brierley, J. and Larcher, V. (2010) Lest we forget ... Research ethics in children: perhaps onerous, yet absolutely necessary. *Archives of Diseases in Childhood*, 95(11): 863–866.

Brinkman, S. and Kvale, S. (2005) Confronting the ethics of qualitative research. *Journal of Constructivist Psychology*, 18(2):157–181.

Brinkman, S. and Kvale, S. (2008) Ethics in qualitative psychological research, in C. Willig and W. Stainton-Rogers (eds), *Handbook of Qualitative Research in Psychology*. London: Sage. pp. 261–279.

Brown, D. (2002) Going digital and staying qualitative: Some alternative strategies for digitizing the qualitative research process. *Forum: Qualitative Social Research*, 3(2): art. 12.

Brydon-Miller, M., Greenwood, D. and Maguire, P. (2003) Why action research? *Action Research*, 1(1): 9–28.

Bryman, A. (1982) The debate about quantitative and qualitative research: A question of method or epistemology? *British Journal of Sociology*, 35(1): 75–92.

Bryman, A. (1992) Quantitative and qualitative research: Further reflections on their integration, in J. Brannen (ed.), *Mixing Methods: Qualitative and Quantitative Research*. Aldershot: Avebury. pp. 57–78.

Bryman, A. (2006) Paradigm peace and implications for quality. *International Journal of Social Research Methodology*, 9(2): 111–126.

Bryman, A. (2007) The research question in social research: What is its role? *International Journal of Social Research Methodology*, 10(1): 5–20.

Bryman, A. (2008a) *Social Research Methods* (3rd edition). Oxford: Oxford University Press.

Bryman, A. (2008b) The end of the paradigm wars? In P. Alasuutari, L. Bickman and J. Brannen (eds), *The SAGE Handbook of Social Research Methods*. London: Sage. pp. 13–25.

Buchanan, D. and Bryman, A. (2007) Contextualizing method choice in organizational research. *Organizational Research Methods*, 10(3): 483–501.

Burck, C. (2005) Comparing qualitative research methodologies for systemic research: The use of grounded theory, discourse analysis and narrative analysis. *Journal of Family Therapy*, 27(3): 237–262.

Burnard, P. and Hannigan, B. (2000) Qualitative and quantitative approaches in mental health nursing: Moving the debate forward. *Journal of Psychiatric and Mental Health Nursing*, 7(1): 1–6.

Burr, V. (2003) *Social Constructionism* (2nd edition). London: Routledge.

Caelli, K., Ray, L. and Mill, J. (2003) 'Clear as mud': Toward greater clarity in generic qualitative research. *International Journal of Qualitative Methods*, 2(2): art. 1. http://www.ualberta.ca/iiqm/backissues/pdf/caellietal.pdf (accessed 31 May 2014).

Cannella, G. and Lincoln, Y. (2004) Dangerous discourses II: Comprehending and countering the redeployment of discourses (and resources) in the generation of liberatory inquiry. *Qualitative Inquiry*, 10(2): 165–174.

Cargo, M. and Mercer, S. (2008) The value and challenges of participatory research: Strengthening its practice. *Annual Review of Public Health*, 29: 325–350.

Carneiro, R. (2000) *The Muse of History and the Science of Culture*. New York: Kluwer Academic/Plenum Press.

Carter, S. and Little, M. (2007) Justifying knowledge, justifying method, taking action: Epistemologies, methodologies, and methods in qualitative research. *Qualitative Health Research*, 17(10): 1316–1328.

Cave, E. and Holm, S. (2002) New governance arrangements for research ethics committees: Is facilitating research achieved at the cost of participants' interest? *Journal of Medical Ethics*, 28(5): 318–321.

Charmaz, K. (1994) 'Discovering' chronic illness: Using grounded theory, in B. Glaser (ed.), *More Grounded Theory: A Reader*. Mill Valley, CA: Sociology Press. pp. 65–94.

Charmaz, K. (1995) Grounded theory, in J. A. Smith, R. Harré and I. van Langenhove (eds), *Rethinking Methods in Psychology*. London: Sage. pp. 27–49.

Charmaz K. (2000) Grounded theory: Objectivist and constructivist methods, in N. Denzin and Y. Lincoln (eds), *Handbook of Qualitative Research* (2nd edition). Thousand Oaks, CA: Sage. pp. 509–535.

Charmaz, K. (2005) Grounded theory in the 21st century: Applications for advancing social justice studies, in N. Denzin and Y. Lincoln (eds), *The SAGE Handbook of Qualitative Research* (3rd edition). London: Sage. pp. 507–535.

Charmaz, K. (2006) *Constructing Grounded Theory: Practical Guide through Qualitative Analysi*s. London: Sage.

Chávez, V., Duran, B., Baker, Q., Avila, M. and Wallerstein, N. (2008) The dance of race and privilege in CBPR, in M. Minkler and N. Wallerstein (eds), *Community-Based Participatory Research for Health: Process to Outcomes* (2nd edition). San Francisco: Jossey-Bass. pp. 91–105

Cheek, J. (2007) Qualitative inquiry, ethics, and politics of evidence: Working within these spaces rather than being worked over by them. *Qualitative Inquiry*, 13: 1051–1059.

Chen, P., Diaz, N., Lucas, G. and Rosenthal, M. (2010) Dissemination of results in community-based participatory research. *American Journal of Preventative Medicine*, 39(4): 372–378.

Chen, X. (1997) Thomas Kuhn's latest notion of incommensurability. *Journal for General Philosophy of Science*, 28(2): 257–273.

Chen, Y. Y., Shek, D. and Bu, F.-F. (2011) Applications of interpretive and constructionist research methods in adolescent research: Philosophy, principles and examples. *International Journal of Adolescent Medicine and Health*, 23(3): 129–139.

Chenitz, C. and Swanson, J. (eds) (1986) *From Practice to Grounded Theory: Qualitative Research in Nursing*. Menlo Park, CA: Addison-Wesley.

Christensen, C. (2004) Children's participation in ethnographic research: Issues of power and representation. *Children and Society*, 18(2): 165–176.

Clandinin, D. J. and Rosiek, J. (2007) Mapping a landscape of narrative inquiry: Borderland spaces and tensions, in D. J. Clandinin (ed.), *Handbook of Narrative Inquiry: Mapping Methodology*. Thousand Oaks, CA: Sage. pp. 35–75.

Cleary, M. and Walter, G. (2004) Apportioning our time and energy: Oral presentation, poster, journal article or other? *International Journal of Mental Health Nursing*, 13(3): 204–207.

Cleary, M., Walter, G. and Luscombe, G. (2007) Spreading the word: Disseminating research results to patients and carers. *Acta Neuropsychiatrica*, 19(4): 224–229.

Coles, J. and Mudlay, N. (2010) Staying safe: Strategies for qualitative child abuse researchers. *Child Abuse Review*, 19(1): 56–69.

Collingridge, D. and Gantt, E. (2008) The quality of qualitative research. *American Journal of Medical Quality*, 23(5): 389–395.

Colyar, J. (2009) Becoming writing, becoming writers. *Qualitative Inquiry*, 15(2): 421–436.

Connolly, K. and Reilly, R. (2007) Emergent issues when researching trauma: A confessional tale. *Qualitative Inquiry*, 13(4): 522–540.

Corbin, J. and Morse, J. (2003) The unstructured interactive interview: Issues of reciprocity and risks when dealing with sensitive topics. *Qualitative Inquiry*, 9(3): 335–354.

Corbin, J. and Strauss, A. (2008) *Basics of Qualitative Research: Techniques and Procedures for Developing Grounded Theory* (3rd edition). Los Angeles: Sage.

Corden, A. and Sainsbury, R. (2006) Exploring 'quality': Research participants' perspectives on verbatim quotations. *International Journal of Social Research Methodology*, 9(2): 97–110.

Cornwall, A. and Jewkes, R. (1995) What is participatory research? *Social Science and Medicine*, 41(12): 1667–1676.

Corti, L. and Thompson, P. (2004) Secondary analysis of archived data, in C. Seale, G. Gobo, J. Gubrium and D. Silverman (eds), *Qualitative Research Practice*. London: Sage. pp. 327–343.

Cox-White, B. and Zimbelman, J. (1998) Abandoning informed consent: An idea whose time has not yet come. *Journal of Medicine and Philosophy*, 23(5): 477–499.

Craswell, G. (2005) *Writing for Academic Success: A Postgraduate Guide*. London: Sage.

Creswell, J. (1998) *Qualitative Inquiry and Research Design: Choosing among Five Traditions*. Thousand Oaks, CA: Sage.

Crossley, M. (2000) *Introducing Narrative Psychology: Self, Trauma and the Construction of Meaning*. Buckingham: Open University Press.

Crotty, M. (2003) *The Foundations of Social Research: Meaning and Perspective in the Research Process*. London: Sage.

Crowell, S. (2010) Existentialism, in E. N. Zalta (ed.), *Stanford Encyclopedia of Philosophy* (Winter 2010 edition). http://plato.stanford.edu/archives/win2010/entries/existentialism/ (accessed 3 October 2014).

Daly, J., Willis, K., Small, R., Green, J., Welch, N., Kealy, M. and Huges, E. (2007) A hierarchy of evidence for assessing qualitative health research. *Journal of Clinical Epidemiology*, 60(1): 43–49.

Davidson, C. (2009) Transcription: Imperatives for research. *International Journal of Qualitative Research*, 8 (2): 35 –52.

Davidson, C. (2010) Transcription matters: Transcribing talk and interaction to facilitate conversation analysis of the taken-for-granted in young children's interactions. *Journal of Early Childhood Research*, 8(2): 115–131.

Davies, D. and Dodd, J. (2002) Qualitative research and the question of rigor. *Qualitative Health Research*, 12(2): 279–289.

Davies, K. and Heaphy, B. (2011) Interactions that matter: Researching critical associations. *Methodological Innovations Online*, 6(3): 5–16.

Denscombe, M. (2008) Communities of practice: A research paradigm for the mixed methods approach. *Journal of Mixed Methods Research*, 2(3): 270–283.

Denscombe M. (2010) *Good Research Guide: For Small-Scale Social Research Projects* (4th edition). Maidenhead: Open University Press.

Denzin, N. (1992) *Symbolic Interactionism and Cultural Studies: The Politics of Interpretation*. Malden, MA: Blackwell.

Denzin, N. (2008) The new paradigm dialogs and qualitative inquiry. *International Journal of Qualitative Studies in Education*, 21(4): 315–325.

Denzin, N. (2010) Moments, mixed-methods, and paradigm dialogs. *Qualitative Inquiry*, 16(6): 419–427.

Denzin, N. and Giardina, M. (2007) *Decolonizing and Politics of Knowledge: Ethical Futures in Qualitative Research*. Walnut Creek, CA: Left Coast Press.

Denzin, N. and Lincoln, Y. (2000) *Handbook of Qualitative Research*. Thousand Oaks, CA: Sage.

Denzin, N. and Lincoln, Y. (2005) Introduction: The discipline and practice of qualitative research, in N. Denzin and Y. Lincoln (eds), *The Sage Handbook of Qualitative Research*. Thousand Oaks, CA: Sage.

Devers, K. (1999) How will we know 'good' qualitative research when we see it? Beginning the dialogue in health services research. *Health Services Research*, 34(5): 1153–1188.

Dickson-Swift, V., James, E., Kippen, S. and Liamputtong, P. (2006) Blurring boundaries in qualitative health research on sensitive topics. *Qualitative Health Research*, 16(6): 853–871.

Dickson-Swift, V., James, E., Kippen, A. and Liamputtong, L. (2007) Doing sensitive research: What challenges do qualitative researchers face? *Qualitative Research*, 7(3): 327–353.

Dickson-Swift, V., James, E., Kippen, S. and Liamputtong, P. (2008) Risk to researchers in qualitative research on sensitive topics: Issues and strategies. *Qualitative Health Research*, 18(1): 133–144.

Dickson-Swift, V., James, E., Kippen, S. and Liamputtong, P. (2009) Researching sensitive topics: Qualitative research as emotion work. *Qualitative Research*, 9(1): 61–79.

Diesing, P. (1965) Objectivism vs. subjectivism in the social sciences. *Philosophy of Science*, 33(1/2): 124–133.

Dingwall, R. (1999) 'Risk society': The cult of theory and the millennium? *Social Policy and Administration*, 33(4): 474–491.

Dixon-Woods, M. and Ashcroft, R. E. (2008) Regulation and the social licence for medical research. *Medicine, Health Care and Philosophy*, 11(4): 381–391.

Dixon-Woods, M. and Bosk, C. (2011) Defending rights or defending privileges? *Public Management Review*, 13(2): 257–272.

Dixon-Woods, M. and Tarrant, C. (2009) Why do people cooperate with medical research? Findings from three studies. *Social Science and Medicine*, 68(12): 2215–2222.

Dixon-Woods, M., Agarwal, S., Young, B., Jones, D. and Sutton, A. (2004a) *Integrative Approaches to Qualitative and Quantitative Evidence*. London: Health Development Agency.

Dixon-Woods, M., Shaw, R., Agarwal, S. and Smith, J. (2004b) The problem of appraising qualitative research. *Quality Safety and Health Care*, 13(3): 223–225.

Dixon-Woods, M., Jackson, C., Windridge, K. and Kenyon, S. (2006a) Receiving a summary of the results of a trial: Qualitative study of participants' views. *British Medical Journal*, 332(7535): 206–209.

Dixon-Woods, M., Young, B. and Ross, E. (2006b) Researching chronic childhood illness: The example of childhood cancer. *Chronic Illness*, 2(3): 165–177.

Dixon-Woods, M., Angell, E., Ashcroft, R. and Bryman, A. (2007) Written work: The social functions of Research Ethics Committee letters. *Social Science and Medicine*, 65(4): 792–802.

Dixon-Woods, M., Tarrant, C., Jackson, C., Jones, D. and Kenyon, S. (2011) Providing the results of research to participants: A mixed-method study of the benefits and challenges of a consultative approach. *Clinical Trials*, 8(3): 330–341.

Doucet, A. and Mauthner, N. (2006) Feminist methodologies and epistemology, in C. Bryant and D. Peck (eds), *Handbook of 21st Century Sociology*. Thousand Oaks, CA: Sage. pp. 36–45.

Duffy, M. (2000) The Internet as a research and dissemination resource. *Health Promotion International*, 15(4): 349–353.

Duncan, R., Drew, S., Hodgson, J. and Sawyer, S. (2009) Is my mum going to hear this? Methodological and ethical challenges in qualitative health research with young people. *Social Science and Medicine*, 69(11): 1691–1699.

Duncombe, J. and Jessop, J. (2002) 'Doing rapport' and the ethics of 'faking friendship', in M. Mauthner, M. Birch, J. Jessop and T. Miller, (eds), *Ethics in Qualitative Research*. London: Sage. pp. 107–122.

Duranti, A. (2007) Transcripts, like shadows on a wall. *Mind, Culture, and Activity*, 13(4): 301–310.

Easterby-Smith, M., Golden-Biddle, K. and Locke, K. (2008) Working with pluralism: Determining quality in qualitative research. *Organizational Research Methods*, 11(3): 419–429.

Eddy, D. (1990) Designing a practice policy: Standards, guidelines, and options. *Journal of the American Medical Association*, 263(22): 3077–3084.

Edwards, D. and Potter, J. (1992) *Discursive Psychology*. London: Sage.

Edwards, D., Ashmore, M. and Potter, J. (2003) Death and furniture: Arguments against relativism, in M. Gergen and K. Gergen (eds), *Social Construction: A Reader*. London: Sage. pp. 231–236.

Elliott, T. (2004) Research bureaucracy in the United Kingdom: Time has come to face research governance. *British Medical Journal*, 329(7466): 623–624.

Emanuel, E. J., Wendler, D. and Grady, C. (2000) What makes clinical research ethical. *Journal of the American Medical Association*, 283(20): 2701–2711.

Ensign, J. (2003) Ethical issues in qualitative health research with homeless youths. *Journal of Advanced Nursing*, 43(1): 43–50.

Etherington, K. (2001) Research with ex-clients: A celebration and extension of the therapeutic process. *British Journal of Guidance and Counselling*, 29(1): 5–19.

Etherington, K. (2007) Working with traumatic stories: From transcriber to witness. *International Journal of Social Research Methodology*, 10(2): 85–97.

European Commission (2010) *European Textbook on Ethics in Research*. Luxembourg: Publications Office of the European Union.

Evans, D. (2003) Hierarchy of evidence: A framework for ranking evidence evaluating healthcare interventions. *Journal of Clinical Nursing*, 12: 77–84.

Fernandez, C., Gao, J., Strahlendorf, C., Moghrabi, A., Davis Pentz, R., Barfield, R., et al. (2009) Providing research results to participants: Attitudes and needs of adolescents and parents of children with cancer. *Journal of Clinical Oncology*, 27(6): 878–883.

Fetterman, D. (2010) *Ethnography, Step-by-Step* (2nd edition).Thousand Oaks, CA: Sage.

Field, M. and Behrman, R. (eds) (2004) *Ethical Conduct of Clinical Research Involving Children*. Washington, DC: National Academies Press.

Fielding, N. (2004) Getting the most from archived qualitative data: Epistemological, practical and professional obstacles. *International Journal of Social Research Methodology*, 7(1): 97–104.

Finch, J. (2004) Feminism and qualitative research. *International Journal of Social Research Methodology*, 7 (1): 61–64.

Fincham, B., Scourfield, J. and Langer, S. (2008) The impact of working with disturbing secondary data: Reading suicide files in a coroner's office. *Qualitative Health Research*, 18(6): 853–862.

Fine, G. (1993) The sad demise, mysterious disappearance, and glorious triumph of symbolic interactionism. *Annual Review of Sociology*, 19: 61–87.

Finlay, L. (2002) 'Outing' the researcher: The provenance, process, and practice of reflexivity. *Qualitative Health Research*, 12(4): 531–545.

Finlay, L. (2003) The reflexive journey: Mapping multiple routes, in L. Finlay and B. Gough (eds), *Reflexivity: A Practical Guide for Researchers in Health and Social Sciences*. Oxford: Blackwell Publishing. pp. 3–20.

Fiss, O. M. (1994) What is feminism? *Faculty Scholarship Series*, paper 1331, pp 413–428. Yale Law School Legal Scholarship Repository. http://digitalcommons.law.yale.edu/fss_papers/1331

Flewitt, R. (2005) Conducting research with young children: Some ethical considerations. *Early Child Development and Care*, 175(6): 553–565.

Fonow, M. M. and Cook, J. (2005) Feminist methodology: New applications in the academy and public policy. *Signs: Journal of Women in Culture and Society*, 30(4): 2211–2236.

Fontana, A. and Frey, J. H. (2003) The interview: From structured questions to negotiated text, in N. Denzin and Y. Lincoln (eds), *Collecting and Interpreting Qualitative Materials* (2nd edition). London: Sage. pp. 61–106.

Fossey, E., Harvey, C., McDermott, F. and Davidson, L. (2002) Understanding and evaluating qualitative research. *Australian and New Zealand Journal of Psychiatry*, 36(6): 717–732.

Foster, A. (2004) A nonlinear model of information-seeking behavior. *Journal of the American Society for Information Science and Technology*, 55(3): 228–237.

Fox, N. (2003) Practice-based evidence: Towards collaborative and transgressive research. *Sociology*, 37(1): 81–102.

Franklin, C. (1998) Distinctions between social constructionism and cognitive constructivism: Practice applications, in C. Franklin and P. Nurius (eds), *Constructivism in Practice: Methods and Challenges*. Milwaukee, WI: Families International Press. pp. 57–94.

Fraser, M., Hindmarsh, J., Best, K., Heath, C., Biegel, G., Greenhalgh, C. and Reeves, S. (2006) Remote collaboration over video data: Towards real-time e-social science. *Computer Supported Cooperative Work*, 15: 257–279.

Fraser, S. and Robinson, C. (2003) Paradigms and philosophy, in S. Fraser, V. Lewis, S. Ding, M. Kellett and C. Robinson (eds), *Doing Research with Children and Young People*. London: Sage. pp. 59–77.

Freeman, M., deMarrais, K., Preissle, J., Roulston, K. and St. Pierre, E. (2007) Standards of evidence in qualitative research: An incitement to discourse. *Educational Researcher*, 36(1): 25–32.

Freshwater, D. (2005) Reading mixed methods research: Contexts for criticism. Paper presented at Mixed Methods in Health and Social Care, July Conference, Cambridge.

Freshwater, D. (2007) Reading mixed methods research: Contexts for criticism. *Journal of Mixed Methods Research*, 1(2): 134–146.

Freshwater, D., Cahill, J., Walsh, E. and Muncey, T. (2010) Qualitative research as evidence: Criteria for rigour and relevance. *Journal of Research in Nursing*, 15(6): 497–508.

Friedman, M., Metelerkamp, J. and Posel, R. (1987) What is feminism? And what kind of feminist am I? *Agenda: Empowering Women for Gender Equity*, 1: 3–24.

Frost, N. (2011) Interpreting data pluralistically, in N. Frost (ed.), *Qualitative Research Methods in Psychology: Combining Core Approaches*. Maidenhead: Open University Press. pp. 145–160.

Frost, N. A., Holt, A., Shinebourne, P., Esin, C., Nolas, S. M., Mehdizadeh, L. and Brooks-Gordon, B. (2011) Collective findings, individual interpretations: An illustration of a pluralistic approach to qualitative data analysis. *Qualitative Research in Psychology*, 8(1): 93–113.

Fry, C. and Dwyer, R. (2001) For love or money? An exploratory study of why injecting drug users participate in research. *Addiction*, 96(9): 1319–1325.

Gee, J. (1991) A linguistic approach to narrative. *Journal of Narrative and Life History*, 1(1): 15–39.

George, V. (1996) Field-workers' sense of coherence and perception of risk when making home visits. *Public Health Nursing*, 13(4): 244–252.

Gergen, K. (2009) *An Invitation to Social Constructionism* (2nd edition). Thousand Oaks, CA: Sage.

Gibbs, G. R., Friese, S. and Mangabeira, W. C. (2002) The use of new technology in qualitative research. Introduction to issue 3(2) of FQS. *Forum: Qualitative Social Research*. http://www.qualitative-research.net/fqs-texte/2-02/2-02hrsg-e.htm (accessed 21 August 2013).

Giglio, M. (2012) Boston College's secret tapes could bring IRA exposure and retribution. *Daily Beast*, 10 July. http://www.thedailybeast.com/articles/2012/07/10/boston-college-s-secret-tapes-could-bring-ira-exposure-and-retribution.html (accessed 21 August 2013).

Gilgun, J. (2005) 'Grab' and good science: Writing up the results of qualitative research. *Qualitative Health Research*, 15(2): 256–262.

Gillies, V. and Edwards, R. (2005) Secondary analysis in exploring family and social change: Addressing the issue of context. *Forum: Qualitative Social Research*, 6(1): art. 44.

Giordano, J., O'Reilly, M., Taylor, H. and Dogra, N. (2007) Confidentiality and autonomy: The challenge(s) of offering research participants a choice of disclosing their identity. *Qualitative Health Research*, 17(2): 264–275.

Glaser, B. (2007) Constructivist grounded theory? *Historical Social Research, Supplement* no. 19: 93–105.

Glaser, B. and Strauss, A. (1967) *The Discovery of Grounded Theory: Strategies for Qualitative Research.* New York: Aldine.

Golafshani, N. (2003) Understanding reliability and validity in qualitative research. *The Qualitative Report,* 8(4): 597–606.

Goldblatt, H., Karnieli-Miller, O. and Neumann, M. (2011) Sharing qualitative research findings with participants: Study experiences of methodological and ethical dilemmas. *Patient Education and Counseling,* 82(3): 389–395.

Gough, B. (2003) Deconstructing reflexivity, in L. Finlay and Gough, B. (eds), *Reflexivity: A Practical Guide for Researchers in Health and Social Sciences.* Oxford: Blackwell. pp. 21–36.

Grant, J. and Luxford, Y. (2009) Video: A decolonising strategy for intercultural communication in child and family health within ethnographic research. *International Journal of Multiple Research Approaches,* 3(3): 218–232.

Grbich, C. (2013) *Qualitative Data Analysis: An Introduction* (2nd edition). London: Sage.

Green, J. and Thorogood, N. (2004) *Qualitative Methods for Health Research.* London: Sage.

Green, J., Franquiz, M. and Dixon, C. (1997) The myth of the objective transcript: Transcribing as a situated act. *TESOL Quarterly,* 31(1): 172–176.

Green, L. (2006) Public health asks of systems science: to advance our evidence-based practice, can you help us get more practice-based evidence? *American Journal of Public Health,* 96(3): 406–409.

Green, L. (2008) Making research relevant: If it is an evidence-based practice, where's the practice-based evidence? *Family Practice,* 25(1): i20–i24.

Gregory, D., Russell, C. and Phillips, L. (1997) Beyond textual perfection: Transcribers as vulnerable persons. *Qualitative Health Research,* 7(2): 294–300.

Grimshaw, A. (1982) Sound-image data records for research on social interaction: Some questions and answers. *Sociological Methods and Research* 11(2): 121–144.

Grossman, J. and Mackenzie, F. (2005) The randomised controlled trial: Gold standard, or merely standard? *Perspectives in Biology and Medicine,* 48(4): 516–534.

Guba, E. (1990) The alternative paradigm dialog, in E. Guba (ed.), *The Paradigm Dialog.* Newbury Park, CA: Sage. pp. 17–30.

Guba, E. and Lincoln, Y. (1981) *Effective Evaluation: Improving the Usefulness of Evaluation Results through Responsive and Naturalistic Approaches.* San Francisco: Jossey-Bass.

Guba, E. and Lincoln, Y. (1989) *Fourth Generation Evaluation.* Newbury Park, CA: Sage.

Guba, E. and Lincoln, Y. (1994) Competing paradigms in qualitative research, in N. Denzin and Y. Lincoln (eds), *Handbook of Qualitative Research.* London: Sage. pp. 105–117.

Guba, E. and Lincoln, Y. (2004) Competing paradigms in qualitative research: Theories and issues, in S. N. Hesse-Biber and P. Leavy (eds), *Approaches to Qualitative Research: A Reader on Theory and Practice.* Oxford: Oxford University Press. pp. 17–38.

Guba, E. and Lincoln, Y. (2005) Paradigmatic controversies, contradictions and emerging confluences, in N. Denzin and Y. Lincoln (eds), *The Sage Handbook of Qualitative Research* (3rd edition). Thousand Oaks, CA: Sage. pp. 191–216.

Gubrium, J. F. and Holstein, J. A. (2008) The constructionist mosaic, in J. A. Holstein and J. F. Gubrium (eds), *Handbook of Constructionist Research*. New York: Guilford. pp. 3–12.

Guest, G., Bruce, A. and Johnson, L. (2006) How many interviews are enough? An experiment with data saturation and variability. *Field Methods*, 18(1): 59–82.

Gunsalus, C., Bruner, E., Burbules, N., Dash, L. D., Finkin, M., Goldberg, J., et al. (2007) The Illinois white paper: Improving the system for protecting human subjects: Counteracting IRM 'mission creep'. *Qualitative Inquiry*, 13(5): 617–649.

Guyatt, G., Cairns, J., Churchill, D., Cook, D., Haynes, B., Hirsh, J., et al. (1992) Evidence-based medicine: A new approach to teaching the practice of medicine. *Journal of the American Medical Association*, 268(17): 2420–2425.

Hadjistavropoulos, T. and Smythe, W. (2001) Elements of risk in qualitative research. *Ethics and Behaviour*, 1(2): 163–174.

Hagen, P., Robertson, T., Kan, M. and Sadler, K. (2005) Emerging research methods for understanding mobile technology use. In *Proceedings of the 17th Australian Conference on Computer–Human Interaction: Citizens Online: Considerations for Today and the Future*. Baulkham Hills, NSW: CHISIG.

Halcomb, E. and Davidson, P. (2006) Is verbatim transcription of interview data always necessary? *Applied Nursing Research*, 19: 38–42.

Halse, C. and Honey, A. (2007) Rethinking ethics review as institutional discourse. *Qualitative Inquiry*, 13(3): 336–352.

Hammersley, M. (1996) The relationship between qualitative and quantitative research: Paradigm loyalty versus methodological eclecticism, in J. Richardson (ed.), *Handbook of Qualitative Research Methods for Psychology and the Social Sciences*. Leicester: BPS Books. pp. 159–174.

Hammersley, M. (1997) Qualitative data archiving: Some reflections on its prospects and problems. *Sociology*, 31(1):131–142.

Hammersley, M. (2007) The issue of quality in qualitative research. *International Journal of Research and Method in Education*, 30(3): 287–305.

Hammersley, M. (2009) Against the ethicists: On the evils of ethical regulation. *International Journal of Social Research Methodology*, 12(3): 211–225.

Hammersley, M. (2010a) Reproducing or constructing? Some questions about transcription in social research. *Qualitative Research*, 10(5): 553–569.

Hammersley, M. (2010b) Can we re-use qualitative data via secondary analysis? Notes on some terminological and substantive issues. *Sociological Research Online*, 15(1): 5. doi: 10.5153/sro.2076.

Hammersley, M. and Atkinson, P. (1993) Ethics, in M. Hammersley and P. Atkinson (eds), *Ethnography: Principles in Practice*. London: Routledge. pp. 263–287.

Hammersley, M. and Atkinson, P. (2007) *Ethnography: Principles in Practice* (3rd edition). New York: Routledge.

Hamo, M., Blum-Kulka, S. and Hacohen, G. (2004) From observation to transcription and back: Theory, practice, and interpretation in the analysis of children's naturally occurring discourse. *Research on Language and Social Interaction*, 37(1): 71–92.

Harcourt, B. (2007) *An Answer to the Question: 'What is Poststructuralism?'* Public Law & Legal Theory Working Papers No. 156, University of Chicago Law School.

Harding, S. (1987) Introduction: Is there a feminist method? in S. Harding (ed.), *Feminism and Methodology: Social Science Issues*. Bloomington: Indiana University Press. pp. 1–14.

Harris, M. (1976) History and significance of the emic/etic distinction. *Annual Review of Anthropology*, 5: 329–350.

Hart, N. and Crawford-Wright, A. (1999) Research as therapy, therapy as research: Ethical dilemmas in new-paradigm research. *British Journal of Guidance and Counselling*, 27(2): 205–214.

Hart, S. (1971) Axiology – theory of values. *Philosophy and Phenomenological Research*, 32(1): 29–41.

Harter, S. and Ford, C. (2000) Web-based analyses of e-journal impact: Approaches, problems, and issues. *Journal of the American Society for Information Science*, 79(5): 1159–1176.

Hartman, R. (1967) *The Structure of Value: Foundations of Scientific Axiology*. Carbondale: Southern Illinois University Press.

Hatch, A. (2006) Qualitative studies in an era of scientifically-based research: Musings of a former QSE editor. *International Journal of Qualitative Studies in Education*, 19(4): 403–409.

Hayashi, M. (2004) Discourse within a sentence: An exploration of postpositions in Japanese as an interactional resource. *Language in Society*, 33(03): 343–376.

Hazelgrove, J. (2002) The old faith and the new science: The Nuremberg Code and human experimentation ethics in Britain 1946–73. *Social History of Medicine*, 15: 109–135.

Headland, T. (1990) A dialogue between Kenneth Pike and Marvin Harris on emics and etics, in T. Headland, K. Pike and M. Harris (eds), *Emics and Etics: The Insider/Outsider Debate*. Newbury Park, CA: Sage. pp. 13–27.

Heath, C. (2004) Analysing face-to-face interaction: Video, the visual and material, in D. Silverman (ed.), *Qualitative Research: Theory, Method and Practice* (2nd edition). London: Sage. pp. 266–282.

Heath, C. (2011) Embodied action: Video and the analysis of social interaction, in D. Silverman (ed.), *Qualitative Research* (3rd edition). London: Sage. pp. 250–270.

Heath, C. and Hindmarsh, J. (2002) Analysing interaction: Video, ethnography and situated conduct, in T. May (ed.), *Qualitative Research in Practice*. London: Sage. pp. 99–121.

Heath, C. and Luff, P. (2008) Video and the analysis of work and interaction, in P. Alasuutari, L. Bickman and J. Brannen (eds), *The SAGE Handbook of Social Research Methods*. London: Sage.

Heath, C., Luff, P. and Svensson, M. (2007) Video and qualitative research: Analysing medical practice and interaction. *Medical Education*, 41: 109–116.

Heath, C., Hindmarsh, J. and Luff, P. (2010) *Video in Qualitative Research: Analysing Social Interaction in Everyday Life*. London: Sage.

Heath, H. and Cowley, S. (2004) Developing a grounded theory approach: A comparison of Glaser and Strauss. *International Journal of Nursing Studies*, 41(2): 141–150.

Heaton, J. (1998) Secondary analysis of qualitative data. *Social Research Update*, 22. http://sru.soc.surrey.ac.uk/SRU22.html (accessed 31 May 2014).

Heaton, J. (2004) *Reworking Qualitative Data*. London: Sage.

Heaton, J. (2008) Secondary analysis of qualitative data: An overview. *Historical Social Research*, 33(3): 33–45.

Hedgecoe, A. (2008) Research ethics review and the sociological research relationship. *Sociology*, 42(5): 873–886.

Hedgecoe, A. (2009) 'A form of practical machinery': The origins of Research Ethics Committees in the UK, 1967–1972. *Medical History*, 53(3): 331–350.

Hepburn, A. and Bolden, G. (2013) The conversation analytic approach to transcription, in T. Stivers and J. Sidnell (eds), *The Blackwell Handbook of Conversation Analysis*. Oxford: Blackwell. pp. 57–76.

Hernick, A. D., Brown, M. K., Pinney, S. M., Biro, F. M., Ball, K. M. and Bornschein, R. L. (2011) Sharing unexpected biomarker results with study participants. *Environmental Health Perspectives*, 119(1): 1–5.

Heron, D. (1989) Secondary data analysis: Research method for the clinical nurse specialist. *Clinical Nurse Specialist*, 3(2): 66–99.

Hesse-Biber, S. and Leavy, P. (2004) Distinguishing qualitative research, in S. Hesse-Biber and P. Leavy (eds), *Approaches to Qualitative Research: A Reader on Theory and Practice*. Oxford: Oxford University Press. pp. 1–17.

Hewitt, J. (2007) Ethical components of researcher–researched relationships in qualitative interviewing. *Qualitative Health Research*, 17(8): 1149–1159.

Hill, M. (1984) Epistemology, axiology, and ideology in sociology. *Mid-American Review of Sociology*, 9(2): 59–77.

Hinchcliffe, V. and Gavin, H. (2009) Social and virtual networks: Evaluating synchronous online interviewing using Instant Messenger. *The Qualitative Report*, 14(2): 318–340.

Hindmarsh, J. (2008) Distributed video analysis in social research, in N. Fielding, R. Lee and G. Blank (eds), *The SAGE Handbook of Internet of Online Research Methods*. London: Sage. pp. 343–361.

Hinds, P., Vogel, R. and Clarke-Steffen, L. (1997) The possibilities and pitfalls of doing a secondary analysis of a qualitative data set. *Qualitative Health Research*, 7(3): 408–424.

Hjørland, B. (2005) Empiricism, rationalism and positivism in library and information science. *Journal of Documentation*, 61(1): 130–155.

Hoagwood, K., Jensen, P. and Fisher, C. (1996) Toward a science of ethics in research on child and adolescent mental disorders, in K. Hoagwood, P. Jensen and C. Fisher (eds), *Ethical Issues in Mental Health Research with Children and Adolescents*. Mahwah, NJ: Lawrence Erlbaum Associates. pp. 3–14.

Honan, E., Knobel, M., Baker, C. and Davies, B. (2000) Producing possible Hannahs: Theory and the subject of research. *Qualitative Inquiry*, 6(1): 9–32.

Hornsby-Smith, M. (1993) Gaining access, in N. Gilbert (ed.), *Researching Social Life*. London: Sage. pp. 52–67.

Howe, K. (1988) Against the quantitative–qualitative incompatibility thesis, or, Dogmas die hard. *Educational Researcher*, 17: 10–16.

Howitt, D. (2010) *Introduction to Qualitative Methods in Psychology* (2nd edition). Harlow: Pearson Education.

Huang, H. (2010) What is good action research? Why the resurgent interest? *Action Research*, 8 (1): 93–109.

Hubbard, G., Backett-Milburn, K. and Kemmer, D. (2001) Working with emotion: Issues for the researcher in fieldwork and teamwork. *International Journal of Social Research Methodology*, 4(2): 119–137.

Hunter, D. (2008) The ESRC research ethics framework and research ethics review at UK universities: Rebuilding the tower of Babel REC by REC. *Journal of Medical Ethics*, 34(11): 815–820.

Husserl, E. (1970) *The Crisis of European Sciences and Transcendental Phenomenology*. Evanston, IL: Northwestern University Press.

Hutchby, I. and Wooffitt, R. (2008) *Conversation Analysis* (2nd edition). Cambridge: Polity Press.

Hyde, K. (2000) Recognising deductive processes in qualitative research. *Qualitative Market Research*, 3(2): 82–89.

Iedema, R., Long, D., Forsyth, R. and Lee, B. (2006) Visibilising clinical work: Video ethnography in the contemporary hospital. *Health Sociology Review*, 15(2): 156–168.

Iedema, R., Forsyth, R., Georgiou, A., Braithwaite, J. and Westbrook, J. (2007) Video research in health: Visibilising the effects of computerising clinical care. *Qualitative Research Journal*, 6(2): 15–30.

James, T. and Platzer, H. (1999) Ethical considerations in qualitative research with vulnerable groups: Exploring lesbians' and gay men's experiences of healthcare – a personal perspective. *Nursing Ethics*, 6(1): 73–81.

Jefferson, G. (1979) A technique for inviting laughter and its subsequent acceptance declination, in G. Psathas (ed.), *Everyday Language: Studies in Ethnomethodology*. New York: Irvington. pp. 79–96.

Jefferson, G. (1983) Issues in the transcription of naturally-occurring talk: Caricature versus capturing pronunciational particulars. *Tilburg Papers in Language and Literature*, 34: 1–12. Tilburg: Tilburg University.

Jefferson, G. (1984) Notes on some orderlinesses of overlap onset, in V. D'Urso and P. Leonardi (eds), *Discourse Analysis and Natural Rhetoric*. Padua: Cleup Editore. pp. 11–38.

Jefferson, G. (1996) A case of transcriptional stereotyping. *Journal of Pragmatics*, 26: 159–170.

Jefferson, G. (2004) Glossary of transcript symbols with an introduction, in G. H. Lerner (ed.), *Conversation Analysis: Studies from the First Generation*. Amsterdam: John Benjamins. pp. 13–31.

Joffe, H. and Yardley, L. (2004) Content and thematic analysis, in D. Marks and L. Yardley (eds), *Research Methods for Clinical and Health Psychology*. London: Sage. pp. 56–68.

Johnson, B. and Macleod Clark, J. (2003) Collecting sensitive data: The impact on researchers. *Qualitative Health Research*, 13(3): 421–434.

Johnson, B. and Onwuegbuzie, A. (2004) Mixed methods research: A research paradigm whose time has come. *Educational Researcher*, 33(7): 14–26.

Johnson, B., Onwuegbuzie, A. and Turner, L. (2007) Toward a definition of mixed methods research. *Journal of Mixed Methods Research*, 1(2): 112–133

Jootun, D., McGhee, G. and Marland, G. (2009) Reflexivity: Promoting rigour in qualitative research. *Nursing Standard*, 23: 42–46.

Kaiser, K. (2009) Protecting respondent confidentiality in qualitative research. *Qualitative Health Research*, 19(11): 1632–1641.

Kaufmann, W. (1975) *Existentialism: From Dostoevsky to Sartre*. New York: Plume (Penguin).

Keen, S. and Todres, L. (2007) Strategies for disseminating qualitative research findings: Three exemplars. *Forum: Qualitative Social Research*, 8(3): art 17. http://www.qualitative-research.net/index.php/fqs/article/view/285/625 (accessed 31 May 2014).

Kelly, A. (2009) In defence of anonymity: Rejoining the criticism. *British Educational Research Journal*, 35(3): 431–445.

Kerner, J., Rimer, B. and Emmons, K. (2005) Dissemination research and research dissemination: How can we close the gap? *Health Psychology*, 24(5): 443–446.

King, N. (2004) Using templates in the thematic analysis of text, in C. Cassell and G. Symon (eds), *Essential Guide to Qualitative Methods in Organisational Research*. London: Sage. pp. 256–270.

King, N. (2012) Doing template analysis, in G. Symon and C. Cassell (eds), *Qualitative Organizational Research*. London: Sage. pp. 426–450.

Kisely, S. and Kendall, E. (2011) Critically appraising qualitative research: A guide for clinicians more familiar with quantitative techniques. *Australasian Psychiatry*, 19(4): 364–367.

Kiyimba, N., and O'Reilly, M. (in press). The risk of secondary traumatic stress in the qualitative transcription process: A research note. *Qualitative Research*.

Koo, M. and Skinner, H. (2005) Challenges of internet recruitment: A case study with disappointing results. *Journal of Medical Internet Research*, 7(1): e6.

Koshy, E., Koshy, V. and Waterman, H. (2010) *Action Research in Healthcare*. London: Sage.

Koski, G. (2007) Healthcare research: Can patients trust physician scientists? In D. Shore (ed.), *The Trust Crisis in Healthcare: Causes, Consequences and Cures*. New York: Oxford University Press. pp. 89–100.

Kuhn, T. (1962) *The Structure of Scientific Revolutions*. Chicago: University of Chicago Press.

Kuhn, T. (1982) Commensurability, comparability, communicability. In *PSA: Proceedings of the Biennial Meeting of the Philosophy of Science Association, Volume 2: Symposia and Invited Papers*. Chicago: University of Chicago Press. pp. 669–688.

Kuhn, T. (1996) *The Structure of Scientific Revolutions* (3rd edition). Chicago: University of Chicago Press.

Kuyper, B. (1991) Bringing up scientists in the art of critiquing research. *BioScience*, 41(4): 248–251.

Kuzel, A. (1992) Sampling in qualitative inquiry, in B. Crabtree and W. Miller (eds), *Doing Qualitative Research*. Newbury Park, CA: Sage. pp. 31–44.

Kvale, S. (1992) Introduction: From archaeology of the psyche to the architecture of cultural landscapes, in S. Kvale (ed.), *Psychology and Postmodernism*. London: Sage. pp. 1–17

Kvale, S. (1992) Qualitative inquiry between scientistic evidentialism, ethical subjectivism and the free market. *International Review of Qualitative Research*, 1(1): 5–18.

Kvale, S. (1996) *Interviews: An Introduction to Qualitative Research Interviewing*. Thousand Oaks, CA: Sage.

Kylmä, J., Vehviläinen-Julkunen, K. and Lähdevirta, J. (1999) Ethical considerations in a grounded theory study on the dynamics of hope in HIV-positive adults and their significant others. *Nursing Ethics*, 6(3): 224–239.

Lal, S., Suto, M. and Ungar, M. (2012) Examining the potential of combining the methods of grounded theory and narrative inquiry: A comparative analysis. *The Qualitative Report*, 17(41): 1–22.

Lalor, J., Begley, C. and Devane, D. (2006) Exploring painful experiences: Impact of emotional narratives on members of a qualitative research team. *Journal of Advanced Nursing*, 56(6): 607–616.

Lambert, S. and Loiselle, C. (2008) Combining individual interviews and focus groups to enhance data richness. *Journal of Advanced Nursing*, 62(2): 228–237.

Lapadat, J. (2000) Problematizing transcription: Purpose, paradigm and quality. *International Journal of Social Research Methodology*, 3(3): 203–219.

Lapadat, J. and Lindsay, A. (1999) Transcription in research and practice: From standardization of technique to interpretive positioning. *Qualitative Inquiry*, 5(1): 64–86.

Lasker, R., Weiss, E. and Miller, R. (2001) Partnership synergy: A practical framework for studying and strengthening the collaborative advantage. *Milbank Quarterly*, 79: 179–205.

Law, S. (2007) *The Great Philosophers: The Lives and Ideas of History's Greatest Thinkers*. London: Quercus.

Lee, R. (1995) *Dangerous Fieldwork*. London: Sage.

Lee-Treweek, G. and Linkogle, S. (2000) Putting danger in the frame, in G. Lee-Treweek and S. Linkogle (eds), *Danger in the Field: Risk and Ethics in Social Research*. London: Routledge. pp. 8–25.

Lester, J. and O'Reilly, M. (2015) Is evidence-based practice a threat to the progress of the qualitative community? Arguments from the bottom of the pyramid. *Qualitative Inquiry*. DOI: 10.1177/1077800414563808.

Lett, J. (1990) Emics and etics: Notes on the epistemology of anthropology, in T. Headland, K. Pike and M. Harris (eds), *Emics and Etics: The Insider/Outsider Debate*. Newbury Park, CA: Sage. pp. 127–142.

Lewis J. and Ritchie, J. (2003) Generalising from qualitative research, in J. Ritchie and J. Lewis (eds), *Qualitative Research Practice: A Guide for Social Science Students and Researchers*. London: Sage. pp. 263–286.

Liamputtong, P. (2007) *Researching the Vulnerable: A Guide to Sensitive Research Methods*. Thousand Oaks, CA: Sage.

Lincoln, Y. (2010) 'What a long strange trip it's been...' Twenty-five years of qualitative and new paradigm research. *Qualitative Inquiry*, 16(1): 3–9.

Lincoln, Y. and Cannella, G. (2004) Dangerous discourses: Methodological conservatism and governmental regimes of truth [special issue]. *Qualitative Inquiry*, 10(1): 5–14.

Lincoln, Y. and Guba, E. (1985) *Naturalistic Inquiry*. Beverly Hills, CA: Sage.

Lincoln, Y. and Tierney, W. (2004) Qualitative research and institutional review boards. *Qualitative Inquiry*, 10(2): 219–234.

Lingard, L., Albert, M. and Levinson, W. (2008) Grounded theory, mixed methods and action research. *British Medical Journal*, 337: 459–461.

Loyd, D. (2013) Obtaining consent from young people with autism to participate in research. *British Journal of Learning Disabilities*, 41(2): 133–140.

Lucas, K. (2010) A waste of time? The value and promise of researcher completed qualitative data transcribing. *Northeastern Educational Research Association Conference Proceedings*, Paper 24. http://digitalcommons.uconn.edu/nera_2010/24 (accessed 5 May 2012).

Lucy, N. and Mickler, S. (2008) The war on English: An answer to the question, what is postmodernism? *Transformations*, 16(1). http://transformationsjournal.org/journal/issue_16/article_01.shtml (accessed 3 October 2014).

Luff, P. and Heath, C. (2012) Some 'technical challenges' of video analysis: Social actions, objects, material realities and the problems of perspective. *Qualitative Research*, 12(3): 255–279.

Lux, A. L., Edwards, S. W. and Osborne, J. P. (2000) Responses of local research ethics committees to a study with approval from a multicentre research ethics committee. *British Medical Journal*, 320: 1182–1183.

Macionis, J. (2012) *Sociology* (14th edition). Boston: Pearson.

Macquarrie, J. (1972) *Existentialism*. Philadelphia: Westminster.

Madill, A., Jordan, A. and Shirley, C. (2000) Objectivity and reliability in qualitative analysis: Realist, contextualist and radical constructionist epistemologies. *British Journal of Psychology*, 91(1): 1–20.

Malacrida, C. (2007) Reflexive journaling on emotional research topics: Ethical issues for team researchers. *Qualitative Health Research*, 17(10): 1329–1339.

Mann, H. (2002) Research ethics committees and public dissemination of clinical trial results. *The Lancet*, 360(9330): 406–408.

Markham, M. (2006) Providing research participants with findings from completed cancer-related clinical trials: Not quite as simple as it sounds. *Cancer*, 106(7): 1421–1424.

Marks, D. (2002) Perspectives on evidence-based practice. Health development agency: Public Health Evidence steering group. http://admin.nice.org.uk/aboutnice/whoweare/aboutthehda/evidencebase/publichealthevidencesteeringgroupproceedings/perspectives_on_evidence_based_practice.jsp (accessed 29 April 2013).

Martin, E. and Martin, P. (1984) The reactions of patients to a video camera in the consulting room. *Journal of the Royal College of General Practice*, 34(268): 607–610.

Marvasti, A. (2011) Three aspects of writing qualitative research: Practice, genre, and audience, in D. Silverman (ed.), *Qualitative Research* (3rd edition). London: Sage. pp. 382–396.

Mason, J. (2006) Mixing methods in a qualitatively driven way. *Qualitative Research*, 6(1): 9–25.

Mason, J. (2011) Facet methodology: The case for an inventive research orientation. *Methodological Innovations Online*, 6(3): 75–92.

Massey, C., Alpass, F., Flett, R., Lewis, K., Morriss, S. and Sligo, F. (2006) Crossing fields: The case of a multi-disciplinary research team. *Qualitative Research*, 6(2): 131–149.

Masterman, M. (1970) The nature of a paradigm, in I. Lakatos and A. Musgrave (eds), *Criticism and the Growth of Knowledge*. Cambridge: Cambridge University Press. pp. 59–90.

Mauthner, N. and Doucet, A. (2003) Reflexive accounts and accounts of reflexivity in qualitative data analysis. *Sociology*, 37(3): 413–431.

Mauthner, N., Parry, O. and Backett-Milburn, K. (1998) The data are out there, or are they? Implications for archiving and revisiting qualitative data. *Sociology*, 32(4): 733–745.

Maxwell, J. (2005) *Qualitative Research Design: An Interactive Approach* (2nd edition). Thousand Oaks, CA: Sage.

Maxwell, J. (2012) *A Realist Approach for Qualitative Research*. Thousand Oaks, CA: Sage.

Mays, N. and Pope, C. (2000) Quality in qualitative health research, in C. Pope and N. Mays (eds), *Qualitative Research in Health Care*. London: BMJ Books. pp. 89–102.

Mays, N., Roberts, E. and Popay, J. (2001) Synthesising research evidence, in N. Fulop, P. Allen, A. Clarke and N. Black (eds), *Studying the Organization and Delivery of Health Services*. London: Routledge. pp. 188–220.

Mazeland, H. (2006) Conversation analysis, in *Encyclopaedia of Language and Linguistics* (2nd edition, Vol. 3). Oxford: Elsevier Science. pp. 153–162.

McCosker, H., Barnard, A. and Gerber, R. (2001) Undertaking sensitive research: Issues and strategies for meeting the safety needs of all participants. *Forum: Qualitative Social Research*, 2(1): art. 22. http://www.qualitative-research.net/index.php/fqs/article/view/983/2142 (accessed 31 May 2013).

McGuinness, S. (2008) Research ethics committees: The role of ethics in a regulatory authority. *Journal of Medical Ethics*, 34(9): 695–700.

McIntosh, M. and Morse, J. M. (2009) Institutional review boards and the ethics of emotion, in N. K. Denzin and M. D. Gardina (eds), *Qualitative Inquiry and Social Justice*. Walnut Creek, CA: Left Coast Press. pp. 81–107.

McLellan, E., MacQueen, K. and Neidig, J. (2003) Beyond the qualitative interview: Data preparation and transcription. *Field Methods*, 15(1): 63–84.

McNeill, T. (2006) Evidence-based practice in an age of relativism: Toward a model for practice. *Social Work*, 51(2): 147–156.

Merriam, S. (2002) Assessing and evaluating qualitative research. In S. Merriam et al. (eds), *Assessing and Evaluating Qualitative Research in Practice*. San Francisco: Jossy-Bass. pp. 18–33.

Metzler, M., Higgins, D., Beeker, C., Freudenberg, N., Lantz, P. et al. (2003) Addressing urban health in Detroit, New York City, and Seattle through community-based participatory research partnerships. *American Journal of Public Health*, 93: 803–811.

Meyer, J. (2000) Using qualitative methods in health-related action research. *British Medical Journal*, 320: 178–181.

Meyrick, J. (2006) What is good qualitative research? A first step towards a comprehensive approach to judging rigour/quality. *Journal of Health Psychology*, 11(5): 799–808.

Miles, B. (2006) Moving out of the dark ages: An argument for the use of digital video in social work research. *Journal of Technology in Human Services*, 24(2/3): 181–196.

Miller, T. and Boulton, M. (2007) Changing constructions of informed consent: Qualitative research and complex social worlds. *Social Science and Medicine*, 65(11): 2199–2211.

Mishna, F., Antle, B. and Regehr, C. (2004) Tapping the perspectives of children: Emerging ethical issues in qualitative research. *Qualitative Social Work*, 3(4): 449–468.

Mitchell, J. C. (1983) Case and situational analysis. *Sociological Review*, 31(2): 187–211.

Moccia, P. (1988) A critique of compromise: Beyond the methods debate. *Advances in Nursing Science*, 10(4): 1–9.

Moe, H. (2008) Dissemination and dialogue in the public sphere: A case for public service media online. *Media, Culture and Society*, 30(3): 319–336.

Mondada, L. (2007) Commentary: Transcript variations and the indexicality of transcribing practices. *Discourse Studies*, 9(6): 809–821.

Moore, N. (2007) (Re)using qualitative data. *Sociological Research Online*, 12(3).

Moreira, V. (2012) From person-centered to humanistic-phenomenological psychotherapy: The contribution of Merleau-Ponty to Carl Rogers's thought. *Experiential Psychotherapies*, 11(1): 48–63.

Morgan, D. (2005) Triangulation and its discontents: Developing pragmatism as an alternative justification for combining qualitative and quantitative methods. Paper presented at Mixed Methods in Health and Social Care, July Conference, Cambridge.

Morgan, D. (2007) Paradigms lost and pragmatism regained: Methodological implications of combining qualitative and quantitative methods. *Journal of Mixed Methods Research*, 1(1): 48–76.

Morris, M., Leung, K., Ames, D. and Lickel, B. (1999) Views from inside and outside: Integrating emic and etic insights about culture and justice judgement. *Academy of Management Review*, 24(4): 781–796.

Morse, J. (1997) 'Perfectly healthy, but dead': The myth of inter-rater reliability. *Qualitative Health Research*, 7 (4): 445–447.

Morse, J. (2000) Researching illness and injury: Methodological considerations. *Qualitative Health Research*, 10(4): 538–546.

Morse, J. (2001) Are there risks in qualitative research? *Qualitative Health Research*, 11(1): 3–4.

Morse, J. (2003) A review committee's guide for evaluating qualitative proposals. *Qualitative Health Research*, 13(6): 833–851.

Morse, J. (2006a) The politics of evidence. *Qualitative Health Research*, 16(3): 395–404.

Morse, J. (2006b) Is it time to revise the Cochrane criteria? [editorial] *Qualitative Health Research*, 16(3): 315–317.

Morse, J. (2007) Ethics in action: Ethical principles for doing qualitative health research. *Qualitative Health Research*, 17(8): 1003–1005.

Morse, J. (2009) Mixing qualitative methods. *Qualitative Health Research*, 19(11): 1523–1524.

Morse, J. (2010) Simultaneous and sequential qualitative mixed method designs. *Qualitative Inquiry*, 16(6): 483–491.

Morse, J., Barrett, M., Mayan, M., Olson, K. and Spiers J. (2002) Verification strategies for establishing reliability and validity in qualitative research. *International Journal for Qualitative Methods*, 1(2): 1–19.

Morse, J., Niehaus, L., Varnhagen, S., Austin, W. and McIntosh, M. (2008) Qualitative researchers' conceptualizations of the risks inherent in qualitative interviews, in N. Denzin and M. Giardina (eds), *Qualitative Inquiry and the Politics of Evidence*. Walnut Creek, CA: Left Coast Press.

Moss, D. (2001) The roots and genealogy of humanistic psychology, in K. Schneider, J. Bugental and J. Pierson (eds), *Handbook of Humanistic Psychology*. Thousand Oaks, CA: Sage. pp. 5–20.

Muecke, M. (1994) On the evaluation of ethnographies, in J. Morse (ed.), *Critical Issues in Qualitative Research Methods*. Thousand Oaks, CA: Sage. pp. 187–209.

Murray, M. (2003) Narrative psychology, in J. A. Smith (ed.), *Qualitative Psychology: A Practical Guide to Research Methods*. London: Sage. pp. 111–131.

Murthy, D. (2008) Digital ethnography: An examination of the use of new technologies for social research. *Sociology*, 42(5): 837–855.

Nikander, P. (2008) Working with transcripts and translated data. *Qualitative Research in Psychology*, 5(3): 225–231.

Nolas, S. (2011) Pragmatics of pluralistic qualitative research, in N. Frost (ed.), *Qualitative Research Methods in Psychology: Combining Core Approaches*. Maidenhead: Open University Press. pp. 121–144.

O'Cathain, A. and Thomas, K. (2006) Combining qualitative and quantitative methods, in C. Pope and N. Mays (eds), *Qualitative Research in Health Care* (3rd edition). Oxford: Blackwell; London: BMJ Books. pp. 102–111.

Ochs, E. (1979) Transcription as theory, in E. Ochs and B. Schiefflin (eds), *Developmental Pragmatics*. New York: Academic Press. pp. 43–72.

O'Connell, D. and Kowal, S. (1995) Basic principles of transcription, in J. A. Smith, R. Harré and L. Van Langenhove (eds), *Rethinking Methods in Psychology*. London: Sage. pp. 93–105.

Oliver, D., Serovich, J. and Mason, T. (2005) Constraints and opportunities with interview transcription: Towards reflection in qualitative research. *Social Forces*, 84(2): 1273–1289.

Onwuegbuzie, A. and Leech, N. (2007) Validity and qualitative research: An oxymoron? *Quality and Quantity*, 41(2): 233–249.

Orb, A., Eisenhouer, L. and Wynaden, D. (2001) Ethics in qualitative research. *Journal of Nursing Scholarship*, 33(1): 93–96.

O'Reilly, M. (2005) Active noising: The use of noises in talk, the case of onomatopoeia, abstract sounds and the functions they serve in therapy. *Text*, 25(6): 745–761.

O'Reilly, M. and Parker, N. (2013) 'Unsatisfactory saturation': A critical exploration of the notion of saturated sample sizes in qualitative research. *Qualitative Research*, 13(2): 190–197.

O'Reilly, M. and Parker, N. (2014) *Doing Mental Health Research with Children and Adolescents: A Guide to Qualitative Methods*. London: Sage.

O'Reilly, M., Armstrong, N. and Dixon-Woods, M. (2009a) Subject positions in research ethics committee letters: A discursive analysis. *Clinical Ethics*, 4(4): 187–194.

O'Reilly, M., Dixon-Woods, M., Angell, E., Ashcroft, R. and Bryman, A. (2009b) Doing accountability: A discourse analysis of research ethics committee letters. *Sociology of Health and Illness*, 31(2): 246–291.

O'Reilly, M., Parker, N. and Hutchby, I. (2011) Ongoing processes of managing consent: The empirical ethics of using video-recording in clinical practice and research. *Clinical Ethics*, 6(4): 179–185.

O'Reilly, M., Karim, K., Taylor, H. and Dogra, N. (2012) Parent and child views on anonymity: 'I've got nothing to hide'. *International Journal of Social Research Methodology*, 15(3): 211–224.

O'Reilly, M., Ronzoni, P. and Dogra, N. (2013) *Research with Children: Theory and Practice*. London: Sage.

Ormston, R., Spencer, L., Barnard, M. and Snape, D. (2014) The foundations of qualitative research, in J. Ritchie, J. Lewis, C. McNaughton-Nicholls and R. Ormston (eds), *Qualitative Research Practice: A Guide for Social Science Students and Researchers*. London: Sage. pp. 1–26.

Padgett, D. (2008) *Qualitative Methods in Social Work* (2nd edition). Thousand Oaks, CA: Sage.

Parker, L. and Lynn, M. (2002) What's race got to do with it? Critical race theory's conflicts with and connections to qualitative research methodology and epistemology. *Qualitative Inquiry*, 8(1): 7–22.

Parker, N. and O'Reilly, M. (2013) 'We are alone in the house': A case study addressing researcher safety and risk. *Qualitative Research in Psychology*, 10(4): 341–354.

Partridge, A. and Winer, E. (2009) Sharing study results with trial participants: Time for action. *Journal of Clinical Oncology*, 27(6): 838–839.

Paterson, B., Gregory, D. and Thorne, S. (1999) A protocol for researcher safety. *Qualitative Health Research*, 9(2): 259–269.

Patton, M. Q. (1990) *Qualitative Evaluation and Research Methods* (2nd edition). Newbury Park, CA: Sage.

Paulus, T., Lester, J. N. and Dempster, P. (2013) *Digital Tools for Qualitative Research*. London: Sage.

Payne, G. and Williams, M. (2005) Generalization in qualitative research. *Sociology*, 39(2): 295–314.

Peräkylä, A. (1997) Reliability and validity in research based on tapes and transcripts, in D. Silverman (ed.), *Qualitative Research: Theory, Method and Practice*. London: Sage. pp. 201–220.

Peters, M. (2001) *Poststructuralism, Marxism, and Neo-liberalism: Between Theory and Politics*. Lanham, MD: Rowman and Littlefield.

Plowman, L. and Stephen, C. (2008) The big picture? Video and the representation of interaction. *British Educational Research Journal*, 34(4): 541–565.

Poland, B. D. (1995) Transcription quality as an aspect of rigor in qualitative research. *Qualitative Inquiry*, 1(3): 290–310.

Ponterotto, J. (2005) Qualitative research in counseling psychology: A primer on research paradigms and the philosophy of science. *Journal of Counseling Psychology*, 52(2): 126–136.

Pope, C. and Mays, N. (1995) Qualitative research: Reaching the parts other methods cannot reach: An introduction to qualitative methods in health and health services research. *British Medical Journal*, 311(6996): 42–45.

Post, J., Preston, L. and Sachs, S. (2002) Managing the extended enterprise: The new stakeholder view. *California Management Review*, 45(1): 6–28.

Poster, M. (1989) *Critical Theory and Poststructuralism: In Search of a Context*. New York: Cornell University Press.

Potter, J. (1996) *Representing Reality: Discourse, Rhetoric and Social Construction*. London: Sage.

Potter, J. (1997) Discourse analysis as a way of analysing naturally occurring talk, in D. Silverman (ed.), *Qualitative Research: Theory, Method and Practice*. London: Sage. pp. 144–160.

Potter, J. (1998) Discursive social psychology: From attitudes to evaluative practices. *European Review of Social Psychology*, 9(1): 233–266.

Potter, J. (2002) Two kinds of natural. *Discourse Studies*, 4(4): 539–542.

Potter, J. (2003) Discursive psychology: Between methods and paradigm. *Discourse and Society*, 14(6): 783–794.

Potter, J. (2004a) Discourse analysis as a way of analysing naturally occurring talk, in D. Silverman (ed.), *Qualitative Research: Theory, Method and Practice* (2nd edition). London: Sage. pp. 200–221.

Potter, J. (2004b) Discourse analysis, in M. Hardy and A. Bryman (eds), *Handbook of Data Analysis*. London: Sage. pp. 607–624.

Potter, J. (2012) Discourse analysis and discursive psychology, in H. Cooper (ed.), *APA Handbook of Research Methods in Psychology, Volume 2. Quantitative, Qualitative, Neuropsychological and Biological*. Washington, DC: American Psychological Association. pp. 119–138.

Potter, J. and Hepburn, A. (2012) Eight challenges for interview researchers, in J. F. Gubrium and J. A. Holstein (eds), *Handbook of Interview Research* (2nd edition). London: Sage. pp. 555–570.

Prasad, P. (2005) *Crafting Qualitative Research: Working in the Post Positivist Traditions*. New York: ME Sharpe.

Psathas, G. and Anderson, T. (1990) The practices of transcription in conversation analysis. *Semiotica*, 78(1/2): 75–99.

Raento, M., Oulasvirta, A. and Eagle, N. (2009) Smartphones: An emerging tool for social scientists. *Sociological Methods and Research*, 37(3): 426–454.

Rahman, M. A. and Fals-Borda, O. (1991) A self-review of PAR, in O. Fals-Borda and M. A. Rahman, *Action and Knowledge: Breaking the Monopoly with Participatory Action Research*. London: Intermediate Technology Publications.

Ratner, C. (2002) Subjectivity and objectivity in qualitative methodology. *Forum: Qualitative Social Research*, 3(3): art. 16. http://www.qualitative-research.net/index.php/fqs/article/view/829/1800 (accessed 31 May 2014).

Ravitch, S. and Riggan, M. (2012) *Reason & Rigour: How Conceptual Frameworks Guide Research*. Thousand Oaks, CA: Sage.

Raymond, G. and Heritage, J. (2006) The epistemics of social relationships: Owning grandchildren. *Language in Society*, 35(5): 677–705.

Reason, M. (2010) *Mind Maps, Presentational Knowledge and the Dissemination of Qualitative Research*. NCRM Working Paper Series, ESRC National Centre for Research Methods.

Reason, P. and Bradbury, H. (2001). Introduction: Inquiry and participation in search of a world worthy of human aspiration, in P. Reason and H. Bradbury (eds), *Handbook of Action Research: Participative Inquiry and Practice*. London: Sage. pp. 1–14.

Rennie, D. (1999) *Using Qualitative Methods in Psychology*. Thousand Oaks, CA: Sage.

Rhodes, P. (2011) Why clinical psychology needs process research: An examination of four methodologies. *Clinical Child Psychology*, 17(4): 495–504.

Richards, H. and Emslie, C. (2000) The 'doctor' or the 'girl for the university'? Considering the influence of professional roles on qualitative interviewing. *Family Practice*, 17(10): 71–75.

Richards, H. and Schwartz, L. J. (2002) Ethics of qualitative research: Are there special issues for health services research? *Family Practice*, 19(2): 135–139.

Richardson, L. (1994) Writing: A method of inquiry, in N. Denzin and Y. Lincoln (eds), *Handbook of Qualitative Research*. Thousand Oaks, CA: Sage.

Riessman, C. K. (2008) *Narrative Methods for the Human Sciences*. Thousand Oaks, CA: Sage.

Roberts, F. and Robinson, J. (2004) Interobserver agreement on first-stage conversation analytic transcription. *Health Communication Research*, 30(3): 376–410.

Robins, B., Dickerson, P., Stribling, P. and Dautenhahn, K. (2004) Robot-mediated joint attention in children with autism: A case study in robot–human interaction. *Interaction Studies*, 5(2): 161–198.

Robinson, I. (1991) Confidentiality for whom? *Social Science and Medicine*, 32(3): 279–286.

Robinson, L., Murdoch-Eaton, D. and Carter, Y. (2007) NHS research ethics committees. *British Medical Journal*, 335(7609): 6.

Robinson, O. C. (2011) The ideographic/nomothetic dichotomy: Tracing historical origins of contemporary confusions. *History & Philosophy of Psychology*, 13(2): 32–39.

Robson, C. (2011) *Real World Research* (3rd edition). Oxford: Blackwell.

Rolfe, G. (1998) The theory–practice gap in nursing: From research-based practice to practitioner-based research. *Journal of Advanced Nursing*, 28(3): 672–679.

Rolfe, G. (2006) Validity, trustworthiness and rigour: Quality and the idea of qualitative research. *Methodological Issues in Nursing Research*, 53(3): 304–310.

Rolfe, G. (2010) Back to the future: Challenging hard science approaches to care, in T. Warne and S. McAndrew (eds), *Creative Approaches to Health and Social Care Education*. Basingstoke: Palgrave.

Rosen, A., Proctor, E. and Staudt, M. (1999) Social work research and the quest for effective practice. *Social Work Research*, 23(1): 4–14.

Rosenau, P. (2004) *Postmodernism and the Social Sciences: Insights, Inroads and Intrusions*. Princeton, NJ: Princeton University Press.

Rychetnik, L., Bauman, A., Laws, R., King. L., Rissel, C., Nutbeam, D., et al. (2012) Translating research for evidence-based public health: Key concepts and future directions. *Journal of Epidemiology and Community Health*, 66(12): 1187–1192.

Rycroft-Malone, J., Harvey, G., Seers, K., Kitson, A., McCormack, B. and Titchen, A. (2004) An exploration of the factors that influence the implementation of evidence into practice. *Issues in Clinical Nursing*, 13(8): 913–924.

Sackett, D., Rosenberg, W., Gray, J.,Haynes, R. and Richardson, W. (1996) Evidence-based medicine: What it is and what it isn't. *British Medical Journal*, 312: 71–72.

Sacks, H., Schegloff, E. and Jefferson, G. (1974) A simplest systematics for the organization of turn-taking for conversation. *Language*, 50(4): 696–735.

Salvatore, S. and Valsiner, J. (2010) Between the general and the unique: overcoming the nomothetic versus idiographic opposition. *Theory & Psychology*, 20(6): 817–833.

Sampson, H., Bloor, M. and Fincham, B. (2008) A price worth paying? Considering the 'cost' of reflexive research methods and the influence of feminist ways of 'doing'. *Sociology*, 42(5): 919–933.

Sandberg, J. (2005) How do we justify knowledge produced within interpretive approaches? *Organizatonal Research Methods*, 8(1): 41–68.

Sandelowski, M. (1993) Rigor or rigor mortis: The problem of rigor in qualitative research revisited. *Advances in Nursing Science*, 16(2): 1–8.

Sandelowski, M. (1998) Writing a good read: Strategies for re-presenting qualitative data. *Research in Nursing and Health*, 21(4): 375–382.

Sandelowski, M. and Barroso, J. (2002) Reading qualitative studies. *International Journal of Qualitative Methods*, 1(1): art. 5.

Sandelowski, M. and Leeman, J. (2012) Writing usable qualitative health research findings. *Qualitative Health Research*, 22(10): 1404–1413.

Sass, L. (1989) Humanism, hermeneutics and humanistic psychoanalysis: Differing conceptions of subjectivity. *Psychoanalysis and Contemporary Thought*, 12(3): 433–504.

Schegloff, E. (1987) Analyzing single episodes of interaction: An exercise in conversation analysis. *Social Psychology Quarterly*, 50(2): 101–114.

Schegloff, E. (1997) Whose text? Whose context? *Discourse and Society*, 8(2): 165–185.

Schwandt, T. (1996) Farewell to criteriology. *Qualitative Inquiry*, 2(1): 58–72.

Schwandt, T. (1997) *Qualitative Inquiry: A Dictionary of Terms*. Thousand Oaks, CA: Sage.

Schwandt, T. (2001) Three epistemological stances for qualitative inquiry, in N. Denzin and Y. Lincoln (eds), *Handbook of Qualitative Research*. Thousand Oaks, CA: Sage. pp. 189–214.

Seale, C. (1999) Quality in qualitative research. *Qualitative Inquiry*, 5(4): 465–478.

Seale, C. (2004) Quality in qualitative research, in C. Seale, G. Gobo, J. Gubrium and D. Silverman (eds), *Qualitative Research Practice*. London: Sage. pp. 409–419.

Shaw, S. and Barrett, G. (2006) Research governance: Regulating risk and reducing harm? *Journal of the Royal Society of Medicine*, 99(1): 14–19.

Shrum, W., Duque, R. and Brown, T. (2005) Digital video as research practice: Methodology for the millennium. *Journal of Research Practice*, 1(1): art. M4.

Sieber, J. (1992) *Planning Ethically Responsible Research: A Guide for Students and Internal Review Boards*. Newbury Park, CA: Sage.

Silverman, D. (2011) *Interpreting Qualitative Data: Methods for Analysing Talk, Text and Interaction* (4th edition). London: Sage.

Silverman, D. (2013) *Doing Qualitative Research: A Practical Handbook*. London: Sage.

Sinding, C. and Aronson, J. (2003) Exposing failures, unsettling accommodations: Tensions in interview practice. *Qualitative Research*, 3(1): 95–117.

Skukauskaite, A. (2012) Transparency in transcribing: Making visible theoretical bases impacting knowledge construction from open-ended interview records. *Forum: Qualitative Social Research*, 13(1): art. 14.

Smith, J. (1983) Quantitative versus qualitative research: An attempt to clarify the issue. *Educational Researcher* 12(3): 6–13.

Smith, J. (1984) The problem of criteria for judging interpretative inquiry. *Educational Evaluation and Policy Analysis*, 6(4): 379–391.

Smith, J. (1990) Goodness criteria: Alternative research paradigms and the problem of criteria, in E. Guba (ed.), *The Paradigm Dialog*. London: Sage. pp. 167–187.

Smith, J. (2004) Reflecting on the development of interpretative phenomeno-logical analysis and its contribution to qualitative research in psychology. *Qualitative Research in Psychology*, 1(1): 39–54.

Smith, J. and Heshusius, L. (1986) Closing down the conversation: The end of the quantitative–qualitative debate among educational inquirers. *Educational Researcher*, 15(1): 4–12.

Smith, J., Flowers, P. and Larkin, M. (2009) *Interpretative Phenomenological Analysis: Theory, Method and Research*. London: Sage.

Smith, L. (2008) How ethical is ethical research? Recruiting marginalised, vulner-able groups into health services research. *Journal of Advanced Nursing*, 62(2): 248–257.

Social Research Association (SRA) (2010) *A Code of Practice for the Safety of Social Researchers*. http://the-sra.org.uk/wp-content/uploads/safety_code_of_practice.pdf (accessed 31 May 2014).

Soini, H. and Kronqvist, E.-L. (2011) Epistemology – A tool or a stance? In H. Soini, E.-L. Kronqvist and G. L. Huber (eds), *Epistemologies for Qualitative Research*. Tübingen: Center for Qualitative Psychology. pp. 6–9.

Sokolowski, R. (2000) *Introduction to Phenomenology*. New York: Cambridge University Press.

Sorrell, J. and Redmond, G. (1995) Interviews in qualitative nursing research: Differing approaches for ethnographic and phenomenological studies. *Journal of Advanced Nursing*, 21(6): 1117–1122.

Sparrman, A. (2005) Video recording as interaction: Participant observation of children's everyday life. *Qualitative Research in Psychology*, 2(3): 241–255.

Speer, S. (2002) Transcending the 'natural/contrived' distinction: A rejoinder to Ten Have, Lynch and Potter. *Discourse Studies*, 4(4): 543–548.

Speer, S. and Hutchby, I. (2003) From ethics to analytics: Aspects of participants' orientations to the presence and relevance of recording devices. *Sociology*, 37(2): 315–337.

Spencer, L., Ritchie, J., Lewis, J. and Dillon, L. (2003) *Quality in Qualitative Evaluation: A Framework for Assessing Research Evidence*. London: Government Chief Social Researcher's Office, Prime Minister's Strategy Unit. http://www.civilservice.gov.uk/wp-content/uploads/2011/09/a_quality_framework_tcm6-38740.pdf (accessed 31 May 2014).

Stacey, J. and Thorne, B. (1985) The missing feminist revolution in sociology. *Social Problems*, 32 (4): 301–316

Staller, K. (2013) Epistemological boot camp: The politics of science and what every qualitative researcher needs to know to survive in the academy. *Qualitative Social Work*, 12(4): 395–413.

Starks, H. and Trinidad, S. (2007) Choose your method: A comparison of phenomenology, discourse analysis, and grounded theory. *Qualitative Health Research*, 17(10): 1372–1380.

Stein, A. (2010) Sex, truths, and audiotape: Anonymity and the ethics of public exposure in ethnography. *Journal of Contemporary Ethnography*, 39(5): 554–568.

Steinke, E. (2004) Research ethics, informed consent and participant recruitment. *Clinical Nurse Specialist*, 18(2): 88–95.

Stenbacka, C. (2001) Qualitative research requires quality concepts of its own. *Management Decision*, 39(7): 551–555.

Stiles, W. (1993) Quality control in qualitative research. *Clinical Psychology Review*, 13: 593–618.

Strauss, A. and Corbin, J. (1998) *Basics of Qualitative Research: Techniques and Procedures for Developing Grounded Theory*. Thousand Oaks, CA: Sage.

Strong, T., Busch, R. and Couture, S. (2008) Conversational evidence in therapeutic dialogue. *Journal of Marital and Family Therapy*, 34(3): 388–405.

Suchman, L. (1987) *Plans and Situated Actions: The Problem of Human–Machine Communication*. Cambridge: Cambridge University Press.

Suddaby, R. (2006) What grounded theory is not. *Academy of Management Journal*, 49(4): 633–642.

Sullivan, C., Gibson, S. and Riley, S. (2012) Introduction and aims of the book, in C. Sullivan, Gibson, S. and Riley, S (eds), *Doing Your Qualitative Psychology Project*. London: Sage. pp. 1–22.

Swanson-Kauffman, K. (1986) A combined qualitative methodology for nursing research. *Advances in Nursing Science*, 8(3): 58–69.

Szasbo, V. and Strang, V. (1997) Secondary analysis of qualitative data. *Advances in Nursing Science*, 20(2): 66–74.

Tadajewski, M. (2009) The debate that won't die? Values incommensurability, antagonism and theory choice. *Organization*, 16(4): 467–485.

Teddlie, C. and Tashakkori, A. (2003) Preface, in A. Tashakkori and C. Teddlie (eds), *Handbook of Mixed-Methods in Social and Behavioral Research*. Thousand Oaks, CA: Sage. pp. 3–50.

Tee, S. and Lathlean, J. (2004) The ethics of conducting a cooperative inquiry with vulnerable people. *Journal of Advanced Nursing*, 47(5): 536–543.

Ten Have, P. (2002) Ontology or methodology? Comments on Speer's 'natural' and 'contrived' data: a sustainable distinction? *Discourse Studies*, 4(4): 527–530.

Thelwall, M. (2002) Research dissemination and invocation on the web. *Online Information Review*, 26(6): 413–420.

Themessl-Huber, M., Humphris, G., Dowell, J., Macgillivray, S., Rushmer, R. and Williams, B. (2008) Audio-visual recording of patient–GP consultations for research purposes: A literature review on recruiting rates and strategies. *Patient Education and Counseling*, 71(2): 157–168.

Thompson, P. (1991) *Pilot Study of Archiving Qualitative Data: Report to the ESRC*. Department of Sociology, University of Essex.

Thorne, S. (1994) Secondary analysis in qualitative research: Issues and implications, in J. Morse (ed.), *Critical Issues in Qualitative Research Methods*. Thousand Oaks, CA: Sage. pp. 263–279.

Thorne, S. (2000) Data analysis in qualitative research. *Evidence Based Nursing*, 3(3): 68–70.

Thorne, S. and Darbyshire, P. (2005) Land mines in the field: A modest proposal for improving the craft of qualitative of qualitative health research. *Qualitative Health Research*, 15(8): 1105–1113.

Thorne, S. E., Kazanjian, A. and MacEntee, M. I. (2001) Oral health in long-term care: The implications of organizational culture. *Journal of Aging Studies*, 15(3): 271–283.

Tilley, L. and Woodthorpe, K. (2011) Is it the end for anonymity as we know it? A critical examination of the ethical principle of anonymity in the context of 21st century demands on the qualitative researcher. *Qualitative Research*, 11(2): 197–212.

Tilley, S. (2003) Transcription work: Learning through coparticipation in research practices. *Qualitative Studies in Education*, 16(6): 835–851.

Tilley, S. and Powick, K. (2002) Distanced data: Transcribing other people's research tapes. *Canadian Journal of Education*, 27(2/3): 291–310.

Tracy, S. (2010) Qualitative quality: Eight 'big-tent' criteria for excellent qualitative research. *Qualitative Inquiry*, 16(10): 837–851.

Trinder, L. (2000) Evidence-based practice in social work and probation, in L. Trinder (ed.), *Evidence-Based Practice*. Oxford: Blackwell. pp. 138–162.

Turner, J. R. (2013) Hierarchy of evidence, in M. D. Gellman and J. R. Turner, *Encyclopedia of Behavioral Medicine*. New York: Springer. pp. 963–964.

van Dijk, T. (1993) Principles of critical discourse analysis. *Discourse and Society*, 4(2): 249–283.

van Dijk, T. (2008) *Discourse and Power*. Basingstoke: Palgrave.

Vannini, P. (2012) Introduction to popularizing research, in P. Vannini (ed.), *Popularizing Research: Engaging New Genres, Media and Audiences*. New York: Peter Lang. pp. 1–12.

Vom Lehn, D., Heath, C. and Hindmarsh, J. (2002) Video-based field studies in museums and galleries. *Visitor Studies Today*, V(III): 15–23.

Waddell, C. and Godderis, R. (2005) Rethinking evidence-based practice for children's mental health. *Evidence-Based Mental Health*, 8(3): 60–62.

Wallerstein, N., Oetzel, J., Duran, B., Tafoya, G., Belone, L. and Rae, R. (2008) What predicts outcomes in CBPR? in M. Minkler and N. Wallerstein (eds), *Community-Based Participatory Research for Health: Process to Outcomes* (2nd edition). San Francisco: Jossey-Bass. pp. 371–392.

Warr, D. (2004) Stories in the flesh and voices in the head: Reflections on the context and impact of research with disadvantaged populations. *Qualitative Health Research*, 14(4): 578–587.

Waterman, H., Tillen, D., Dickson, R. and de Koning, K. (2001) Action research: A systematic review and guidance for assessment. *Health Technology Assessment* [programme report], 5(23): 1–166.

Watson, M., Jones, D. and Burns, L. (2007) Internet research and informed consent: An ethical model using archived emails. *International Journal of Therapy and Rehabilitation*, 14(9): 396–403.

Webb, S. (2001) Some considerations on the validity of evidence-based practice in social work. *British Journal of Social Work*, 31(1): 57–79.

Weiss, G. and Wodak, R. (2003) Introduction: Theory, interdisciplinarity and critical discourse analysis, in G. Weiss and R. Wodak (eds), *Critical Discourse Analysis: Theory and Interdisciplinarity*. Basingstoke: Palgrave. pp. 1–34.

Welsh, B. and Farrington, D. (2001) Toward an evidence-based approach to preventing crime. *The ANNALS of the American Academy of Political and Social Science*, 578(1): 158–173.

White, C., Woodfield, K., Ritchie, J. and Ormston, R. (2014) Writing up qualitative research, in J. Ritchie, J. Lewis, C. McNaughton Nicholls and R. Ormston (eds), *Qualitative Research Practice: A Guide for Social Science Students and Researchers*. London: Sage. pp. 367–400.

Whittemore, R., Chase, S. and Mandle, C. (2001) Validity in qualitative research. *Qualitative Health Research*, 11(4): 522–537.

Wiles, R., Crow, G., Heath, S. and Charles, V. (2008) The management of confidentiality and anonymity in social research. *International Journal of Social Research Methodology*, 11(5): 417–428.

Wilkes, L., Cummings, J. and Haigh, C. (2014) Transcriptionist saturation: Knowing too much about sensitive health and social data. *Journal of Advanced Nursing*, DOI: 10.111/jan.12510.

Wilkes, M. (1997) The public dissemination of medical research: Problems and solutions. *Journal of Health Communication*, 2: 3–16.

Wilkes, M. and Kravitz, R. (1992) Medical researchers and the media: Attitudes toward public dissemination of research. *Journal of the American Medical Association*, 268(8): 999–1003.

Wilkinson, S., Joffe, H. and Yardley, L. (2004) Qualitative data collection: Interviews and focus groups, in D. Marks and L. Yardley (eds), *Research Methods for Clinical and Health Psychology*. London: Sage. pp. 38–55.

Williams, M. (2000) Interpretivism and generalization. *Sociology*, 34(2): 209–224.

Willig, C. (2008) *Introducing Qualitative Research in Psychology* (2nd edition). Maidenhead: Open University Press.

Wilson, H. and Hutchinson, S. (1991) Triangulation of qualitative methods: Heideggerian hermeneutics and grounded theory. *Qualitative Health Research*, 1(2): 263–276.

Wimpenny, P. and Gass, J. (2000) Interviewing in phenomenology and grounded theory: Is there a difference? *Methodological Issues in Nursing Research*, 31(6): 1485–1492.

Wodak, R. (2002) Aspects of critical discourse analysis. *Zeitschrift für Angewandte Linguistik*, 36: 5–31.

Wong, J. P.-H. and Poon, M. K.-L. (2010) Bringing translation out of the shadows: Translation as an issue of methodological significance in cross-cultural qualitative research. *Journal of Transcultural Nursing*, 21(2): 151–158.

Woodby, L., Williams, B., Wittich, A. and Burgio, K. (2011) Expanding the notion of researcher distress: The cumulative effects of coding. *Qualitative Health Research*, 21(6): 830–838.

Wooffitt, R. (2005) *Conversation Analysis and Discourse Analysis: A Comparative and Critical Introduction*. London: Sage.

Wray, N., Markovic, M. and Manderson, L. (2007) 'Researcher saturation': The impact of data triangulation and intensive-research practices on the researcher and qualitative research process. *Qualitative Health Research*, 17(10): 1392–1402.

Yancher, S. and Williams, D. (2006) Reconsidering the compatibility thesis and eclecticism: Five proposed guidelines for method use. *Educational Researcher*, 35(9): 3–12.

Young, L. and Barrett, H. (2001) Adapting visual methods: Action research with Kampala street children. *Area*, 33(2): 141–152.

Young, R. and Collin, A. (2004) Introduction: Constructivism and social constructionism in the career field. *Journal of Vocational Behavior*, 64: 373–388.

Zezima, K. (2011) College fights subpoena of interviews tied to I.R.A. *New York Times*, 9 June. http://www.nytimes.com/2011/06/10/us/10irish.html (accessed 21 August 2013).

Index